CREATING FICTION
A WRITER'S COMPANION

FRED LEEBRON
The Fine Arts Work Center in Provincetown

ANDREW LEVY
Butler University

Harcourt Brace College Publishers

Fort Worth Philadelphia San Diego New York Orlando Austin San Antonio
Toronto Montreal London Sydney Tokyo

Publisher	Ted Buchholz
Senior Acquisitions Editor	Stephen T. Jordan
Developmental Editor	Camille Adkins
Project Editor	Christopher Nelson
Production Manager	Jane Tyndall Ponceti
Art Directors	Peggy Young and Pat Bracken
Cover Illustration	Craig B. McCormick

ISBN: 0-15-501414-5

Library of Congress Catalog Card Number: 94-78050

Address for Editorial Correspondence: Harcourt Brace College Publishers, 301 Commerce Street, Suite 3700, Fort Worth, TX 76102.

Address for Orders: Harcourt Brace & Company, 6277 Sea Harbor Drive, Orlando, FL 32887-6777. 1-800-782-4479, or 1-800-433-0001 (in Florida).

Printed in the United States of America

4 5 6 7 8 9 0 1 2 3   016   10 9 8 7 6 5 4 3 2 1

PREFACE

Ten years ago, we were two of ten fiction writers in the graduate program of the Writing Seminars at Johns Hopkins University. Since then, we have continued a conversation as friends and as teachers, as we've sought ways to understand better the art of fiction and the nature of its creation. We now hope that *Creating Fiction* will serve you as a companion in the process of learning to write fiction. We offer a comprehensive discussion of the elements of fiction and a range of writing strategies, as well as straightforward talk about the life of a writer, including the role of the fiction workshop. A selection of short stories and novel excerpts accompanies most chapters.

In combining the most constructive aspects of a textbook and anthology with stories, novel excerpts, interviews, and essays from celebrated writers, *Creating Fiction* offers you a conversation about writing fiction. You may write fiction for a semester or a lifetime; your writing may take place in a classroom or at home. We address all fiction writers who care deeply about craft and vision. We hope *Creating Fiction* will lead you to an open-minded approach to the art of fiction, in which all styles and forms are welcome, and in which you become knowledgeable about the traditional conventions of writing, but also begin to feel a sense of confidence and imagination in attempting to transcend such conventions.

The characteristics that make up a story, such as plot, character, and dialogue, are discussed in the opening chapter, "Elements." We not only explore the critical need for these elements, but also provide examples of fiction that eschew the use of one or more such elements because the nature of the story has demanded something else. In the second chapter, "Approaches to the Short Story," we present models for reading and writing short fiction that have worked for many writers as they strive to understand and improve the shape and style of their narratives. We explore a number of strategies, including a broad examination of how to start writing and a detailed presentation of the construction of a piece of fiction, from the opening sentence through the body of the story to the ending. Both of these chapters define and discuss fiction writing thoroughly, and present a range of techniques to increase the approaches you can take in making short stories.

We present "rules" of fiction writing because they are important to know, but also because they are important to break. These pieces of traditional wisdom about writing fiction—we call them *axioms*—have been handed down from writer to writer so consistently that they have become institutions themselves. Such rules as "Show, don't tell," "Write what you know," and "Don't waste a word" are essential to know, as tools for effective writing, but they are not always applicable. We discuss eight such axioms to show how they apply—to follow the crucial logic that has made them rules—and to illustrate particular instances in story writing where fiction creates its own rules. We encourage you to allow the power of your ideas and your distinctive approaches to transcend axioms or to work within them.

While we present useful approaches to rethinking your fiction in virtually every chapter, "Revision" treats the specific subject of how you can challenge yourself to re-see and better your own work. Our discussion of voice explores a variety of literary voices, and explains in detail strategies for creating and enhancing voice in fiction while retaining the distinctive sound of your writing. Novels and short-short fictions are discussed as alternative forms, with ideas suggested for experimentation. Strong fiction of any form has common attributes, and the practice of one form can lead you to greater achievement in another form.

In two chapters, "First Workshops" and "Advanced Workshops," we present and discuss the role of participants in the fiction workshop. As will always be the case, more writers come to the craft of fiction from outside the classroom than from inside it; but the undeniable fact is that creative writing is the fastest growing discipline in the American university system today, and that, even in towns and cities where there are no workshops offered by local colleges and universities, workshops flourish through libraries, community centers, and arts organizations. It is not only crucial to recognize the advent of the workshop in the practice of fiction writing; it is essential that the nature and the requirements of the workshop be detailed in such a way that you come to the table with a set of realistic expectations. We discuss the differences between workshops and the kinds of student-to-student relations found in more traditional classrooms. We explore how to give helpful criticism in a workshop, and also how to use the criticism you receive. Issues such as choosing what to submit to a workshop, what to do when your story is being workshopped, and how best to use teacher conferences are also discussed.

Whether or not you join a fiction workshop, you will certainly write outside of a workshop. Throughout *Creating Fiction*, our discussions of writing strategies treat fiction writing as part of living, because we believe that writing does not occur in a vacuum. In "Writing Without a Workshop," we include essays and stories in which writers talk about how fiction works in their lives. Ways to find space and time to write, to find inspiration and support, and issues concerning family as well as finances are all explored. A bibliography offers a thorough, annotated list of books that may be useful to you as you continue writing.

The stories and novel excerpts appear here because we consider them stories that can inspire, and because our students have enjoyed them. The stories are placed in their particular chapters to exemplify possibilities discussed in the chapters, to show how a particular approach or vision can work. Although we discuss critical aspects of the fiction that we include, we hope that the excellence of each story speaks for itself, and speaks to you in the same way each story has spoken to us—to illuminate a world, and to inspire us as writers to try to live up to its example.

Overall, our greatest hope for *Creating Fiction* is that it encourages you to invent and pursue your own writing methods. We hope that you will leave this book with an admiration for good stories, a desire to write, and an awareness of the choices you have in enlarging and enriching your own particular talents.

In our careers as writers and teachers, we've participated in and taught numerous workshops, and have benefitted from the companionship and instruction of many teachers, peers, and students. For helping us with this particular book, we thank Butler University, Alan Watahara and the University of California at Berkeley, Melinda Knight and the University of San Francisco, Camille Adkins, George Angel, Richard Burgin, Frank Conroy, Henry Dunow, Marshall Gregory, Leslie Hawke, Jeff Insko, Stephen T. Jordan, Laurie Kirszner, James Linville, Christopher Nelson, Susan Neville, Deb West, and Josh Weiner. We want to especially thank Kathryn Rhett, for her enormous and irreplaceable contributions to this work.

CONTENTS

PART II *Writing in the Workshop* 285

7 *First Workshops* 287

8 *Advanced Workshops* 297

PART III *On Your Own* 305

9 *Writing Without a Workshop* 307

PART

I

WRITING STRATEGIES

1

ELEMENTS

The "elements of fiction" are a vocabulary for discussing the technical aspects of stories and novels. The notion of "elements" derives from Aristotle's *Poetics,* a fourth-century B.C. guidebook for Greek dramatists. Aristotle divided his essay into chapters (or perhaps had it divided into this format by students or later translators) devoted to aspects of playwriting such as "character," "plot," and "diction." In doing so, he implied that a story could be considered as a whole made up of elements, and that an author could work on one aspect (character, for instance) without touching or affecting the other aspects of the story, the way an athlete might exercise certain muscle groups while maintaining others.

In the twentieth century, a second way of talking about the "elements of fiction" evolved, one which borrowed from the science of chemistry. Just as air, for instance, is composed of the elements of nitrogen, oxygen, and so on, a story is composed of elements such as dialogue, plot, and character in amounts and proportions that are unique to that story. These elements exist in a complex and subtle relationship that cannot be reproduced mechanically, and cannot be divided without causing injury or fatality to the body they constitute. In the human body, for instance, oxygen, hydrogen, and carbon create a sum greater than their individual parts, and this sum cannot be divided. In the story, character, plot, and language create a sum greater than *their* parts, and this sum also does not obey the simple rules of addition and deletion.

You can choose between these two models of the elements of fiction. You can also find a language for talking about stories without talking about "elements" at all. Aristotle's elements are different from the ones that most twentieth-century authors and teachers discuss; he devoted chapters to "nouns," and "pity and fear," among others. In the field of creative writing, elements can change, century by century, person by person. The elements can be mechanical: diction, sentence structure, plotting. Or they can be impressionistic: emotion, passion, intellectual courage. This chapter defines and discusses the most prominent elements of fiction to be found in contemporary discussions of creative writing. But you should use our list as a launching point for a personal "elements of fiction": such a list, thoughtfully constructed, would constitute a record of what matters most to you in good stories.

PLOT

"Plot" refers to the events and actions that take place in a story, and the chain of causality that creates links between them. "Plot" is different from story: if, for instance, you choose to tell a story backwards (as Martin Amis does in *Time's Arrow*), with the last event occurring first, the plot of the story will be the events described in the proper chronological order, with an explanation of how one event leads to the following event. The "structure" of the story refers to the technical details of how the author builds the story. In *Time's Arrow,* Amis builds the story backwards, with the ending first and the beginning last, and every event in the story taking place in reverse:

> This business with the yellow cabs, it surely looks like an unimprovable deal. They're always there when you need one, even in the rain or when the theaters are closing. They pay you up front, no questions asked. They always know where you're going. They're great. No wonder we stand there, for hours on end, waving goodbye, or saluting—saluting this fine service. The streets are full of people with their arms raised, drenched and weary, thanking the yellow cabs. Just the one hitch: they're always taking me places I don't want to go.

Plot is a line of action plucked out of the flux of reality. Plot is important because you want your reader to have a compelling reason to turn the page and read more. This reason might be the faith that a reader develops in you because of three inventive pages you wrote ten pages ago, or it might be the curiosity you create by devising a suspenseful plot, or it might be the simple fact that every page you write introduces something new that maintains the reader's interest. A successful story may or may not have slow patches and false notes; but it creates better reasons for being read than for being put down. A good plot can support a story even when the language goes flat or the characters cease developing.

However, a tightly wound plot is not a prerequisite to writing a successful story. The idea of plot is more important to some writers than to others. Edgar Allan Poe believed (or claimed to believe) that an author should know every turn of a story's plot before applying pen to paper. On the other hand, numerous writers, such as Sherwood Anderson, have believed that plot was "poison," and that mapping out a blueprint before writing denied the author the opportunity to let characters and story grow spontaneously and take on lives of their own. Still other writers hardly care about plot at all: Sandra Cisneros' "My Lucy Friend Who Smells Like Corn" has little plot, little conflict, and little resolution. When "Lucy" affects readers, it does so because of Cisneros' verbal energy, because she writes with affection about an original character, and because of her feel for description. In other words, "plot" is simply a tool that the writer can use to make a good story, but not all good stories have plots. Or good plots.

In standard discussions of plot, teachers and students attempt to find ways to map story structure: arrows on the chalkboard, intersecting lines, overlapping circles. The most famous of story diagrams, Freytag's Triangle (which will be discussed at greater length in Chapter 2), divides the typical story into three loose sections: a ground situation, in which the author first describes the issue or problem that will create tension and require resolution; a period of "rising action," in which the tension created by the initial conflict increases in suspense and energy; and a period of "resolution," in which the major conflict is concluded. Freytag's Triangle, like many plot models, can be used to describe everything from African folktales to television situation comedies and Harlequin romances, and it can be twisted, flattened, or bent to accommodate the idiosyncrasies of an individual story. It can be used to describe Yukio Mishima's "Patriotism," for instance: the conflict is introduced when the lieutenant announces that he must commit ritual suicide rather than choosing between fighting the mutiny or joining it. The rising action consists of the preparations for suicide of the lieutenant and his wife, Reiko. The resolution consists of the suicides themselves, which bring the reader to the very last word in the story.

Like most plot diagrams, Freytag's Triangle is most useful as a building block, or an after-the-fact method of analyzing a story that already works. Plot diagrams can remind you that stories must be *constructed* sometimes, and that on first drafts they rarely emerge perfectly paced and completely focused. A diagram, however, cannot express the suppleness of the plot of "Patriotism": the tantalizingly slow rising action, or the small transitions and shifts in pace as the couple moves from heated scenes of lovemaking to their extraordinarily stoic final preparations to the suicides themselves. And while "Patriotism" clearly illustrates Freytag's plot diagram, its most unusual plot device also defies that classic triangle: Mishima tells us *in the first sentence* of the story what will happen at the end, but still builds a story of great and moving tension. It is hard to imagine the plot diagram that could inspire that particular touch.

Similarly, plot diagrams cannot help you create surprising, memorable plot devices. In "Prue," for instance, Alice Munro delivers a primer on how to shift speeds within a story, varying scenes portrayed in real, dawdling time with very short passages in which she covers years:

> Prue used to live with Gordon. This was after Gordon left his wife and before he went back to her—a year and four months in all. Some time later, he and his wife were divorced. After that came a period of indecision, of living off and on; then the wife went away to New Zealand, most likely for good.

In "Girl," Jamaica Kincaid creates a device—the entire story consists of a mother figure offering a set of lessons to her nameless daughter—so compressed and rhythmic that you may not notice that the first instructions are addressed to a child ("Wash the white clothes on Monday"), while the final instructions could only be addressed to a young woman ("This is how to love a man"), and that Kincaid has actually narrated an entire upbringing in two short pages. In "Seizing Control," Mary Robison's young, unnamed narrator seems uninterested in conventional plot. While you could claim that the nonsense recitation uttered by Hazel at the end of the story echoes themes raised throughout the story, you could also describe that haunting ending as purely intuitive on the author's part—a loose, inexplicable piece of dialogue that works precisely because it floats beyond interpretation.

There are writers who coolly evaluate their own work-in-progress, and say things like, "I need to introduce this conflict earlier," or "This part of the story goes too long." Some writers don't plan plot. They plot as they write, maybe knowing in advance what will happen on the next page, but not the page after, or perhaps putting words on paper in the hope that a plot will emerge. You can write two great pages to begin a story during a period of energy and inspiration, and follow with three slow pages written while inspiration was lacking. Similarly, while you can tack on a situation-comedy ending to a realistic story for ironic effect, it is more likely that when you pull a plot twist from a movie, television show, or popular novel, you are doing it because your inspiration ran dry or you lost interest. Experienced writers find work habits that catch them in their best writing trim (they write only at night, they write to music, they write hungry), and almost always create the effect of consistent verbal energy or inspiration through hard work and frequent revision.

In other words, good story structure comes from good planning, good luck, real effort, and some measure of self-knowledge. It is important to remember that "plot," despite its technical connotations, is not detached from the emotional and everyday aspects of storywriting: who you are, and where you are when you write. Isaac Babel, explaining why his stories took their particular form, once noted that

> Tolstoy was able to describe what happened to him minute by minute, he remembered it all, whereas I, evidently, only have it in me to describe the most interesting five minutes in twenty-four hours.

"My First Goose" does much to illustrate Babel's tongue-in-cheek "five minutes in twenty-four hours" theory: it takes place in the course of one day and one night, and is comprised of several short, memorable scenes bound together by the narrator's overwhelming but understated mood of heartbreak.

In his essay "Fires," Raymond Carver also argues against the traditional notion that a writer's most important influences are literary. He tells us instead that he developed his terse writing style, and chose to focus on the short story form, for the rather unromantic reasons that he had children, and little money, during the early stages of his writing career:

> The short things I could sit down and, with any luck, write quickly and have done with. . . . Time and again I reached the point where I couldn't see or plan any further ahead than the first of next month and gathering together enough money, by hook or crook, to meet the rent and provide the children's school clothes. This is true.

What is most interesting, however, is that when the conditions of Carver's life changed, he couldn't (or didn't want to—he is deliberately ambiguous) change his writing style:

> The circumstances of my life are much different now, but now I *choose* to write short stories and poems. Or at least I think I do. . . .

As Carver's quote suggests, plot and story structure ideas might come from the personality of the author, or from the conditions of the author's life, or from conscious decision making; but they come from somewhere, and they are not necessarily controllable choices.

Overall, the structure of a story is dictated from the same part of your consciousness that creates the characters, the language, and the other seemingly more spontaneous and organic aspects of writing. While we have found an expressive language for talking about characters, however (largely because it is the same language that we use to talk about real individuals), we have difficulty referring to plots as being "nice" (the plot that treats its characters with generosity), "mean-spirited" (the story structure where bad things happen to well-intentioned characters), or "haphazard" (a plot where events fail to represent a single emotional viewpoint). Plots have their own kind of character, however, created by your character, and your vision about the essence of storytelling. The voice that takes you to the precipice of your deepest fascinations, and makes the first ten pages of your story crackle with tension, is the same voice that will lead you to attach a superficial ending. Or, more subtly, you will start to find your language getting denser, and harder to understand, the closer you get to the truth of your story. These are positive signs, indicating that you are writing about something so important that it is difficult to bear its moral and emotional weight.

Writing Strategies

1. Select a story from this book. Make a list of the individual extended sequences that comprise that story. An extended sequence may include an individual scene, an individual dialogue, or an extended description of a setting, object, or person. Construct this list in the order in which the scenes occur. Do all of the sequences on this list advance the story toward its ending, or provide information, or set the tone in such a way that the ending becomes more meaningful? If some do not, do you believe these passages add to the pleasure of reading the story for other reasons?

Do the same exercise for one of your own stories.

2. Select a story from this book. Write a different ending. Reread the entire story: did your changes make any of the earlier sections of the story unnecessary, irrelevant, or misleading?

Do the same for one of your own stories.

3. Write a one-page story that, like certain passages from Alice Munro's "Prue," covers a large amount of time and action in very short paragraphs.

Review the story. Which events seem to justify more expanded treatment? Select one, and write a one- to two-page scene describing it in detail. Select two others, and provide half- to one-page treatments.

4. Using one of your own stories, construct the same kind of list of "extended sequences" as in the first writing strategy, but instead make this list a diary that describes *how* the story was written, not what was written.

    a. Which sequences were written first?
    b. Which sequences were written at a single sitting? At what time? With (or without) what distractions?
    c. Which sequences were written in a state of emotional cool? Which sequences were written in a state of emotional pique?

After others read your story, compare the comments you receive to the comments in this diary. Does it provide insight into when, and how, you do your best writing?

5. Using one of your own stories, repeat strategies 1 and 4, but this time make a list of sequences that describes the sources of the material.

a. Which sequences came from real life?
b. Which sequences came completely from your imagination?
c. Which sequences were borrowed, or seem to be borrowed, from other narrative mediums (like television, movies, other books, stories you have heard)?

After others read your story, compare the comments you receive to the results of this list. Do your readers' responses provide insight into which sources inspire your best writing?

CHARACTER

The word *character* connotes several different meanings. First, "character" can describe any person who has a role in the story being discussed. There are "round characters," who possess complex, three-dimensional personality traits. There are also "flat characters," who are defined by one or two major personality traits; "main characters," who play major roles; and "secondary characters," who don't. "Round characters" are usually also "main characters," although there is no reason that main characters cannot be flat instead of round. An animal can be a character, if it has a personality, or acts like it does. A piece of furniture can be a character, although it is very likely to be a flat one. A dead person can be a character: "Justina seemed to be waiting for me and changing from an inert into a demanding figure," the narrator of John Cheever's "The Death of Justina" imagines.

A second way to talk about "character" refers to the qualities that make up any individual who has a part to play in your story, and also refers to how (or whether) you have manipulated those qualities to create a "likable character," a "memorable character," a "humorous character," or even just a "character who steals the story away from the major characters." "Character," in this case, refers to the intersection of plot, voice, and character that most stories have at their heart: you don't want your characters to do anything that is not in character, and where your characters go, your plot must follow. "Character," in this broader definition, doesn't just describe the people you put in your story; it describes how well you made them, and how well they fit together. Not every story must have good characters, or characters at all. But, inversely, there are stories, like Eudora Welty's "Old Mr. Marblehall," in which every paragraph either introduces a new character, or introduces a new facet of an existing character; the story possesses no plot *per se,* but rather is sustained by the aggregation of complications about characters who were striking and fantastical in the first place.

While it is useful to write crisp descriptions of a character's physical appearance and actions, it is more essential to communicate character with subtle, accidental, or semiconscious strokes, or by accumulating the kind of complexities that cannot fit in a newspaper's columns. Consider, for instance, this description of the Commander from the first paragraph of Isaac Babel's "My First Goose":

> He rose, the purple of his riding-breeches and the crimson of his little tilted cap and the decorations stuck on his chest cleaving the hut as a standard cleaves the sky. . . .

The writing is pointed, almost journalistic, and the passage provides scattered physical details about its subject. At the same time, the description is decidedly subjective: the "little" in "little tilted cap" and the decorations "stuck" on his chest make the Commander seem ridiculous, just as the rich colors, the image of "rising," and the comparison to a flag held high in battle make him seem imposing. But what do these metaphorical structures mean? Do we interpret them as being about the narrator, telling us that he feels himself superior to, and frightened by, the Commander? Or do we read them as careful editorialization on the part of the author, who wants us to see the Commander as a ridiculous yet imposing figure? Or do we read them as a combination of these two things? There is no way to answer these questions, to understand the shape and reasoning behind Babel's first paragraph, without reading the rest of the story—to see what the Commander says and does, and what kind of person the narrator turns out to be.

In "Genesis," the opening chapter to her autobiographical novel, *Oranges Are Not the Only Fruit,* Jeanette Winterson seems to turn a creative writing exercise into a story by having her narrator describe her mother using a list of her likes and dislikes:

Enemies were: The Devil (in his many forms)

Next Door

Sex (in its many forms)

Slugs

Friends were: God
                 Our dog
                 Auntie Madge
                 The Novels of Charlotte Brontë
                 Slug pellets
and me, at first.

While this list seems like a shortcut, an easy way to describe a character, it is also a serious responsibility for the writer, who must now deliver a character that fits this list as surely as if she had signed a contract to do so. In fact, Winterson does exactly that: not only does the mother parade these friends and enemies throughout "Genesis" (she derides the neighbors next door, practices strict religion, and dislikes sex enough to adopt the narrator rather than bear her own child), but she is portrayed as the kind of person whose worldview is divided into a list of "friends" and "enemies"—she is, as the narrator indicates, a woman without "mixed feelings." Even the "and me, at first" previews the estrangement between adopted daughter and mother that will occur later in the novel. Winterson's list, which appears casual, almost haphazard, on the first page of the novel, in fact provides a careful blueprint for the character that will follow. But it is the intensity of the conception of the mother—the narrator's attention fixed closely upon her throughout the chapter—that makes the character memorable. And that kind of success in characterization is difficult to make part of any conscious plan.

There are three sources that you can go to find the material from which to build a character: first, your real life; second, your imagination; third, other stories. Many writers do not plan their characters beforehand, beyond one or two broad strokes (a mass murderer, a stoic lieutenant); characters come bubbling up as the next turn in the story seems to require, and they are capable of disappearing just as quickly. Similarly, characters never exist in a vacuum: change the personality of one character, and it may make another character appear in a different light, or it may make a plot turn that made sense in a first draft look odd and implausible in a second.

Readers can help you find the sources of your best characters. They can tell you, for instance, which characters moved them, and you can then study your own writing habits to determine whether their compliments create a pattern. Perhaps they are telling you that the characters you drew from real life are the most evocative, or the least convincing. Perhaps they are telling you that the characters you created at 3:00 A.M. are more original than the ones you wrote about in the afternoon. Perhaps they are telling you that your characters do not stay in character, do not develop, or act and sound exactly like each other.

Or perhaps they are simply telling you when you are inspired and when you are not. It is a chief irony of fiction writing (and writing in general) that the story you write in white heat, convinced of the worth of your own words, is sometimes the story that no one else likes. This can be a crushing experience, but it can also be a learning experience. If your readers all tell you that a certain character is lifeless and uninteresting, and you find you agree with them, then you should change that character. But when your readers don't like a character about whom you truly care, then you must make a small (but nontrivial) decision about who is right, and who you are writing for. Sophisticated and experienced writers have complex relationships with their characters, but those relationships are based upon the experience of a thousand tiny failures, a thousand tiny successes, and a thousand tiny choices. Your characters will mature as long as you continue to write.

Writing Strategies

1. Select a story from this book. Make a list of the characters in the story and describe, in approximate terms, the amount of attention each character receives from the author.

Does the proportion of the amount of attention each character receives seem appropriate to you? Are there characters who do not seem to belong for any reason, who are introduced and then dropped, or who seem to be onstage for more time than they deserve?

Do the same exercise for one of your own stories.

2. Using one of your own stories, make a list of the characters.

   a. Which characters came from real life?
   b. Which characters came from your imagination?
   c. Which characters were borrowed, or seemed to be borrowed, from other narrative mediums (like television, movies, other books, stories you have heard)?

After others read your story, compare the comments you receive to the results of this list. Do your readers' responses provide insight into the sources of your best characters?

3. In the course of a story, characters evolve incrementally; every action and reaction allows the reader to see further complexities in their personalities.

Select a character from a story included in this anthology. Change a central feature of that character by changing his or her response in a specific situation. How does it change the remainder of the story?

Do the same for one of your own stories.

VOICE

"Voice" refers to one of three possible (and overlapping) definitions of the term. First, "voice" is used to describe the point of view from which a story is told:

A *first-person* story is told from the point of view of a narrator who is also a character within the story, and who uses "I" in the narration to describe himself or herself.

A *second-person* story contains a narrator who addresses the reader as "you," and transforms the reader into a character within the story by doing so. (In "How to Become a Writer," Lorrie Moore writes, "You wake up in the morning. You hate the sound of your alarm.")

A *third-person* story contains a narrator who stands apart from the action, and describes the characters within the story as "he," "she," and "they." This point of view may be *third-person omniscient,* which means that the narrator can look into the minds of all the characters and tell us what they are thinking; or this point of view may be *third-person limited,* which means that the narrator can only look into the mind of some of the characters, one of the characters, or none of the characters.

Second, "voice" describes the quality and tone of the point of view of a given story. The "voice" of a story is analogous to the voice of a speaker in conversation. Just as every sentence spoken by a person in conversation bears similarities to every other sentence—the speaker may talk fast, the speaker may use a broad vocabulary, the speaker may seem obsessed with certain issues—"voice" in fiction can be defined as the set of style traits that distinguishes *the way* one story is told from any other.

Similarly, "voice" can describe those style traits, psychological fascinations, and thematic concerns that carry over from one story to another in a single author's works, and which distinguish the work of that author from any other. In this third definition, "authorial voice" is simply another word for "personality": your personality not as it appears in everyday life, but as it appears in your writing. For this reason, "voice" is misnamed as an element of fiction; it permeates every written word that you compose, and can rarely be easily described.

A fuller discussion of the many aspects of "voice" can be found in Chapter 5.

Writing Strategies

See Chapter 5.

SETTING

"Setting" is where the action in a given story takes place. "Setting" can refer specifically to the physical environment where a scene (or an entire story) occurs: the first scene in Edith Wharton's "Roman Fever" takes place in a restaurant in Rome in the 1930s, and the second scene takes place on a veranda in the same hotel where the restaurant is situated. Within "Roman Fever," however, there are several flashbacks: these flashbacks are *set* within the minds (mental settings, if not physical ones) of the two women who are the main characters of the story. The flashbacks themselves also have settings of their own: the Roman Colosseum, their homes in New York, and the past, which can also be called a setting, although of a different sort.

"Setting" can also refer more broadly to the cultural environment where a story occurs. It would not be difficult to describe the physical setting of Kate Chopin's "The Story of an Hour," for instance: the story takes place in a woman's house around the turn of the century. Nevertheless, the cultural setting is more relevant to the drama that the story creates. "The Story of an Hour" is set within a regional culture and during a time period where even the most successful marriages were viewed by both husband and wife as dull and restrictive; it is our understanding of this culture and its main features that allows us to respond emotionally to the story's protagonist. "Cultural" setting, in this case, refers to the set of spoken and unspoken rules by which the society within a story plays, and the extent to which the reader understands those rules.

It is difficult to compose a story that has no setting: there are few ways to describe the actions of human beings without incidentally describing the physical or cultural environment where those actions take place. Since you will probably describe some aspects of setting whenever you write about human action, then, a more central question might be: Do you need to *consciously* develop settings, by installing descriptions of place into a story? And will these conscious attempts to conjure the spirit and feel of a place enhance the experience of reading, or will they feel forced?

Many writers, because they want their readers to be able to fully and vividly imagine the smallest details of their stories, work carefully to describe physical settings. In Tobias Wolff's *This Boy's Life*, for instance, the narrator describes setting with a clear reportorial eye and simple, unmannered language. In one scene where the narrator returns to a farm to apologize for stealing gasoline the night before, he finds

> The Welch farmyard was all mud, a wallow without hogs. Nothing grew there. And nothing moved, no cats, no chickens, no mutts running out to challenge us. The house was small, ash gray and decrepit. Moss grew thickly on the shingle roof. There was no porch, but a tarpaulin had been stretched from one wall to give shelter to a washtub with a mangle and a clothesline that drooped with dull flannel shirts of different sizes, and dismal sheets.

On one level, this excerpt serves as an example of how setting interacts with the other elements of fiction. The fact that the farm is in bad shape communicates to the reader and to the protagonist that the family is poor, and that the act of stealing from them was particularly cruel: "These people weren't making it," the narrator tells us. "They were near the edge, and I had nudged them that much farther along." In turn, this realization drives plot, and reveals character: seeing the condition of the farm and its residents, the protagonist is unable to apologize, struck dumb by the mix of self-hatred and repression that has resulted from his recognition that he has done real harm.

At the same time, setting can be a powerful aspect of a story even when it is not described with any great clarity, and often exactly because it is not described with great clarity. A story like Eudora Welty's "Old Mr. Marblehall" does not contain a concrete physical environment where the action of the story takes place, because the action of the story is described in a swift and nonlinear monologue. Despite this fact, the setting of "Old Mr. Marblehall"—the small Southern town where Mr. Marblehall lives with his two wives—is powerfully described in the course of the story in the kind of casual but precise detail that would be used by one town member speaking to another. By treating the reader like someone already familiar with the town (in a perfect example of how voice works with setting and tone, Welty uses aspects of second-person voice in narrating the story, occasionally addressing readers as though they were neighbors), Welty creates a level of intimacy that might otherwise be absent if she had treated the reader like a tourist.

Overall, setting is not an inert backdrop against which characters and plot play themselves out. It is also not an obligation. It is completely possible to compose a moving piece of fiction where you thinly describe setting, and where you make little if any effort to consciously describe the settings where the action occurred. In Milan Kundera's "The Hitchhiking Game," for instance, settings are described in perfunctory detail: "It was a narrow room with two beds, a small table, a chair, and a washbasin." But there are many other stories where setting is a live, fluid aspect of how fiction communicates meaning and emotion. In Edith Wharton's "Roman Fever," the city of Rome, where ruins have been built upon ruins, is a metaphorical equivalent for the memories of the two middle-aged women who inhabit the story. Likewise, the Roman setting, and the sunset that gradually shrouds it during the course of the story, inspires the two women to make statements that no other city could have drawn from them. In Italo Calvino's "The Distance of the Moon," the setting—a primitive yet strangely sublime civilization, and a younger version of our own moon that passes within feet of the earth's surface once a month—are surreal reconstructions of things that are familiar to us from everyday life. In describing this setting, Calvino's scientific background (he graduated from the University of Turin with a degree in agronomy in 1947), as well as his self-deprecating intellectual manner, emerge in passages that seem to be built of a cross between geometry and poetry: "Orbit?

Oh, elliptical, of course: for a while it would huddle against us and then it would take flight for a while." And while Calvino's story contains characters of substance, it is the moon—the setting itself— that is the active agent. It is the moon that "was so strong that it pulled you up"; it is the moon that draws Little Xlthlx, the child, above the surface of the sea in a scene of eerie beauty; it is the moon that separates lovers, and brings them together; and it is the moon that most readers remember.

Writing Strategies

1. Select a story from this book. Make a list of the settings in the story and describe, in approximate terms, the amount of page length and level of detail the author devotes to describing each setting. Does the proportion of the amount of attention each setting receives seem appropriate to you?

Do the same exercise for one of your own stories.

2. Make a list of settings that you can remember clearly *from memory*—a childhood bedroom or an old workplace, for example.

    a. Select one setting, and describe it in one detailed, reportorial paragraph.

    b. Select another setting, and attempt to describe it in one paragraph. Unlike the previous paragraph, however, this paragraph should not be objective, or objective-seeming, but clearly subjective: the setting should be portrayed as a frightening place, a warm place, a place clearly hated or loved by the narrator.

3. Describe the setting of a place you have never seen, but have always wanted to see: a Creole dance hall, a room in the Beverly Wilshire Hotel, Bermuda at sunset.

DIALOGUE

Dialogue constitutes the spoken utterances of characters. It is standard form to contain dialogue within quotation marks:

> "Do I look like a liar?"

and to begin a new paragraph every time a different character speaks:

"Do I look like a liar?"
"You look like you enjoy lying to women."

In addition, most authors provide dialogue "tags," phrases placed at the end of the quotation to indicate who is speaking. Authors do not provide tags every time a character speaks, but only when the reader might be confused if the dialogue tag is not provided:

"Do I look like a liar?"
"You look like you enjoy lying to women," said the girl.

Frequently, authors extend the dialogue tag, using it as an opportunity to explain how the words were said, and perhaps even to provide a short description of why they were said that way:

"Do I look like a liar?"
"You look like you enjoy lying to women," said the girl, and into her words there crept unawares a touch of the old anxiety, because she really did believe that her young man enjoyed lying to women.

Alternately, authors use a piece of dialogue as the tag for a description of a character's motives, providing a cause-and-effect explanation for why an individual chooses to make a particular statement:

The girl was grateful to the young man for every bit of flattery; she wanted to linger for a moment in its warmth and so she said, "You're very good at lying."
"Do I look like a liar?"

Lastly, authors frequently combine action and dialogue, to provide the reader with a visual image of how a scene appeared as a piece of dialogue was spoken:

He smiled at her and said: "I'm lucky today. I've been driving for five years, but I've never given a ride to such a pretty hitchhiker."
The girl was grateful to the young man for every bit of flattery; she wanted to linger for a moment in its warmth and so she said, "You're very good at lying."

Not every author uses the standard format for dialogue. James Joyce did not use quotation marks, but used a single dash to indicate the beginning of a quotation:

–It's when it's all over that you'll miss him, said my aunt.
–I know that, said Eliza.

Stephen Dixon, author of over four hundred short stories, does not use new paragraph indentations:

> "But just last week or the week before that you said you loved me more than you ever have, or as much as you ever have, you said." "I was lying." "You wouldn't lie about something like that." "I'm telling you, I was lying," she said.

Other authors place quotations in italics, or paraphrase dialogue to speed plot and create a distancing effect: "The young man replied that he wasn't worried. . . . The girl objected. . . ." In each of these cases, however, the author creates a consistent style, so that readers will not be confused by sudden changes, but simply adjust to a new set of rules about what quotations on the page look like. Few authors want to place barriers between their readers and their dialogue; Dixon's style, for instance, may be briefly disorienting, but it creates a sense of urgency that more than compensates for any momentary confusion.

The purpose of dialogue in fiction is unambiguous: conversation is a vital part of human interaction, and few stories exist without one character speaking to another character at some point. Dialogue is a separate element of fiction, however, because it is a special form of language. When readers read a story, they judge that story by the standards of other stories they have read; when they read dialogue, however, they judge that dialogue not only by the standard of dialogue in other stories, but also by the standard of how real people speak. Readers expect dialogue to be a reproduction of authentic speech, or an interesting and vivid variation. Authors, on the other hand, can draw upon the real-life speech of people they have known, or draw upon literary examples, or edit "real" speech into different forms. Most authors are mindful that their dialogue does not exist in a vacuum, separate from the other elements of a story: dialogue shapes character (for characters are best judged by what they say, and how they say it), provides exposition (through the common trick of having characters, rather than the third-person narrator, describe actions that have taken place offstage), and provides linguistic contrast to the author's voice. If dialogue is a special language, it is one that presents you with extraordinary opportunities.

Realism is one of two models for good dialogue. In realistic dialogue, you recreate the sound of authentic speech on the page; if there is a third-person narrator telling your story, that narration will perhaps sound strikingly distinct from the way that the characters speak. Mark Twain, angered by literature in which characters did not sound like their real-life counterparts—and did not even sound like themselves from sentence to sentence—savaged the early-nineteenth-century American author James Fenimore Cooper in an essay entitled "Fenimore Cooper's Literary Offences." Among Twain's nineteen rules for good fiction were

> 5. . . . when the personages of a tale deal in conversation, the talk shall sound like human talk, and be talk such as human beings would be likely to talk in the given circumstances, and have a discoverable purpose, and a show of relevancy, and remain in the neighborhood of the subject at hand, and be interesting to the reader, and help out the tale, and stop when the people cannot think of anything more to say. . . .
>
> 6. . . . when the author describes the character of a personage in his tale, the conduct and conversation of the personage shall justify said description. . . .

Twain's rules are relatively easy to learn. Above all else, he recommended that authors listen to the way real individuals speak in specific situations, and use those examples as a standard for fictional dialogue. There is simply no substitute for a good "ear" for dialogue, and the only way to get a good ear is to be a good, even compulsive, listener. As important, Twain recommended that characters behave with an inner consistency, that characters who speak in slang on page one continue to speak in slang throughout the story, unless they have compelling reasons to change. The best method for creating consistently in-character dialogue is to have a clear vision of your characters before they even speak. If you are putting together your characters in bits and pieces throughout a first draft, however, you can wait until the conclusion of that draft to get a better view of those characters, and what they have said. In this case, an essential part of revision is to review dialogue—character by character, or scene by scene—to make sure that it is internally consistent, character by character, scene by scene.

Authorial sympathy is the second model for dialogue. In this kind of dialogue, you can detect indications that the narrative voice and the voices of the character are somewhat similar; while you might feel that the dialogue is not realistic in such stories, you could also discover that the dialogue and authorial voice are working together in creating a clear and unified emotional vision for the reader. In "The Pale Pink Roast," for instance, Grace Paley's third-person narrator appears to feel such appreciation for Peter, the protagonist, that she corroborates his worldview. In one paragraph, for instance, Peter tells Judy, his daughter, that, "I'm glad you still have a pussycat's sniffy nose and a pussycat's soft white fur." In the next paragraph, the narrator refers to Judy's "springy hind" and "smooth front paw," as if to show support for Peter's choice of metaphor. In "Prue," the third-person narrator and the two main characters, Prue and Gordon, speak in the same terse, almost clipped manner, as though they together bore the same impatience with unnecessary words. John Cheever's "The Death of Justina" provides an example of how gradations in tone between dialogue and narration can enrich a story. Here the reader grows so accustomed to the narrator's manic, adjectival style that it is easy to miss that Dr. Hunter speaks in the same manner, but with marginally (and only marginally) more control—as if to suggest, as the rest of the story does on other levels, that the distance between middle-class sanity and breakdown is narrow and tentative.

At other times, authorial sympathy can be more encompassing. The reader of Don DeLillo's contemporary novel, *White Noise*, will quickly recognize that many of the characters—the children, the scholars, the housewives—all sound somewhat alike:

> Housewife: "What is night? It happens seven times a week. Where is the uniqueness in this?"
> Teenager: "What dead? Define the dead."
> Nun: "Saved? What is saved? This is a dumb head, who would come in here to talk about angels."

Using Twain's rules, you could convict DeLillo of the same literary crime for which Twain chastised Cooper. But because DeLillo's characters are consistently engaging, the fact that their voices seem to emanate from the same strong consciousness is an irrelevant complaint to make. In addition, because DeLillo's novels are about the rise of new kinds of communities and their shared languages, it also is a counterproductive complaint to make, one that misses the fact that DeLillo's dialogue is completely consistent with the philosophical content of his books.

Twain's recommendations are as pragmatic and reasonable as legal advice: they even sound like legal advice. But "The Pale Pink Roast," "Prue," "The Death of Justina," and *White Noise* provide you with an opportunity to explore the inner, secret logic of the individual voice, which has little to do with law, and little to do with reason. These works are reminders that dialogue is inextricably linked with the other elements of the story in which it appears. Twain says the same thing, but Twain means, roughly, that any piece of dialogue should be consistent with the character who speaks it, and should be relevant to the plot. The stories described in this chapter suggest other options: that good dialogue is an end in itself, and readers enjoy listening to tangents as long as they are entertaining or relevatory or suspenseful tangents; that dialogue is linked to the other aspects of a story for philosophical and emotional reasons as well as Twain's more practical reasons; that readers are not paying that close attention to the internal consistency of dialogue when they are engaged with the other wonderful things taking place in a story; and finally, that the violation of a reasonable rule for writing fiction is justified if the result is a larger, richer, or more unified story.

Writing Strategies

1. There is a set of grammatical rules that apply to the transcription of dialogue: how to use quotation marks, when to use punctuation, when to capitalize, and when to begin new paragraphs. Create your own personal grammar for transcribing dialogue onto the page (see examples by Stephen Dixon and James Joyce). In your next story, use this grammar. Make sure the rules of the grammar are internally consistent—that is, the way you write dialogue on page one is identical to the way you write dialogue on page five.

2. Apply Mark Twain's rules for writing dialogue to your last story. Did you "violate" any of them? Read the dialogue aloud to yourself, or have friends or classmates read aloud the separate parts. Does your dialogue abide by Twain's rule that "the talk shall sound like human talk, and be talk such as human beings would be likely to talk in the given circumstances"?

If your dialogue does violate Twain's rules, does it do so for a discernible literary purpose? Does your dialogue sound better than "human talk," because it does something especially appealing, from a storytelling perspective?

3. Write a short-short story that is all dialogue, with no dialogue tags; your reader should be able to tell who is talking by the quality

of the voice, word choice, dialect, slang. Make sure your dialogue voices abide by Twain's rules.

Take this same story and add dialogue tags that explain what actions the characters are taking during the course of the story.

4. Write a first-person story in which the language of the narrative and the language of the narrator's dialogue belong on two different levels of literary sophistication—that is, a narrator who thinks complex thoughts, but for some reason cannot make his or her feelings clear to other characters in the story.

Flannery O'Connor

Flannery O'Connor was born in Savannah, Georgia, in March 1925. A graduate of Georgia College and the University of Iowa Writer's Workshop in 1947, O'Connor published two novels, Wise Blood *(1952) and* The Violent Bear It Away *(1960), as well as two major collections of short stories. O'Connor won three O. Henry Awards for her short fiction, and posthumously received the National Book Award in 1972 for* The Complete Short Stories. *"A Good Man Is Hard to Find" first appeared in book form in* A Good Man Is Hard to Find and Other Stories, *published in 1955.*

A Good Man Is Hard to Find

The dragon is by the side of the road, watching those who pass. Beware lest he devour you. We go to the Father of Souls, but it is necessary to pass by the dragon.

St. Cyril of Jerusalem

The grandmother didn't want to go to Florida. She wanted to visit some of her connections in east Tennessee and she was seizing at every chance to change Bailey's mind. Bailey was the son she lived with, her only boy. He was sitting on the edge of his chair at the table, bent over the orange sports section of the *Journal.* "Now look here, Bailey," she said, "see here, read this," and she stood with one hand on her thin hip and the other rattling the newspaper at his bald head. "Here this fellow that calls himself The Misfit is aloose from the Federal Pen and headed toward Florida and you read here what it says he did to these people. Just you read it. I wouldn't take my children in any direction with a criminal like that aloose in it. I couldn't answer to my conscience if I did."

Bailey didn't look up from his reading so she wheeled around then and faced the children's mother, a young woman in slacks, whose face was as broad and innocent as a cabbage and was tied around with a green headkerchief that had two points on the top like a rabbit's ears. She was sitting on the sofa, feeding the baby his apricots out of a jar. "The children have been to Florida before," the old lady said. "You all ought to take them somewhere else for a change so they would see different parts of the world and be broad. They never have been to east Tennessee."

The children's mother didn't seem to hear her but the eight-year-old boy, John Wesley, a stocky child with glasses, said, "If you don't want to go to Florida, why dontcha stay at home?" He and the little girl, June Star, were reading the funny papers on the floor.

"She wouldn't stay at home to be queen for a day," June Star said without raising her yellow head.

"Yes and what would you do if this fellow, The Misfit, caught you?" the grandmother asked.

"I'd smack his face," John Wesley said.

"She wouldn't stay at home for a million bucks," June Star said. "Afraid she'd miss something. She has to go everywhere we go."

"All right, Miss," the grandmother said. "Just remember that the next time you want me to curl your hair."

June Star said her hair was naturally curly.

The next morning the grandmother was the first one in the car, ready to go. She had her big black valise that looked like the head of a hippopotamus in one corner, and underneath it she was hiding a basket with Pitty Sing, the cat, in it. She didn't intend for the cat to be left alone in the house for three days because he would miss her too much and she was afraid he might brush against one of the gas burners and accidentally asphyxiate himself. Her son, Bailey, didn't like to arrive at a motel with a cat.

She sat in the middle of the back seat with John Wesley and June Star on either side of her. Bailey and the children's mother and the baby sat in front and they left Atlanta at eight forty-five with the mileage on the car at 55890. The grandmother wrote this down because she thought it would be interesting to say how many miles they had been when they got back. It took them twenty minutes to reach the outskirts of the city.

The old lady settled herself comfortably, removing her white cotton gloves and putting them up with her purse on the shelf in front of the back window. The children's mother still had on slacks and still had her head tied up in a green kerchief, but the grandmother had on a navy blue straw sailor hat with a bunch of white violets on the brim and a navy blue dress with a small white dot in the print. Her collars and cuffs were white organdy trimmed with lace and at her neckline she had pinned a purple spray of cloth violets containing a sachet. In case of an accident, anyone seeing her dead on the highway would know at once that she was a lady.

She said she thought it was going to be a good day for driving, neither too hot nor too cold, and she cautioned Bailey that the speed limit was fifty-five miles an hour and that the patrolmen hid themselves behind billboards and small clumps of trees and sped out after you before you had a chance to slow down. She pointed out interesting details of the scenery: Stone Mountain; the blue granite that in some places came up to both sides of the highway; the brilliant red clay banks slightly streaked with purple; and the various crops that made rows of green lace-work on the ground. The trees were full of silver-white sunlight and the meanest of them sparkled. The children were reading comic magazines and their mother had gone back to sleep.

"Let's go through Georgia fast so we won't have to look at it much," John Wesley said.

"If I were a little boy," said the grandmother, "I wouldn't talk about my native state that way. Tennessee has the mountains and Georgia has the hills."

"Tennessee is just a hillbilly dumping ground," John Wesley said, "and Georgia is a lousy state too."

"You said it," June Star said.

"In my time," said the grandmother, folding her thin veined fingers, "children were more respectful of their native states and their parents and everything else. People did right then. Oh look at the cute little pickaninny!" she said and pointed to a Negro child standing in the door of a shack. "Wouldn't that make a picture, now?" she asked and they all turned and looked at the little Negro out of the back window. He waved.

"He didn't have any britches on," June Star said.

"He probably didn't have any," the grandmother explained. "Little niggers in the country don't have things like we do. If I could paint, I'd paint that picture," she said.

The children exchanged comic books.

The grandmother offered to hold the baby and the children's mother passed him over the front seat to her. She set him on her knee and bounced him and told him about the things they were passing. She rolled her eyes and screwed up her mouth and stuck her leathery thin face into his smooth bland one. Occasionally he gave her a faraway smile. They passed a large cotton field with five or six graves fenced in the middle of it, like a small island. "Look at the graveyard!" the grandmother said, pointing it out. "That was the old family burying ground. That belonged to the plantation."

"Where's the plantation?" John Wesley asked.

"Gone with the Wind," said the grandmother. "Ha. Ha."

When the children finished all the comic books they had brought, they opened the lunch and ate it. The grandmother ate a peanut butter sandwich and an olive and would not let the children throw the box and the paper napkins out the window. When there was nothing else to do they played a game by choosing a cloud and making the other two guess what shape it suggested. John Wesley took one the shape of a cow and June Star guessed a cow and John Wesley said, no, an automobile, and June Star said he didn't play fair, and they began to slap each other over the grandmother.

The grandmother said she would tell them a story if they would keep quiet. When she told a story, she rolled her eyes and waved her head and was very dramatic. She said once when she was a maiden lady she had been courted by a Mr. Edgar Atkins Teagarden from Jasper, Georgia. She said he was a very good-looking man and a gentleman and that he brought her a watermelon every Saturday afternoon with his initials cut in it, E. A. T. Well, one Saturday, she said, Mr. Teagarden brought the watermelon and there was nobody at home and he left it on the front porch and returned in his buggy to Jasper, but she never got the watermelon, she said, because a nigger boy ate it when he saw the initials, E. A. T.! This story tickled John Wesley's funny bone and he giggled and giggled but June Star didn't think it was any good. She said she wouldn't marry a man that just brought her a watermelon on Saturday. The grandmother said she would have done well to marry Mr. Teagarden because he was a gentleman and had bought Coca-Cola stock when it first came out and that he had died only a few years ago, a very wealthy man.

They stopped at The Tower for barbecued sandwiches. The Tower was a part stucco and part wood filling station and dance hall set in a clearing outside of Timothy. A fat man named Red Sammy Butts ran it and there were signs stuck here and there on the building and for miles up and down the highway saying, TRY RED SAMMY'S FAMOUS BARBECUE. NONE LIKE FAMOUS RED SAMMY'S! RED SAM! THE FAT BOY WITH THE HAPPY LAUGH. A VETERAN! RED SAMMY'S YOUR MAN!

Red Sammy was lying on the bare ground outside The Tower with his head under a truck while a gray monkey about a foot high, chained to a small chinaberry tree, chattered nearby. The monkey sprang back into the tree and got on the highest limb as soon as he saw the children jump out of the car and run toward him.

Inside, The Tower was a long dark room with a counter at one end and tables at the other and dancing space in the middle. They all sat down at a board table next to the nickelodeon and Red Sam's wife, a tall burnt-brown woman with hair and eyes lighter than her skin, came and took their order. The children's mother put a dime in the machine and played "The Tennessee Waltz," and the grandmother said that tune always made her want to dance. She asked Bailey if he would like to dance but he only glared at her. He didn't have a naturally sunny disposition like she did and trips made him nervous. The grandmother's brown eyes were very bright. She swayed her head from side to side and pretended she was dancing in her chair. June Star said play something she could tap to so the children's mother put in another dime and played a fast number and June Star stepped out onto the dance floor and did her tap routine.

"Ain't she cute?" Red Sam's wife said, leaning over the counter. "Would you like to come be my little girl?"

"No I certainly wouldn't," June Star said. "I wouldn't live in a broken-down place like this for a million bucks!" and she ran back to the table.

"Ain't she cute?" the woman repeated, stretching her mouth politely.

"Aren't you ashamed?" hissed the grandmother.

Red Sam came in and told his wife to quit lounging on the counter and hurry up with these people's order. His khaki trousers reached just to his hip bones and his stomach hung over them like a sack of meal swaying under his shirt. He came over and sat down at a table nearby and let out a combination sigh and yodel. "You can't win," he said. "You can't win," and he wiped his sweating red face off with a gray handkerchief. "These days you don't know who to trust," he said. "Ain't that the truth?"

"People are certainly not nice like they used to be," said the grandmother.

"Two fellers come in here last week," Red Sammy said, "driving a Chrysler. It was a old beat-up car but it was a good one and these boys looked all right to me. Said they worked at the mill and you know I let them fellers charge the gas they bought? Now why did I do that?"

"Because you're a good man!" the grandmother said at once.

"Yes'm, I suppose so," Red Sam said as if he were struck with this answer.

His wife brought the orders, carrying the five plates all at once without a tray, two in each hand and one balanced on her arm. "It isn't a soul in this green world of God's that you can trust," she said. "And I don't count nobody out of that, not nobody," she repeated, looking at Red Sammy.

"Did you read about that criminal, The Misfit, that's escaped?" asked the grandmother.

"I wouldn't be a bit surprised if he didn't attack this place right here," said the woman. "If he hears about it being here, I wouldn't be none surprised to see him. If he hears it's two cent in the cash register, I wouldn't be a tall surprised if he. . . ."

"That'll do," Red Sam said. "Go bring these people their Co'-Colas," and the woman went off to get the rest of the order.

"A good man is hard to find," Red Sammy said. "Everything is getting terrible. I remember the day you could go off and leave your screen door unlatched. Not no more."

He and the grandmother discussed better times. The old lady said that in her opinion Europe was entirely to blame for the way things were now. She said the way Europe acted you would think we were made of money and Red Sam said it was no use talking about it, she was exactly right. The children ran outside into the white sunlight and looked at the monkey in the lacy chinaberry tree. He was busy catching fleas on himself and biting each one carefully between his teeth as if it were a delicacy.

They drove off again into the hot afternoon. The grandmother took cat naps and woke up every few minutes with her own snoring. Outside of Toombsboro she woke up and recalled an old plantation that she had visited in this neighborhood once when she was a young lady. She said the house had six white columns across the front and that there was an avenue of oaks leading up to it and two little wooden trellis arbors on either side in front where you sat down with your suitor after a stroll in the garden. She recalled exactly which road to turn off to get to it. She knew that Bailey would not be willing to lose any time looking at an old house, but the more she talked about it, the more she wanted to see it once again and find out if the little twin arbors were still standing. "There was a secret panel in this house," she said craftily, not telling the truth but wishing that she were, "and the story went that all the family silver was hidden in it when Sherman came through but it was never found. . . ."

"Hey!" John Wesley said. "Let's go see it! We'll find it! We'll poke all the woodwork and find it! Who lives there? Where do you turn off at? Hey Pop, can't we turn off there?"

"We never have seen a house with a secret panel!" June Star shrieked. "Let's go to the house with the secret panel! Hey Pop, can't we go see the house with the secret panel!"

"It's not far from here, I know," the grandmother said. "It won't take over twenty minutes."

Bailey was looking straight ahead. His jaw was as rigid as a horseshoe. "No." he said.

The children began to yell and scream that they wanted to see the house with the secret panel. John Wesley kicked the back of the front seat and June Star hung over her mother's shoulder and whined desperately into her ear that they never had any fun even on their vacation, that they could never do what THEY wanted to do. The baby began to scream and John Wesley kicked the back of the seat so hard that his father could feel the blows in his kidney.

"All right!" he shouted and drew the car to a stop at the side of the road. "Will you all shut up? Will you all just shut up for one second? If you don't shut up, we won't go anywhere."

"It would be very educational for them," the grandmother murmured.

"All right," Bailey said, "but get this: this is the only time we're going to stop for anything like this. This is the one and only time."

"The dirt road that you have to turn down is about a mile back," the grandmother directed. "I marked it when we passed."

"A dirt road," Bailey groaned.

After they had turned around and were headed toward the dirt road, the grandmother recalled other points about the house, the beautiful glass over the front doorway and the candle-lamp in the hall. John Wesley said that the secret panel was probably in the fireplace.

"You can't go inside this house," Bailey said. "You don't know who lives there."

"While you all talk to the people in front, I'll run around behind and get in a window," John Wesley suggested.

"We'll all stay in the car," his mother said.

They turned onto the dirt road and the car raced roughly along in a swirl of pink dust. The grandmother recalled the times when there were no paved roads and thirty miles was a day's journey. The dirt road was hilly and there were sudden washes in it and sharp curves on dangerous embankments. All at once they would be on a hill, looking down over the blue tops of trees for miles around, then the next minute, they would be in a red depression with the dust-coated trees looking down on them.

"This place had better turn up in a minute," Bailey said, "or I'm going to turn around."

The road looked as if no one had traveled on it for months.

"It's not much farther," the grandmother said and just as she said it, a horrible thought came to her. The thought was so embarrassing that she turned red in the face and her eyes dilated and her feet jumped up, upsetting her valise in the corner. The instant the valise moved, the newspaper top she had over the basket under it rose with a snarl and Pitty Sing, the cat, sprang onto Bailey's shoulder.

The children were thrown to the floor and their mother, clutching the baby was thrown out the door onto the ground; the old lady was thrown into the front seat. The car turned over once and landed right-side-up in a gulch off the side of the road. Bailey remained in the driver's seat with the cat—gray-striped with a broad white face and an orange nose—clinging to his neck like a caterpillar.

As soon as the children saw they could move their arms and legs, they scrambled out of the car, shouting, "We've had an ACCIDENT!" The grandmother was curled up under the dashboard, hoping she was injured so that Bailey's wrath would not come down on her all at once. The horrible thought she had before the accident was that the house she had remembered so vividly was not in Georgia but in Tennessee.

Bailey removed the cat from his neck with both hands and flung it out the window against the side of a pine tree. Then he got out of the car and started looking for the children's mother. She was sitting against the side of the red gutted ditch, holding the screaming baby, but she only had a cut down her face and a broken shoulder. "We've had an ACCIDENT!" the children screamed in a frenzy of delight.

"But nobody's killed," June Star said with disappointment as the grandmother limped out of the car, her hat still pinned to her head but the broken front brim standing up at a jaunty angle and the violet spray hanging off the side. They all sat down in the ditch, except the children, to recover from the shock. They were all shaking.

"Maybe a car will come along," said the children's mother hoarsely.

"I believe I have injured an organ," said the grandmother, pressing her side, but no one answered her. Bailey's teeth were clattering. He had on a yellow sport shirt with bright blue parrots designed in it and his face was as yellow as the shirt. The grandmother decided that she would not mention that the house was in Tennessee.

The road was about ten feet above and they could only see the tops of the trees on the other side of it. Behind the ditch they were sitting in there were more woods, tall and dark and deep. In a few minutes they saw a car some distance away on top of a hill, coming slowly as if the occupants were watching them. The grandmother stood up and waved both arms dramatically to attract their attention. The car continued to come on slowly, disappeared around a bend and appeared again, moving even slower, on top of the hill they had gone over. It was a big black battered hearse-like automobile. There were three men in it.

It came to a stop just over them and for some minutes, the driver looked down with a steady expressionless gaze to where they were sitting, and didn't speak. Then he turned his head and muttered something to the other two and they got out. One was a fat boy in black trousers and a red sweat shirt with a silver stallion embossed on the front of it. He moved around on the right side of them and stood staring, his mouth partly open in a kind of loose grin. The other had on khaki pants and a blue striped coat and a gray hat pulled very low, hiding most of his face. He came around slowly on the left side. Neither spoke.

The driver got out of the car and stood by the side of it, looking down at them. He was an older man than the other two. His hair was just beginning to gray and he wore silver-rimmed spectacles that gave him a scholarly look. He had a long creased face and didn't have on any shirt or undershirt. He had on blue jeans that were too tight for him and was holding a black hat and a gun. The two boys also had guns.

"We've had an ACCIDENT!" the children screamed.

The grandmother had the peculiar feeling that the bespectacled man was someone she knew. His face was as familiar to her as if she had known him all her life but she could not recall who he was. He moved away from the car and began to come down the embankment, placing his feet carefully so that he wouldn't slip. He had on tan and white shoes and no socks, and his ankles were red and thin. "Good afternoon," he said. "I see you all had you a little spill."

"We turned over twice!" said the grandmother.

"Oncet," he corrected. "We seen it happen. Try their car and see will it run, Hiram," he said quietly to the boy with the gray hat.

"What you got that gun for?" John Wesley asked. "Whatcha gonna do with that gun?"

"Lady," the man said to the children's mother, "would you mind calling them children to sit down by you? Children make me nervous. I want all you all to sit down right together there where you're at."

"What are you telling US what to do for?" June Star asked.

Behind them the line of woods gaped like a dark open mouth. "Come here," said the mother.

"Look here now," Bailey said suddenly, "we're in a predicament! We're in. . . ."

The grandmother shrieked. She scrambled to her feet and stood staring. "You're The Misfit!" she said. "I recognized you at once!"

"Yes'm," the man said, smiling slightly as if he were pleased in spite of himself to be known, "but it would have been better for all of you, lady, if you hadn't of reckernized me."

Bailey turned his head sharply and said something to his mother that shocked even the children. The old lady began to cry and The Misfit reddened.

"Lady," he said, "don't you get upset. Sometimes a man says things he don't mean. I don't reckon he meant to talk to you that-away."

"You wouldn't shoot a lady, would you?" the grandmother said and removed a clean handkerchief from her cuff and began to slap at her eyes with it.

The Misfit pointed the toe of his shoe into the ground and made a little hole and then covered it up again. "I would hate to have to," he said.

"Listen," the grandmother almost screamed, "I know you're a good man. You don't look a bit like you have common blood. I know you must come from nice people!"

"Yes mam," he said, "finest people in the world." When he smiled he showed a row of strong white teeth. "God never made a finer woman than my mother and my daddy's heart was pure gold," he said. The boy with the red sweat shirt had come around behind them and was standing with his gun at his hip. The Misfit squatted down on the ground. "Watch them children, Bobby Lee," he said. "You know they make me nervous." He looked at the six of them huddled together in front of him and he seemed to be embarrassed as if he couldn't think of anything to say. "Ain't a cloud in the sky," he remarked, looking up at it. "Don't see no sun but don't see no cloud neither."

"Yes, it's a beautiful day," said the grandmother. "Listen," she said, "you shouldn't call yourself The Misfit because I know you're a good man at heart. I can just look at you and tell."

"Hush!" Bailey yelled. "Hush! Everybody shut up and let me handle this!" He was squatting in the position of a runner about to sprint forward but he didn't move.

"I pre-chate that, lady," The Misfit said and drew a little circle in the ground with the butt of his gun.

"It'll take a half a hour to fix this here car," Hiram called, looking over the raised hood of it.

"Well, first you and Bobby Lee get him and that little boy to step over yonder with you." The Misfit said, pointing to Bailey and John Wesley, "The boys want to ast you something," he said to Bailey. "Would you mind stepping back in them woods there with them?"

"Listen," Bailey began, "we're in a terrible predicament! Nobody realizes what this is," and his voice cracked. His eyes were as blue and intense as the parrots in his shirt and he remained perfectly still.

The grandmother reached up to adjust her hat brim as if she were going to the woods with him but it came off in her hand. She stood staring at it and after a second she let it fall to the ground. Hiram pulled Bailey up by the arm as if he were assisting an old man. John Wesley caught hold of his father's hand and Bobby Lee followed. They went off toward the woods and just as they reached the dark edge, Bailey turned and supporting himself against a gray naked pine trunk, he shouted, "I'll be back in a minute, Mamma, wait on me!"

"Come back this instant!" his mother shrilled but they all disappeared into the woods.

"Bailey Boy!" the grandmother called in a tragic voice but she found she was looking at The Misfit squatting on the ground in front of her. "I just know you're a good man," she said desperately. "You're not a bit common!"

"Nome, I ain't a good man," The Misfit said after a second as if he had considered her statement carefully, "but I ain't the worst in the world neither. My daddy said I was a different breed of dog from my brothers and sisters. 'You know,' Daddy said, 'it's some that can live their whole life out without asking about it and it's others has to know why it is, and this boy is one of the latters. He's going to be into everything!'" He put on his black hat and looked up suddenly and then away deep into the woods as if he were embarrassed again. "I'm sorry I don't have on a shirt before you ladies," he said, hunching his shoulders slightly. "We buried our clothes that we had on when we escaped and we're just making do until we can get better. We borrowed these from some folks we met," he explained.

"That's perfectly all right," the grandmother said. "Maybe Bailey has an extra shirt in his suitcase."

"I'll look and see terrectly," The Misfit said.

"Where are they taking him?" the children's mother screamed.

"Daddy was a card himself," The Misfit said. "You couldn't put anything over on him. He never got in trouble with the Authorities though. Just had the knack of handling them."

"You could be honest too if you'd only try," said the grandmother. "Think how wonderful it would be to settle down and live a comfortable life and not have to think about somebody chasing you all the time."

The Misfit kept scratching in the ground with the butt of his gun as if he were thinking about it. "Yes'm, somebody is always after you," he murmured.

The grandmother noticed how thin his shoulder blades were just behind his hat because she was standing up looking down at him. "Do you ever pray?" she asked.

He shook his head. All she saw was the black hat wiggle between his shoulder blades. "Nome," he said.

There was a pistol shot from the woods, followed closely by another. Then silence. The old lady's head jerked around. She could hear the wind move through the tree tops like a long satisfied insuck of breath. "Bailey Boy!" she called.

"I was a gospel singer for a while," The Misfit said. "I been most everything. Been in the arm service, both land and sea, at home and abroad, been twict married, been an undertaker, been with the railroads, plowed Mother Earth, been in a tornado, seen a man burnt alive oncet," and he looked up at the children's mother and the little girl who were sitting close together, their faces white and their eyes glassy; "I even seen a woman flogged," he said.

"Pray, pray," the grandmother began, "pray, pray. . . ."

"I never was a bad boy that I remember of," The Misfit said in an almost dreamy voice, "but somewheres along the line I done something wrong and got sent to the penitentiary. I was buried alive," and he looked up and held her attention to him by a steady stare.

"That's when you should have started to pray," she said. "What did you do to get sent to the penitentiary, that first time?"

"Turn to the right, it was a wall," The Misfit said, looking up again at the cloudless sky. "Turn to the left, it was a wall. Look up it was a ceiling, look down it was a floor. I forgot what I done, lady. I set there and set there, trying to remember what it was I done and I ain't recalled it to this day. Oncet in a while, I would think it was coming to me, but it never come."

"Maybe they put you in by mistake," the old lady said vaguely.

"Nome," he said. "It wasn't no mistake. They had the papers on me."

"You must have stolen something," she said.

The Misfit sneered slightly. "Nobody had nothing I wanted," he said. "It was a head-doctor at the penitentiary said what I had done was kill my daddy but I known that for a lie. My daddy died in nineteen ought nineteen of the epidemic flu and I never had a thing to do with it. He was buried in the Mount Hopewell Baptist churchyard and you can see for yourself."

"If you would pray," the old lady said, "Jesus would help you."

"That's right," The Misfit said.

"Well then, why don't you pray?" she asked trembling with delight suddenly.

"I don't want no hep," he said. "I'm doing all right by myself."

Bobby Lee and Hiram came ambling back from the woods. Bobby Lee was dragging a yellow shirt with bright blue parrots in it.

"Throw me that shirt, Bobby Lee," The Misfit said. The shirt came flying at him and landed on his shoulder and he put it on. The grandmother couldn't name what the shirt reminded her of. "No, lady," The Misfit said while he was buttoning it up, "I found out the crime don't matter. You can do one thing or you can do another, kill a man or take a tire off his car, because sooner or later you're going to forget what it was you done and just be punished for it."

The children's mother had begun to make heaving noises as if she couldn't get her breath. "Lady," he asked, "would you and that little girl like to step off yonder with Bobby Lee and Hiram and join your husband?"

"Yes, thank you," the mother said faintly. Her left arm dangled helplessly and she was holding the baby, who had gone to sleep, in the other. "Hep that lady up, Hiram," The Misfit said as she struggled to climb out of the ditch, "and Bobby Lee, you hold onto that little girl's hand."

"I don't want to hold hands with him," June Star said. "He reminds me of a pig."

The fat boy blushed and laughed and caught her by the arm and pulled her off into the woods after Hiram and her mother.

Alone with The Misfit, the grandmother found that she had lost her voice. There was not a cloud in the sky nor any sun. There was nothing around her but woods. She wanted to tell him that he must pray. She opened and closed her mouth several times before anything came out. Finally she found herself saying, "Jesus, Jesus," meaning, Jesus will help you, but the way she was saying it, it sounded as if she might be cursing.

"Yes'm," The Misfit said as if he agreed. "Jesus thown everything off balance. It was the same case with Him as with me except He hadn't committed any crime and they could prove I had committed one because they had the papers on me. Of course," he said, "they never shown me my papers. That's why I sign myself now. I said long ago, you get your signature and sign everything you do and keep a copy of it. Then you'll know what you done and you can hold up the crime to the punishment and see do they match and in the end you'll have something to prove you ain't been treated right. I call myself The Misfit," he said, "because I can't make what all I done wrong fit what all I gone through in punishment."

There was a piercing scream from the woods, followed closely by a pistol report. "Does it seem right to you, lady, that one is punished a heap and another ain't punished at all?"

"Jesus!" the old lady cried. "You've got good blood! I know you wouldn't shoot a lady! I know you come from nice people! Pray! Jesus, you ought not to shoot a lady. I'll give you all the money I've got!"

"Lady," The Misfit said, looking beyond her far into the woods, "there never was a body that give the undertaker a tip."

There were two more pistol reports and the grandmother raised her head like a parched old turkey hen crying for water and called, "Bailey Boy, Bailey Boy!" as if her heart would break.

"Jesus was the only One that ever raised the dead," The Misfit continued, "and He shouldn't have done it. He thrown everything off balance. If He did what He said, then it's nothing for you to do but throw away everything and follow Him, and if He didn't, then it's nothing for you to do but enjoy the few minutes you got left the best you can—by killing somebody or burning down his house or doing some other meanness to him. No pleasure but meanness," he said and his voice had become almost a snarl.

"Maybe He didn't raise the dead," the old lady mumbled, not knowing what she was saying and feeling so dizzy that she sank down in the ditch with her legs twisted under her.

"I wasn't there so I can't say He didn't," The Misfit said. "I wisht I had of been there," he said, hitting the ground with his fist. "It ain't right I wasn't there because if I had of been there I would of known. Listen lady," he said in a high voice, "if I had of been there I would of known and I wouldn't be like I am now." His voice seemed about to crack and the grandmother's head cleared for an instant. She saw the man's face twisted close to her own as if he was going to cry and she murmured, "Why you're one of my babies. You're one of my own children!" She reached out and touched him on the shoulder. The Misfit sprang back as if a snake had bitten him and shot her three times through the chest. Then he put his gun down on the ground and took off his glasses and began to clean them.

Hiram and Bobby Lee returned from the woods and stood over the ditch, looking down at the grandmother who half sat and half lay in a puddle of blood with her legs crossed under her like a child's and her face smiling up at the cloudless sky.

Without his glasses, The Misfit's eyes were red-rimmed and pale and defenseless-looking. "Take her off and throw her where you thrown the others," he said, picking up the cat that was rubbing itself against his leg.

"She was a talker, wasn't she?" Bobby Lee said, sliding down the ditch with a yodel.

"She would of been a good woman," The Misfit said, "if it had been somebody there to shoot her every minute of her life."

"Some fun!" Bobby Lee said.

"Shut up, Bobby Lee," The Misfit said. "It's no real pleasure in life."

Edith Wharton

Edith Wharton was born into an upper-class New York family in 1862. Over the course of her career, she published eighty-six short stories, several volumes of criticism and essays, an autobiography, A Backward Glance *(1934), and fifteen major novels, including* The House of Mirth *(1905) and* The Custom of the Country *(1913). Her novel* The Age of Innocence *received the Pulitzer Prize in 1921, and Wharton herself was the first woman to be awarded the Gold Medal of the National Institute of Arts and Letters. "Roman Fever" was first published in* Liberty *magazine in 1934.*

Roman Fever

I

From the table at which they had been lunching two American ladies of ripe but well-cared-for middle age moved across the lofty terrace of the Roman restaurant and, leaning on its parapet, looked first at each other, and then down on the outspread glories of the Palatine and the Forum, with the same expression of vague but benevolent approval.

As they leaned there a girlish voice echoed up gaily from the stairs leading to the court below. "Well, come along, then," it cried, not to them but to an invisible companion, "and let's leave the young things to their knitting" and a voice as fresh laughed back: "Oh, look here, Babs, not actually *knitting*—" "Well, I mean figuratively," rejoined the first. "After all, we haven't left our poor parents much else to do . . ." and at that point the turn of the stairs engulfed the dialogue.

The two ladies looked at each other again, this time with a tinge of smiling embarrassment, and the smaller and paler one shook her head and colored slightly.

"Barbara!" she murmured, sending an unheard rebuke after the mocking voice in the stairway.

The other lady, who was fuller, and higher in color, with a small determined nose supported by vigorous black eyebrows, gave a good-humored laugh. "That's what our daughters think of us!"

Her companion replied by a deprecating gesture. "Not of us individually. We must remember that. It's just the collective modern idea of Mothers. And you see—" Half guiltily she drew from her handsomely mounted black hand-bag a twist of crimson silk run through by two fine knitting needles. "One never knows," she murmured. "The new system has certainly given us a good deal of time to kill; and sometimes I get tired just looking—even at this." Her gesture was now addressed to the stupendous scene at their feet.

The dark lady laughed again, and they both relapsed upon the view, contemplating it in silence, with a sort of diffused serenity which might have been borrowed from the spring effulgence of the Roman skies. The luncheon-hour was long past, and the two had their end of the vast terrace to themselves. At its opposite extremity a few groups, detained by a lingering look at the outspread city, were gathering up guide-books and fumbling for tips. The last of them scattered, and the two ladies were alone on the air-washed height.

"Well, I don't see why we shouldn't just stay here," said Mrs. Slade, the lady of the high color and energetic brows. Two derelict basket-chairs stood near, and she pushed them into the angle of the parapet, and settled herself in one, her gaze upon the Palatine. "After all, it's still the most beautiful view in the world."

"It always will be, to me," assented her friend Mrs. Ansley, with so slight a stress on the "me" that Mrs. Slade, though she noticed it, wondered if it were not merely accidental, like the random underlinings of old-fashioned letter-writers.

"Grace Ansley was always old-fashioned," she thought; and added aloud, with a retrospective smile: "It's a view we've both been familiar with for a good many years. When we first met here we were younger than our girls are now. You remember?"

"Oh, yes, I remember," murmured Mrs. Ansley, with the same undefinable stress—"There's that head-waiter wondering," she interpolated. She was evidently far less sure than her companion of herself and of her rights in the world.

"I'll cure him of wondering," said Mrs. Slade, stretching her hand toward a bag as discreetly opulent-looking as Mrs. Ansley's. Signing to the head-waiter, she explained that she and her friend were old lovers of Rome, and would like to spend the end of the afternoon looking down on the view—that is, if it did not disturb the service? The head-waiter, bowing over her gratuity, assured her that the ladies were most welcome, and would be still more so if they would condescend to remain for dinner. A full moon night, they would remember. . . .

Mrs. Slade's black brows drew together, as though references to the moon were out-of-place and even unwelcome. But she smiled away her frown as the head-waiter retreated. "Well, why not? We might do worse. There's no knowing, I suppose, when the girls will be back. Do you even know back from *where?* I don't!"

Mrs. Ansley again colored slightly. "I think those young Italian aviators we met at the Embassy invited them to fly to Tarquinia for tea. I suppose they'll want to wait and fly back by moonlight."

"Moonlight—moonlight! What a part it still plays. Do you suppose they're as sentimental as we were?"

"I've come to the conclusion that I don't in the least know what they are," said Mrs. Ansley. "And perhaps we didn't know much more about each other."

"No; perhaps we didn't."

Her friend gave her a shy glance. "I never should have supposed you were sentimental, Alida."

"Well, perhaps I wasn't." Mrs. Slade drew her lids together in retrospect; and for a few moments the two ladies, who had been intimate since childhood, reflected how little they knew each other. Each one, of course, had a label ready to attach to the other's name; Mrs. Delphin Slade, for instance, would have told herself, or any one who asked her, that Mrs. Horace Ansley, twenty-five years ago, had been exquisitely lovely—no, you wouldn't believe it, would you? . . . though, of course, still charming, distinguished. . . . Well, as a girl she had been exquisite; far more beautiful than her daughter Barbara, though certainly Babs, according to the new standards at any rate, was more effective— had more *edge,* as they say. Funny where she got it, with those two nullities as parents. Yes; Horace Ansley was—well, just the duplicate of his wife. Museum specimens of old New York. Good-looking, irreproachable, exemplary. Mrs. Slade and Mrs. Ansley had lived opposite each other—actually as well as figuratively— for years. When the drawing-room curtains in No. 20 East 73rd Street were renewed, No. 23, across the way, was always aware of it. And of all the movings, buyings, travels, anniversaries, ill-nesses—the tame chronicle of an estimable pair. Little of it es-caped Mrs. Slade. But she had grown bored with it by the time her husband made his big *coup* in Wall Street, and when they bought in upper Park Avenue had already begun to think: "I'd rather live opposite a speak-easy for a change; at least one might see it raided." The idea of seeing Grace raided was so amusing that (before the move) she launched it at a woman's lunch. It made a hit, and went the rounds—she sometimes wondered if it had crossed the street, and reached Mrs. Ansley. She hoped not, but didn't much mind. Those were the days when respectability was at a discount, and it did the irreproachable no harm to laugh at them a little.

A few years later, and not many months apart, both ladies lost their husbands. There was an appropriate exchange of wreaths and condolences, and a brief renewal of intimacy in the half-shadow of their mourning; and now, after another interval, they had run across each other in Rome, at the same hotel, each of them the mod-est appendage of a salient daughter. The similarity of their lot had again drawn them together, lending itself to mild jokes, and the mu-tual confession that, if in old days it must have been tiring to "keep up" with daughters, it was now, at times, a little dull not to.

No doubt, Mrs. Slade reflected, she felt her unemployment more than poor Grace ever would. It was a big drop from being the wife of Delphin Slade to being his widow. She had always regarded herself (with a certain conjugal pride) as his equal in social gifts, as contributing her full share to the making of the exceptional couple they were: but the difference after his death was irremediable. As the wife of the famous corporation lawyer, always with an international case or two on hand, every day brought its exciting and unexpected obligation: the impromptu entertaining of eminent colleagues from abroad, the hurried dashes on legal business to London, Paris or Rome, where the entertaining was so handsomely reciprocated; the amusement of hearing in her wake: "What, that handsome woman with the good clothes and the eyes is Mrs. Slade—*the* Slade's wife? Really? Generally the wives of celebrities are such frumps."

Yes; being *the* Slade's widow was a dullish business after that. In living up to such a husband all her faculties had been engaged; now she had only her daughter to live up to, for the son who seemed to have inherited his father's gifts had died suddenly in boyhood. She had fought through that agony because her husband was there, to be helped and to help; now, after the father's death, the thought of the boy had become unbearable. There was nothing left but to mother her daughter; and dear Jenny was such a perfect daughter that she needed no excessive mothering. "Now with Babs Ansley I don't know that I *should* be so quiet," Mrs. Slade sometimes half-enviously reflected; but Jenny, who was younger than her brilliant friend, was that rare accident, an extremely pretty girl who somehow made youth and prettiness seem as safe as their absence. It was all perplexing—and to Mrs. Slade a little boring. She wished that Jenny would fall in love—with the wrong man, even; that she might have to be watched, out-manœuvred, rescued. And instead, it was Jenny who watched her mother, kept her out of draughts, made sure that she had taken her tonic. . . .

Mrs. Ansley was much less articulate than her friend, and her mental portrait of Mrs. Slade was slighter, and drawn with fainter touches. "Alida Slade's awfully brilliant; but not as brilliant as she thinks," would have summed it up; though she would have added, for the enlightenment of strangers, that Mrs. Slade had been an extremely dashing girl; much more so than her daughter, who was pretty, of course, and clever in a way, but had none of her mother's—well, "vividness," someone had once called it. Mrs. Ansley would take up current words like this, and cite them in quotation marks, as unheard-of audacities. No; Jenny was not like her mother. Sometimes Mrs. Ansley thought Alida Slade was disappointed; on the whole she had had a sad life. Full of failures and mistakes; Mrs. Ansley had always been rather sorry for her. . . .

So these two ladies visualized each other, each through the wrong end of her little telescope.

II

For a long time they continued to sit side by side without speaking. It seemed as though, to both, there was a relief in laying down their somewhat futile activities in the presence of the vast Memento Mori which faced them. Mrs. Slade sat quite still, her eyes fixed on the golden slope of the Palace of the Caesars, and after a while Mrs. Ansley ceased to fidget with her bag, and she too sank into meditation. Like many intimate friends, the two ladies had never before had occasion to be silent together, and Mrs. Ansley was slightly embarrassed by what seemed, after so many years, a new stage in their intimacy, and one with which she did not yet know how to deal.

Suddenly the air was full of that deep clangor of bells which periodically covers Rome with a roof of silver. Mrs. Slade glanced at her wristwatch. "Five o'clock already," she said, as though surprised.

Mrs. Ansley suggested interrogatively: "There's bridge at the Embassy at five." For a long time Mrs. Slade did not answer. She appeared to be lost in contemplation, and Mrs. Ansley thought the remark had escaped her. But after a while she said, as if speaking out of a dream: "Bridge, did you say? Not unless you want to. . . . But I don't think I will, you know."

"Oh, no," Mrs. Ansley hastened to assure her. "I don't care to at all. It's so lovely here; and so full of old memories, as you say." She settled herself in her chair, and almost furtively drew forth her knitting. Mrs. Slade took sideway note of this activity, but her own beautifully cared-for hands remained motionless on her knee.

"I was just thinking," she said slowly, "what different things Rome stands for to each generation of travelers. To our grandmothers, Roman fever; to our mothers, sentimental danger—how we used to be guarded!—to our daughters, no more dangers than the middle of Main Street. They don't know it—but how much they're missing!"

The long golden light was beginning to pale, and Mrs. Ansley lifted her knitting a little closer to her eyes. "Yes; how we were guarded!"

"I always used to think," Mrs. Slade continued, "that our mothers had a much more difficult job than our grandmothers. When Roman fever stalked the streets it must have been comparatively easy to gather in the girls at the danger hour; but when you and I were young, with such beauty calling us, and the spice of disobedience thrown in, and no worse risk than catching cold during the cool hour after sunset, the mothers used to be put to it to keep us in—didn't they?"

She turned again toward Mrs. Ansley, but the latter had reached a delicate point in her knitting. "One, two, three—slip two; yes, they must have been," she assented, without looking up.

Mrs. Slade's eyes rested on her with a deepened attention. "She can knit—in the face of *this!* How like her. . . ."

Mrs. Slade leaned back, brooding, her eyes ranging from the ruins which faced her to the long green hollow of the Forum, the fading glow of the church fronts beyond it, and the outlying immensity of the Colosseum. Suddenly she thought: "It's all very well to say that our girls have done away with sentiment and moonlight. But if Babs Ansley isn't out to catch that young aviator—the one who's a Marchese—then I don't know anything. And Jenny has no chance beside her. I know that too. I wonder if that's why Grace Ansley likes the two girls to go everywhere together? My poor Jenny as a foil—!" Mrs. Slade gave a hardly audible laugh, and at the sound Mrs. Ansley dropped her knitting.

"Yes—?"

"I—oh, nothing. I was only thinking how your Babs carries everything before her. That Campolieri boy is one of the best matches in Rome. Don't look so innocent, my dear—you know he is. And I was wondering, ever so respectfully, you understand . . . wondering how two such exemplary characters as you and Horace had managed to produce anything quite so dynamic." Mrs. Slade laughed again, with a touch of asperity.

Mrs. Ansley's hands lay inert across her needles. She looked straight out at the great accumulated wreckage of passion and

splendor at her feet. But her small profile was almost expressionless. At length she said: "I think you overrate Babs, my dear."

Mrs. Slade's tone grew easier. "No; I don't. I appreciate her. And
perhaps envy you. Oh, my girl's perfect; if I were a chronic invalid
I'd—well, I think I'd rather be in Jenny's hands. There must be
times . . . but there! I always wanted a brilliant daughter . . . and
never quite understood why I got an angel instead."

Mrs. Ansley echoed her laugh in a faint murmur. "Babs is an
angel too."

"Of course—of course! But she's got rainbow wings. Well,
they're wandering by the sea with their young men; and here we
sit . . . and it all brings back the past a little too acutely."

Mrs. Ansley had resumed her knitting. One might almost have
imagined (if one had known her less well, Mrs. Slade reflected)
that, for her also, too many memories rose from the lengthening
shadows of those august ruins. But no; she was simply absorbed
in her work. What was there for her to worry about? She knew that
Babs would almost certainly come back engaged to the extremely
eligible Campolieri. "And she'll sell the New York house, and settle down near them in Rome, and never be in their way . . . she's
much too tactful. But she'll have an excellent cook, and just the
right people in for bridge and cocktails . . . and a perfectly peaceful old age among her grandchildren."

Mrs. Slade broke off this prophetic flight with a recoil of self-
disgust. There was no one of whom she had less right to think un-
kindly than of Grace Ansley. Would she never cure herself of
envying her? Perhaps she had begun too long ago.

She stood up and leaned against the parapet, filling her troubled
eyes with the tranquilizing magic of the hour. But instead of tranquilizing her the sight seemed to increase her exasperation. Her
gaze turned toward the Colosseum. Already its golden flank was
drowned in purple shadow, and above it the sky curved crystal
clear, without light or color. It was the moment when afternoon
and evening hang balanced in mid-heaven.

Mrs. Slade turned back and laid her hand on her friend's arm.
The gesture was so abrupt that Mrs. Ansley looked up, startled.

"The sun's set. You're not afraid, my dear?"

"Afraid—?"

"Of Roman fever or pneumonia? I remember how ill you were
that winter. As a girl you had a very delicate throat, hadn't you?"

"Oh, we're all right up here. Down below, in the Forum, it does get deathly cold, all of a sudden . . . but not here."

"Ah, of course, you know because you had to be so careful." Mrs. Slade turned back to the parapet. She thought: "I must make one more effort not to hate her." Aloud she said: "Whenever I look at the Forum from up here I remember that story about a great-aunt of yours, wasn't she? A dreadfully wicked great-aunt?"

"Oh, yes; Great-aunt Harriet. The one who was supposed to have sent her young sister out to the Forum after sunset to gather a night-blooming flower for her album. All our great-aunts and grandmothers used to have albums of dried flowers."

Mrs. Slade nodded. "But she really sent her because they were in love with the same man—"

"Well, that was the family tradition. They said Aunt Harriet confessed it years afterward. At any rate, the poor little sister caught the fever and died. Mother used to frighten us with the story when we were children."

"And you frightened *me* with it, that winter when you and I were here as girls. The winter I was engaged to Delphin."

Mrs. Ansley gave a faint laugh. "Oh, did I? Really frightened you? I don't believe you're easily frightened."

"Not often; but I was then. I was easily frightened because I was too happy. I wonder if you know what that means?"

"I—yes. . . ." Mrs. Ansley faltered.

"Well, I suppose that was why the story of your wicked aunt made such an impression on me. And I thought: 'There's no more Roman fever, but the Forum is deathly cold after sunset—especially after a hot day. And the Colosseum's even colder and damper.'"

"The Colosseum—?"

"Yes. It wasn't easy to get in, after the gates were locked for the night. Far from easy. Still, in those days it could be managed; it was managed, often. Lovers met there who couldn't meet elsewhere. You knew that?"

"I—I daresay. I don't remember."

"You don't remember? You don't remember going to visit some ruins or other one evening, just after dark, and catching a bad chill? You were supposed to have gone to see the moon rise. People always said that expedition was what caused your illness."

There was a moment's silence; then Mrs. Ansley rejoined: "Did they? It was all so long ago."

"Yes. And you got well again—so it didn't matter. But I suppose it struck your friend—the reason given for your illness, I mean—because everybody knew you were so prudent on account of your throat, and your mother took such care of you. . . . You *had* been out late sight-seeing, hadn't you, that night?"

"Perhaps I had. The most prudent girls aren't always prudent. What made you think of it now?"

Mrs. Slade seemed to have no answer ready. But after a moment she broke out: "Because I simply can't bear it any longer—!"

Mrs. Ansley lifted her head quickly. Her eyes were wide and very pale. "Can't bear what?"

"Why—your not knowing that I've always known why you went."

"Why I went—?"

"Yes. You think I'm bluffing, don't you? Well, you went to meet the man I was engaged to—and I can repeat every word of the letter that took you there."

While Mrs. Slade spoke Mrs. Ansley had risen unsteadily to her feet. Her bag, her knitting and gloves, slid in a panic-stricken heap to the ground. She looked at Mrs. Slade as though she were looking at a ghost.

"No, no—don't," she faltered out.

"Why not? Listen, if you don't believe me. 'My one darling, things can't go on like this. I must see you alone. Come to the Colosseum immediately after dark tomorrow. There will be somebody to let you in. No one whom you need fear will suspect'—but perhaps you've forgotten what the letter said?"

Mrs. Ansley met the challenge with an unexpected composure. Steadying herself against the chair she looked at her friend, and replied: "No; I know it by heart too."

"And the signature? 'Only *your* D.S.' Was that it? I'm right, am I? That was the letter that took you out that evening after dark?"

Mrs. Ansley was still looking at her. It seemed to Mrs. Slade that a slow struggle was going on behind the voluntarily controlled mask of her small quiet face. "I shouldn't have thought she had herself so well in hand," Mrs. Slade reflected, almost resentfully. But at this moment Mrs. Ansley spoke, "I don't know how you knew. I burnt that letter at once."

"Yes; you would, naturally—you're so prudent!" The sneer was open now. "And if you burnt the letter you're wondering how on earth I know what was in it. That's it, isn't it?"

Mrs. Slade waited, but Mrs. Ansley did not speak.

"Well, my dear, I know what was in that letter because I wrote it!"

"You wrote it?"

"Yes."

The two women stood for a minute staring at each other in the last golden light. Then Mrs. Ansley dropped back into her chair. "Oh," she murmured, and covered her face with her hands.

Mrs. Slade waited nervously for another word or movement. None came, and at length she broke out: "I horrify you."

Mrs. Ansley's hands dropped to her knee. The face they uncovered was streaked with tears. "I wasn't thinking of you. I was thinking—it was the only letter I ever had from him!"

"And I wrote it. Yes; I wrote it! But I was the girl he was engaged to. Did you happen to remember that?"

Mrs. Ansley's head dropped again. "I'm not trying to excuse myself. . . . I remembered. . . ."

"And still you went?"

"Still I went."

Mrs. Slade stood looking down on the small bowed figure at her side. The flame of her wrath had already sunk, and she wondered why she had ever thought there would be any satisfaction in inflicting so purposeless a wound on her friend. But she had to justify herself.

"You do understand? I'd found out—and I hated you, hated you. I knew you were in love with Delphin—and I was afraid; afraid of you, of your quiet ways, your sweetness . . . your . . . well, I wanted you out of the way, that's all. Just for a few weeks; just till I was sure of him. So in a blind fury I wrote that letter. . . . I don't know why I'm telling you now."

"I suppose," said Mrs. Ansley slowly, "it's because you've always gone on hating me."

"Perhaps. Or because I wanted to get the whole thing off my mind." She paused. "I'm glad you destroyed the letter. Of course I never thought you'd die."

Mrs. Ansley relapsed into silence, and Mrs. Slade, leaning above her, was conscious of a strange sense of isolation, of being cut off from the warm current of human communion. "You think me a monster!"

"I don't know. . . . It was the only letter I had, and you say he didn't write it?"

"Ah, how you care for him still!"

"I cared for that memory," said Mrs. Ansley.

Mrs. Slade continued to look down on her. She seemed physically reduced by the blow—as if, when she got up, the wind might scatter her like a puff of dust. Mrs. Slade's jealousy suddenly leapt up again at the sight. All these years the woman had been living on that letter. How she must have loved him, to treasure the mere memory of its ashes! The letter of the man her friend was engaged to. Wasn't it she who was the monster?

"You tried your best to get him away from me, didn't you? But you failed; and I kept him. That's all."

"Yes. That's all."

"I wish now I hadn't told you. I'd no idea you'd feel about it as you do; I thought you'd be amused. It all happened so long ago, as you say; and you must do me the justice to remember that I had no reason to think you'd ever taken it seriously. How could I, when you were married to Horace Ansley two months afterward? As soon as you could get out of bed your mother rushed you off to Florence and married you. People were rather surprised—they wondered at its being done so quickly; but I thought I knew. I had an idea you did it out of *pique*—to be able to say you'd got ahead of Delphin and me. Girls have such silly reasons for doing the most serious things. And your marrying so soon convinced me that you'd never really cared."

"Yes. I suppose it would," Mrs. Ansley assented.

The clear heaven overhead was emptied of all its gold. Dusk spread over it, abruptly darkening the Seven Hills. Here and there lights began to twinkle through the foliage at their feet. Steps were coming and going on the deserted terrace—waiters looking out of the doorway at the head of the stairs, then reappearing with trays and napkins and flasks of wine. Tables were moved, chairs straightened. A feeble string of electric lights flickered out. Some vases of faded flowers were carried away, and brought back replenished. A stout lady in a dust-coat suddenly appeared, asking in broken Italian if any one had seen the elastic band which held together her tattered Baedeker. She poked with her stick under the table at which she had lunched, the waiters assisting.

The corner where Mrs. Slade and Mrs. Ansley sat was still shadowy and deserted. For a long time neither of them spoke. At length Mrs. Slade began again: "I suppose I did it as a sort of joke—"

"A joke?"

"Well, girls are ferocious sometimes, you know. Girls in love especially. And I remember laughing to myself all that evening at the idea that you were waiting around there in the dark, dodging out of sight, listening for every sound, trying to get in—Of course I was upset when I heard you were so ill afterward."

Mrs. Ansley had not moved for a long time. But now she turned slowly toward her companion. "But I didn't wait. He'd arranged everything. He was there. We were let in at once," she said.

Mrs. Slade sprang up from her leaning position. "Delphin there? They let you in?—Ah, now you're lying!" she burst out with violence.

Mrs. Ansley's voice grew clearer, and full of surprise. "But of course he was there. Naturally he came—"

"Came? How did he know he'd find you there? You must be raving!"

Mrs. Ansley hesitated, as though reflecting. "But I answered the letter. I told him I'd be there. So he came."

Mrs. Slade flung her hands up to her face. "Oh, God—you answered! I never thought of your answering. . . ."

"It's odd you never thought of it, if you wrote the letter."

"Yes. I was blind with rage."

Mrs. Ansley rose, and drew her fur scarf about her. "It is cold here. We'd better go . . . I'm sorry for you," she said as she clasped the fur about her throat.

The unexpected words sent a pang through Mrs. Slade. "Yes; we'd better go." She gathered up her bag and cloak. "I don't know why you should be sorry for me," she muttered.

Mrs. Ansley stood looking away from her toward the dusky secret mass of the Colosseum. "Well—because I didn't have to wait that night."

Mrs. Slade gave an unquiet laugh. "Yes; I was beaten there. But I oughtn't to begrudge it to you, I suppose. At the end of all these years. After all, I had everything; I had him for twenty-five years. And you had nothing but that one letter that he didn't write."

Mrs. Ansley was again silent. At length she turned toward the door of the terrace. She took a step, and turned back, facing her companion.

"I had Barbara," she said, and began to move ahead of Mrs. Slade toward the stairway.

2

APPROACHES TO THE SHORT STORY

DEFINING THE SHORT STORY

I once heard or read somewhere that a novel is a work of fiction of a certain length that has something wrong with it. Perhaps a short story is a work of fiction of a certain (somewhat shorter) length that has nothing wrong with it. I don't mean to evade the question; I think a short story can be any number of things (snapshot, an entire life, a voice coming to me from an interesting place) but the main thing it is, if it succeeds, is true to itself in all its elements.

A hard thing to define. A short story is a brief, growing excitement and lingering recollection and pleasure. Kind of Wordsworthian. A good story should come back on you.

An asterisk in time.

A story is a fully realized world. After passing through this world, the reader sees his own world differently.

A story is a narrative wherein a character absorbs an experience.

I'm not really sure what a short story is. I think it's when something happens in a story that makes the reader feel he's experienced something meaningful by reading it.

A short story is about something unforgettable to the writer for some reason. Otherwise, it shouldn't be written. It has characters, scenes or settings, and usually tension and conflict. It reveals the subtleties of the event by language, order/structure, and portraits. It is about place and feeling and people.

A short story is a slice of life—the thinner the better.

A short story (disregarding the type of fiction that makes comment on itself as "art") should provide some kind of continuous dream which the reader can enter, commune with, and leave having felt something.

Imagining a life you could never have imagined yourself, a life that might've killed you, or made you immeasurably happy, a life that by its very *simple depiction* seems ultimately strange, ultimately imagined, yet true.

Short story—an interesting little tale that is interesting, self-contained, and in some way important.

A short story is a narrative that gives the feeling of being absolutely complete despite its brevity. Its subject is humanity, and the unexpected is a favorite device although it can also march ahead like a firing squad.

—*Students of James Salter's Graduate Fiction Workshop, University of Iowa*

Most of the writers in Salter's workshop are pointing to narrative, the *telling* of something to an audience of readers. Are characters necessary? Must the short story focus on a single event? As these writers suggest, the overriding purpose of short fiction, as in all fiction, is to affect the reader; to take the reader somewhere he or she has never been before; to create a movement in understanding or emotion. If a short story is a form of art, then it can be compared to other forms of art. Like a painting, which might be abstract or representational or multimedial, a short story can create its own rules. It can be written entirely in the first person, or in the third person, or it can switch points of view, or it can lack punctuation, or it can be just twenty words long. But the short story, like all forms of art, is concerned with its audience, and, as in all forms of art, the audience has a set of expectations that writers must consider in order to achieve the primary objective of their art: to affect the audience.

Writing Strategies

1. Define the short story for yourself. Consider stories you have written, and stories you have read and admired. What *is* a short story, as opposed to a newspaper article, or a poem, or a novel? What can a short story accomplish?

2. As you write stories, and read stories, consider your definition, revising it to reflect your observations. A sequence of definitions will be a record of your thoughts about short fiction.

MODELS FOR READING AND WRITING SHORT FICTION

Audience expectations have led to the development of a number of models for reading and writing short fiction. Some of these models focus on a familiar definition of a short story: that it narrates a plot in which characters engage in a conflict that reaches crisis proportions and then resolves at a point where one or more characters is changed.

FREYTAG'S TRIANGLE

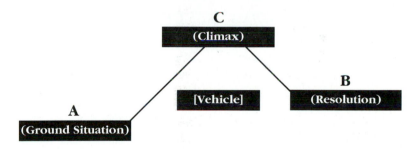

This variation of Freytag's Triangle, a conflict-crisis-resolution model for short fiction, is particularly effective in illuminating movement in a story: a story traces the movement of a character or characters from point A to point B through point C. The means of the movement is called the *vehicle,* because it sets the story in motion and keeps it rolling. The vehicle in Milan Kundera's "The Hitchhiking Game," for example, is the active role-playing the young couple embarks on during their vacation—the hitchhiking game itself. The *ground situation* of the story, the nature and status of the young couple's relationship up to the point that they enter the game, is elucidated in the story's first section; the second section ends with the dramatic change in their relationship as they begin to play the game. The *climax* of the story occurs when the couple's role-playing transcends the boundaries of the psychological and enters their physical relationship. The *resolution* takes place as the young woman attempts to confirm her self-identity, an identity that the game has obscured, if not obliterated, in the young man's eyes. Freytag's Triangle is most helpful in allowing you to keep in mind the issue of movement, of whether characters change, and how that change is brought about. The model also underscores a story's sense of event, that a momentous situation can occur that will change the characters not only within the frame of the story, but also beyond it. It's no coincidence that many stories begin with the arrival of a character at an unfamiliar destination (such as Isaac Babel's "My First Goose"), or the departure of a character on a trip of some import (such as "The Hitchhiking Game" or Flannery O'Connor's "A Good Man Is Hard to Find"). Literal physical movement of character can precipitate the kind of figurative or psychological movement of character that readers expect from fiction.

ASCENDING ARCS OF ENERGY

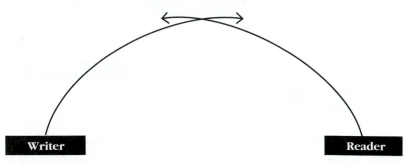

A model for the relationship between writer and reader has been developed by Frank Conroy, author of the memoir, *Stop-Time,* the short story collection *Midair,* and the novel *Body and Soul,* and director of the Writer's Workshop at the University of Iowa. With "Ascending Arcs of Energy," Conroy describes fiction as a contract between the writer and the reader. The writer and the reader both must project energy for this contract to be fulfilled: the writer to get the work done, the reader to receive and assimilate the work. The writer is bound to the principles of meaning and sense; mood, ambiguity, style, and other aspects which Conroy calls "fancy stuff" can and will emerge, but only if meaning and sense are accomplished first. As Mark Twain argues, the writer must "say what he is proposing to say, not merely come near it." The writer is obligated to tell the story in clear, understandable language.

The reader is obligated to read attentively and thoughtfully, with a willingness to enter the created world of a particular story. The reader is also bound to a restraining principle: "Do not pretend to understand in the text that which the text, for one reason or another, only pretends to express." Sometimes, a reader may be tempted to puzzle over a story, making connections where there are none. Both participants need to project adequate but not excessive energy—a reader cannot come to the text with too much expectation or bias, and a writer cannot come to the text wanting to create solely the music of mood, for instance, without covering the basic concerns of meaning and sense, of what words mean and whether they will make equal sense to both the writer and the reader. In "Fenimore Cooper's Literary Offences," Mark Twain argues that "inaccuracy of the details throws a sort of air of fictitiousness and general improbability over" any piece of fiction. This kind of inaccuracy stems from a writer's "inadequacy as an observer." Writing can be faulty because the writer's "ear was satisfied with the approximate word," rather than with precision.

If, for instance, Kundera had chosen to tell "The Hitchhiking Game" in an overwrought, melodramatic style, how would it have affected the reader? His choice of a simple, straightforward style takes into account the idea that a reader presented with too much energy, too much sensory detail, given the psychological focus of the story, might have felt oppressed or bewildered. The reader can pour a significant amount of energy into "The Hitchhiking Game," because the writing style allows the reader in, rather than shutting out the reader. In this sense, "The Hitchhiking Game" fulfills the notion that the reader and the writer are what Conroy calls "co-creators of the text." The reader is alongside, rather than below or above, the writer as he discovers the changing nature in the relationship between his two characters. The prose style of "The Hitchhiking Game" holds back enough energy that it feels as if the reader and writer are discovering the shifting and fundamentally problematic relationship between the two characters just as the characters are discovering it, and that none of the participants in this experience (neither the writer, reader, nor characters) necessarily know the parameters of this dynamic relationship until the characters themselves discover them. Co-creating the text is the activity of the contract between the writer and the reader. The model implies that *something* must happen between the reader and the writer for the short story to have an effect.

Francine Prose, author of several short story collections, has developed the idea that every story must occur in an *arena*—all the characters are interacting, at one point, in a common realm, much like athletes on a playing field. Within this common realm are any number of elements or factors that will be changed or affected by the introduction of new variables. Has the introduction of this set of variables enabled the story to fully create and explore the arena? Here is how Kundera's "The Hitchhiking Game" could be diagrammed:

ARENA

The diagram illustrates that the arena of the story, because the couple is so fully involved in the game, is the relationship. The elements or factors of the relationship include how the couple lives (the general quality of their life), how the couple interacts socially with one another and with the outside world, how the couple exists emotionally or spiritually, and how the couple manages to function on an economic or financial level. The external variable that wreaks havoc with all these factors is their increasing involvement in the game. The diagram implicitly makes the argument that "The Hitchhiking Game" is essentially a story *about* the relationship, not just one character or the other. The last scenes of the story focus on the couple's transformed sexual interplay, and, as such, give credit to the diagram's argument.

As with any model, the diagram has the effect of *reducing* the story. For instance, the diagram makes nothing of the substantial elucidation of each of the two characters that Kundera has achieved. But the arena model is useful in that it allows you to consider a range of issues that arise in a story without limiting yourself to plot or character.

Although no single model can encompass the complexity and diversity of short fiction, models can be used to encourage a close examination of the elements of story, including plot, character, voice, setting, dialogue, and structure. Ultimately, a consideration of these elements evolves into an understanding of the vision of a particular piece of short fiction.

Writing Strategies

1. Choose a story from this book and analyze it in terms of the three models listed above.

   a. For Freytag's Triangle, draw the triangle and note the story's exact ground situation, vehicle, climax, and resolution.

   b. For Ascending Arcs of Energy, write a paragraph about how the writer projects energy (with a certain language or plot focus) and how the reader projects energy (by having to read a type of style or assess a certain suggestion on the part of the writer).

   c. For Arena, draw the arena that the story focuses on, note the new variable that affects it, and list the factors that are affected.

In which areas do these models offer a common assessment of the story? In which areas do they differ? What aspects of the story do all of them miss entirely?

2. Choose a story you have written and analyze it in the same terms as outlined in the above strategy.

WRITING SHORT FICTION

Writers construct their stories in a wide variety of ways. Some writers rely on incidents out of their real lives, while others believe that every detail and character must be culled from the imagination or observation of lives around them. An idea for a story can begin with a character, or an incident, or a strong sensory detail. A sentence may suddenly strike you as a good way to open a story, and you can go from there. You can write with the entire story fully thought out in your head, to the point where you've outlined every instant of plot escalation, or you can create your fiction a sentence at a time, with perhaps only the vaguest idea of where the story might be going. The process of imagination, and the connection between imagination and language, is particular to each writer. Stories have been written over the course of a few hours, or a few years, depending on the temperament and the creative *process* of the writer.

The most important activity for writing fiction is reading fiction. There is no substitute for reading authors whom you like and dislike, becoming cognizant of exactly why you do or don't like them, and reading them as a writer, noting what choices they make, occasionally drawing connections between their choices and the choices you are making in your own fiction. Why that particular point of view? Why that tense? Why that style? Why that pacing? How is the piece a short story? What is the author accomplishing? Could the author have written it better? Some writers critique published stories as if they were going to be discussed in a writer's group or workshop. This exercise may help you improve your own writing by heightening your awareness of fictive choices—of the choices in language, structure, and characterization. It is especially useful to critique stories that you like as well as stories that you don't like.

Almost all authors come to the craft of writing fiction through reading fiction. What is it about fiction that inspires readers to write? Why has a story by another writer moved you to want to sit at a desk by yourself for hours at a time in an effort to create your own fiction? For some writers, getting to the heart of why they want to write in the first place will help them to tell their stories. Gabriel García Márquez and Toni Cade Bambara, for example, share a conscious desire to portray and explore specific social and political issues. In "How to Become a Writer," Lorrie Moore's narrator asks, "Why write? Where does writing come from? These are questions to ask yourself. They are like: Where does dust come from? Or: Why is there war? Or: If there's a God, then why is my brother now a cripple?" Other writers suggest less deliberate reasons for writing. They speak of characters who arrive in their minds and create nagging questions that the writers, only through the act of writing, can discover the answers to; or they speak of characters who arrive all at once, ready to talk, demanding that the inhabited writer set down their words on the page. "I thank everybody in this book for coming," Alice Walker writes at the conclusion of *The Color Purple,* and she signs herself "author and medium."

Often, writers may begin a story by "just writing," or "freewriting," an exercise in which they don't edit or censor themselves at all—they just keep moving the pen across the page as it forms word after word, *whatever comes to mind,* much like what psychiatrists and psychologists refer to as "free associating." You can start with any single word and just go—with a pen, on the typewriter, or at the word processor. Such freewriting can unlock doors to issues and images that interest or even obsess you, and may result in a piece of writing you can work with—a sentence, the notion of a character, a sensory detail that you can associate to another sensory detail that will associate to yet another detail, until something that has the shape of a story emerges. The point to freewriting is to get something on the page, anything, and then see what you've got, with the idea that it is easier to create something from something than it is to create something from nothing. While the apparent lack of discipline in freewriting can seem disconcerting and counterproductive, it certainly has a tonic effect on restrained, self-censoring writing habits.

Writing Strategies

1. Start with an interesting character, any character, someone you know or someone you imagine.

   a. Write a description of that character, beginning with the physical reality of the person, including usual (for example, hair color, the type of clothes he or she wears) and unusual traits (a mole, a scar). What is it about the character's physical being that makes him or her interesting to you?

   b. Write an action involving this character, either something this character does alone (like eating a meal in a small kitchen), or something he or she does with other people (such as being confronted by a mugger on a dark street). The very invention of this action can lead you into the world of a story.

    c. Write a thought involving that character. What's on the character's mind, and why? For example, is she thinking about work, or a doorbell that needs to be replaced in the front hall, or a relationship with another person, or a relationship with a particular object (such as her mother's watch, which she now twirls idly on her wrist)?

2. Start with a single event, either momentous (like a car hitting a bicyclist) or potentially momentous (like a teenager shoplifting a light bulb from a hardware store).

    a. Describe the action of the event. Who is participating, what is happening, and where is it taking place? Envision and write carefully about the characters' precise gestures. A car hits a bicycle on a quiet country road, and a woman climbs from her vehicle . . . or does she drive off without stopping . . . or does the person on the bicycle reach into his jacket as he slumps by the side of the road and . . . ?

    b. Develop a thought involving one of the event's participants. Open your story in the mind of the twelve-year-old girl tucking the light bulb into the interior pocket of her windbreaker, or the elderly woman behind the counter who witnesses the theft.

    c. Begin with the aftermath of the event, with the event only suggested through implication. The thirty-seven-year-old man wakes up in a strange antiseptic room unable to recall why he is there. Or the woman continues to drive down the country road, the right front headlight of the car cracked. The story can proceed from there, with no outright announcement that an accident has just happened.

3. Start with an evocation, a sound or an image or something sensory that attracts or repels you.

    a. Explore the image, what it looks like, feels like, sounds like, what the world around it is like. The image can be as complex or as simple as you want—dusk in the mountains; a rock jutting out from an ocean; a plate of food; a glass of water.

    b. Immediately skip to another image, and see if you want to explore the new image further. Dusk in the mountains can lead to something interesting in the valley.

    c. Connect an image immediately to a character, such as the dour young man who lifts his fork to begin on the liver and beets that have been set before him. Or the hikers climbing diligently up the mountain to try to capture the dusk before it fades into night.

4. Begin with a subject that is absolutely true to your life: a moment you witnessed on the sidewalk, a person you know, something that happened to you. Narrate these circumstances in a voice that allows you to enter them as fully as possible, and stick with the truth until you want to move it elsewhere or the facts have provided the shape of their own story.

5. Require yourself to write about a subject with which you have absolutely no experience.

    a. A scene that you've witnessed in passing may seem so strange to you that writing about it will become a way of understanding it.

    b. You can attempt fiction that is less realistic, such as fantasy, or horror, or fable. Note Calvino's story in this book.

OPENING SENTENCES

Some practitioners of fiction believe that the short story, or the short-short story, or even the novel, has to begin *in medias res*—in the middle of things—to give the reader a feeling of intimacy and immediacy. Other practitioners, such as John Cheever in "The Death of Justina," prefer to take a roundabout entrance, as if the actual beginning of the tale is something to be arrived at later, once the voice has warmed to the telling. Certainly, it can be advantageous if the opening sentence states something inextricably linked to the storyline, if it bears some of the weight of the story in it.

An opening sentence can simply state the conflict, or an aspect of it, as when Alice Munro begins "Prue": "Prue used to live with Gordon." Here, the opening line points to the exact nature of the conflict, that Prue used to live with Gordon but obviously doesn't now, and yet the experience of living with him still figures in her life. An opening sentence may focus on a character who will be a major figure in the story. Eudora Welty's "Old Mr. Marblehall" begins: "Old Mr. Marblehall never did anything, never got married until he was sixty." An opening sentence can describe the situation that will dictate the crucial action of the story, as in "A Good

Man Is Hard to Find" by Flannery O'Connor: "The grandmother didn't want to go to Florida." An opening sentence can also help teach the reader how to read the story by introducing a markedly original style or a striking content detail that the ensuing story will maintain. Italo Calvino's "The Distance of the Moon" begins: "At one time, according to Sir George H. Darwin, the Moon was very close to the Earth." This opening sentence is part of an encyclopedic fragment that ushers us into the "real" story. In "How to Become a Writer," Lorrie Moore begins in such a way that *the title* is virtually the opening sentence.

Regardless of how you choose to start your story, you can always change it by cutting the opening sentence or sentences until you arrive at a sentence in your draft that seems to work better, or by adding the opening sentence to what you've already written. As a writer, though, the "right" opening sentence of a draft can possibly propel you all the way through the story to the end. An opening sentence could serve as a springboard to writing the entire story. The voice that emerges, or the conflict, or the tone, can give you the necessary confidence and energy to finish.

Sometimes, too, you may find that you write a compelling opening sentence or opening paragraph or opening series of paragraphs and are simply unable to continue; the force of what you have written strikes you as impossible to sustain. This stalled situation doesn't mean that you won't ever write the entire story; it just means that you won't continue the story immediately. You can retain good openings in notebooks or on computer disks, and access them when you feel ready to build on them—a day, a week, a month, or even years later.

Writing Strategies

1. Start with a dramatic statement, a statement that carries with it a strong opinion, and then revise it to capture the physical essence from which the drama or opinion has emerged. For example, you can start with:

"Frank was a terrible guy."

This can evolve to:

"I knew Frank was a terrible guy the first day I met him."

Which can lead to:

"The first day Frank came to work, he insulted everyone mercilessly."

And:

"When Frank entered the office for the first time, he wore an olive green double-breasted suit, and his hair was slicked up in a haughty pompadour."

The evolution of your opinion into a sentence that begins to capture its genesis can lead you to develop a story that results in the reader sharing your opinion, without your ever having to state it explicitly.

2. Begin, as Yukio Mishima does in "Patriotism," with a sentence that captures the whole story: "I was there when my brother killed the stockbroker." Then write the story of that sentence. Allow yourself the possibility of examining the most intriguing details and moments that lead up to this ultimate climax.

3. Once you finish a story, examine the opening sentence. Does it set the mood and tone that you're looking for? Does the story begin soon enough? Does it begin too soon? Try taking away or adding to the opening sentence.

THE BODY OF THE STORY

Once you've begun your story, and find yourself moving, it is useful to keep in mind that the reader is moving as well—both physically through the process of turning the page and psychologically as the reader becomes immersed in the world that you have created. To achieve this movement the body of the story has to achieve movement as well. The story, like the left side of Freytag's Triangle, may have an upward movement, with rising tension generated through increasing complication that eventually reaches fruition through the climax. Another story, however, may achieve tension through a rising crescendo of language, or through an experiment in form (such as a story that numbers each of its sections and so achieves upward movement through mere upward numbering—as in Kundera's "The Hitchhiking Game").

The body of the story presents you with the challenge to *get going*, to give your story speed, before it's too late. Eudora Welty's "Old Mr. Marblehall" begins almost like an essay, with a series of paragraphs focusing on defined characters and topics: the first paragraphs describe, respectively, Mr. Marblehall, Mrs. Marblehall, and the ancestral home. But Welty increases the complication, and thereby speeds the pace, with the rapid introduction of the first son, the second wife, and the second son. And while Ida Fink's narrator begins "A Scrap of Time" with a deliberate circling of her topic, the pacing of the story occurs in the increasing specificity of detail that the narrator's memory can pinpoint: the ending of the story is the ultimate specific detail.

Pacing—that sense of a story's forward movement—is crucial to keep your readers with you, but if your story opens at a breakneck speed, the body of your story is your opportunity to slow it down, to vary it so that the reader won't be too breathless to continue. Yukio Mishima's "Patriotism" begins with a shocking climax, then stops to explain how this situation exactly came to pass. A virtue of the story lies in how quickly it is willing to dispense with the necessaries: Reiko's suicide at the end earns only one paragraph. And yet, another virtue of the story emerges in how much it is willing to linger: the actual description of the lieutenant's suicide is excruciatingly and dizzyingly slow. The speed of the opening and closing of "Patriotism" is even more effective in contrast to the extended lingering accomplished within the story's body.

The body of the story also presents an opportunity for you to expand, both in content and in technique. In "A Good Man Is Hard to Find," the story's middle opens up into the minor characters who populate Red Sammy's restaurant, and yet, the focus of the dialogue remains on The Misfit. In Denis Johnson's "Dundun," the deadpan, flat opening gives way to an intriguing emotionalism and the introduction of impressionistic description: "Rather than moving, we were just getting smaller and smaller." And Grace Paley's "The Pale Pink Roast" turns from an accent on dialogue to an accent on compressed descriptive language: "Peter sighed. He turned the palms of his hands up as though to guess at rain. Anna knew him, theme and choreography. The sunshiny spring afternoon seeped through his fingers. He looked up at the witnessing heavens to keep what he could. He dropped his arms and let the rest go."

The challenge of the body of your story is the same as the challenge of fiction writing in general: to make choices, and to carry out these choices so that they become the most successful selections you could make. A body of a story will weave from the general to the specific, or journey from scene to scene, or dramatize and then summarize and repeat the cycle. What are you choosing to focus on, what are you choosing to gloss over or omit entirely, and why? In the closely narrated "The Hitchhiking Game," where so much dialogue is included, the critical dialogue of the "striptease" scene is all summarized. Why does Kundera make this particular choice? Certainly, the story picks up speed as it moves to summary; but also, since the dialogue is merely implied rather than explicitly stated, the characters appear to be moving beyond the borders of language, beyond the borders of acceptable behavior with one another, as the game spirals toward the irreparable damage of their relationship.

Five principles worth considering as you write and read the body of your story are:

Clarity—Is every word clear in its meaning? Does its intent equal this meaning?

Conviction—Is the story told with enough authority to convince the reader of its "truth"? Is it, in a sense, believable?

Interest—Is every movement of the story original, striking, and essential? Does every detail and gesture hold the reader's interest?

Intimacy—Does the story contain enough information and emotion for the reader to feel a sense of closeness to the characters or to what you are trying to convey?

Vision—What is your intellectual or spiritual purpose in telling the story, and is this purpose made somehow worthwhile to the reader?

While these principles are formulaic, they allow you to move past the concerns about formal dexterity in writing fiction to a consideration of why you write and what motivates you. Your answers regarding such issues may be explicit, or intuitive.

When developing the body of your story, it may be useful to actually consider the entire story as *a body*, as James Salter does. In this approach, the skin of the body is the surface—or language—

of the story. The bones of the body are the structure of the story. The soul of the body is the meaning, or the theme of the story. This organic approach is applicable to all kinds of stories. The surface of "The Hitchhiking Game" is matter-of-fact and straightforward, almost unadorned, while the structure (to simplify a bit) examines a relatively short period of time in a variety of summarized and closely described scenes. The story as body allows both reader and writer to consider not only how each of the three elements work, but also how they work together. Does the plain language of "The Hitchhiking Game" serve its meaning? How does the story's length and carefully controlled structure work with both language and meaning? The "body" approach helps readers and writers view the story as a whole, without categorizing it as a distinct type of story, whether it be a story with a traditional plot or a story without characters.

Writing Strategies

1. Draw or sketch a model of your story-in-progress. The model can be of your own making, but you may want to consider a model that:

    a. addresses what the story is trying to accomplish;
    b. analyzes which arena the story is exploring, and how it is exploring that arena;
    c. shows which characters you are working with and how they change over the course of the story.

How does your model apply to your story, and what does it fail to show about it? What strengths or weaknesses or gaps does the model reveal in the story?

2. As you write the story, keep an extra notebook or scratch paper available for jotting down details and interactions that may occur later in the narrative.

3. Introduce new characters and new scenes as you pursue the storyline. If your story up to this point takes place in a house or an office, push the characters out into the yard or the street or the supermarket. Who do they meet, and how does the interaction define both the main characters and the minor characters?

ENDINGS

Novelist and short story writer Paula Fox once said that a short story begins with a small question mark and ends with a large question mark. A short story, in a relatively short space, creates a total world, and by its end manages to extend itself, to reach beyond the small world of its creation to the larger world in which the small world must exist. Chekhov's characters, for example, are so thoroughly developed that by the end of his stories they are on virtual "railroad tracks"—you can see the tracks of their lives beyond the story leading off the page. Consequently, a reader of Chekhov has a fair sense of how characters are fated to endure; the reader isn't told, but knows, by everything that has come before.

One technique that Chekhov employs to help create this transcendence in his short stories is the very subtle and slight shift of the camera eye at the story's end. In "Gusev," for example, we follow the life of a sailor to his death, and then, in the absolutely final shot of the story, we see the character as a dead body being toyed with by creatures of the sea, and the sea itself becomes a character. The camera shift extends the story and allows for the largeness of the external world to creep into the small world of the story itself. John Barth calls this technique the "Chekhovian spin-out." Possibilities within this technique include: a subtle shift in focus concerning one character (such as in "Gusev"); a shift in the tense of the story (as in "Old Mr. Marblehall"); a shift in the camera eye from one setting (for example, in a story set entirely within a particular house or neighborhood) to another (outside the house or outside the neighborhood); or a shift in the camera eye from a main character to a relatively minor character. At the conclusion of "A Good Man Is Hard to Find," for example, O'Connor switches deftly to a scene that no member of the family could be privy to, because they've all been killed.

Another useful philosophy toward endings is to take the same approach when ending a story as you do when starting it. In story openings, you pour all your energy into creating a new world. If you look at the ending as simply another beginning, as the opportunity to open further the fictive world rather than begin to shut it down, then chances are you will open that world. When you begin to do the work of shutting down a story, you are closing the bag, sealing it up, leaving a neat package, as Jane Smiley begins to do in "Lily," the story of an awkward reunion among three old friends:

> After a long silence Nancy said, "I don't suppose any of us are going to be friends after this." Lily shrugged, but really she didn't suppose so either.

But like a rhymed couplet at the end of a poem, the closing gesture may imply that your fictive world is sealable, resolvable. In "Lily," for example, Smiley reopens the world of the story through a change in tone:

> Her throat closed over, as if she were about to cry. Across the room Nancy picked up one of her hairbrushes with a sigh—and she was, after all, uninjured. Lily said, "Ten years ago he might have killed you."

Although an approach that "opens" an ending does not necessarily mean that you will create new characters or new conflicts in the final paragraphs of your work, it can mean that you will suggest the possibility for new changes or new choices for the character.

Richard Ford, author of the story collection *Rock Springs* and several novels, likes to talk about "muscling up" for an ending, creating a rising crescendo in both the language and the intellectual musings of his characters. In "Dundun," Denis Johnson begins a poetic elevation in the last two paragraphs, by expanding the scope of the story: "Glaciers had crushed this region in the time before history." Yet, Johnson's last line turns the story abruptly *on* the reader: "If I opened up your head and ran a hot soldering iron around in your brain, I might turn you into someone like that." The muscling up Johnson gives "Dundun" allows his narrator to transcend the limitations of his own character, and permits the reader to glimpse the future beyond the story. The crescendo also gives the reader a sense of thematic and rhythmic closure; it creates a kind of grand finale, when the music is at its loudest and all the main characters are on stage, providing a satisfying spectacle before the curtain comes down. There is, however, a fine line between effective elevation of language and character perception that manages to open the story, and elevation that wraps up the story a bit too tightly. In the silence after the grand ending, is your reader thinking? Or is your reader more than ready to close the book, all questions answered?

The "hand test" is useful to improving story endings. Take any story you've written, and block out—with your hand—the entire last sentence or even the entire last paragraph, and read the story as if it ended that much earlier. What effect does the test have on the meaning and the sound of the ending?

When reaching the conclusion of a story you are working on, you can also try writing through the ending, not bothering to stop where you thought the ending would be, but pushing on, just to see what comes of it. Perhaps these additional paragraphs will wreck your story, but you can always cut them. You cannot cut what you don't have down on paper, however; perhaps writing through the ending will open up the world of the story a bit more. Consider, again, the endings of "Dundun," "Gusev," and "Lily." New details of your characters may emerge, and even if you don't use the extra paragraphs as the ending, you can always incorporate the good material of these paragraphs into the story at an earlier point. As Charles Baxter, author of the story collections *Through the Safety Net* and *Harmony of the World,* says, "You cannot be afraid of looking like a fool on a first draft."

Writing Strategies

1. Experiment with the Chekhovian "camera shift" for one of your story endings. You can do this by switching setting, or perspective, or tense, or even tone.

2. Take the ending of a finished story and try to write beyond it. Make your characters interact more, or make yourself further develop the landscape of the story.

3. Take the ending of a finished story, and cut it to a place earlier in the tale that sounds like an ending as well. What is lost by the cutting? What is gained?

4. Take the final paragraph of any story included in this book, and eliminate it from the story. How does the story read without it? What exactly is the last paragraph accomplishing?

Isaac Babel

Isaac Babel was born in the Jewish ghetto in Odessa, Russia, in 1894. Babel moved to Kiev at the age of sixteen. After graduating from the Kiev Institute of Finance and Business Studies in 1915, he moved to St. Petersburg, where Maxim Gorky supported his first publications. He served in the Russian Army during World War I, and as a war correspondent during the Russian revolution. After gaining literary celebrity for his short fiction during the 1920s, Babel was censored, and entered a period of self-censorship during which he refused to write propaganda for the Soviet government. He was eventually arrested in 1939, and it is believed that he died in prison in 1941. "My First Goose" appeared in the collection Konarmiia, *published in English as* Red Calvary *in 1929.*

My First Goose*

Savitsky, Commander of the VI Division, rose when he saw me, and I wondered at the beauty of his giant's body. He rose, the purple of his riding breeches and the crimson of his little tilted cap and the decorations stuck on his chest cleaving the hut as a standard cleaves the sky. A smell of scent and the sickly sweet freshness of soap emanated from him. His long legs were like girls sheathed to the neck in shining riding boots.

He smiled at me, struck his riding whip on the table, and drew toward him an order that the Chief of Staff had just finished dictating. It was an order for Ivan Chesnokov to advance on Chugunov-Dobry-vodka with the regiment entrusted to him, to make contact with the enemy and destroy the same.

"For which destruction," the Commander began to write, smearing the whole sheet, "I make this same Chesnokov entirely responsible, up to and including the supreme penalty, and will if necessary strike him down on the spot; which you, Chesnokov, who have been working with me at the front for some months now, cannot doubt."

The Commander signed the order with a flourish, tossed it to his orderlies and turned upon me gray eyes that danced with merriment.

Translated by Walter Morison.

I handed him a paper with my appointment to the Staff of the Division.

"Put it down in the Order of the Day," said the Commander. "Put him down for every satisfaction save the front one. Can you read and write?"

"Yes, I can read and write," I replied, envying the flower and iron of that youthfulness. "I graduated in law from St. Petersburg University."

"Oh, are you one of those grinds?" he laughed. "Specs on your nose, too! What a nasty little object! They've sent you along without making any enquiries; and this is a hot place for specs. Think you'll get on with us?"

"I'll get on all right," I answered, and went off to the village with the quartermaster to find a billet for the night.

The quartermaster carried my trunk on his shoulder. Before us stretched the village street. The dying sun, round and yellow as a pumpkin, was giving up its roseate ghost to the skies.

We went up to a hut painted over with garlands. The quartermaster stopped, and said suddenly, with a guilty smile:

"Nuisance with specs. Can't do anything to stop it, either. Not a life for the brainy type here. But you go and mess up a lady, and a good lady too, and you'll have the boys patting you on the back."

He hesitated, my little trunk on his shoulder; then he came quite close to me, only to dart away again despairingly and run to the nearest yard. Cossacks were sitting there, shaving one another.

"Here, you soldiers," said the quartermaster, setting my little trunk down on the ground. "Comrade Savitsky's orders are that you're to take this chap in your billets, so no nonsense about it, because the chap's been through a lot in the learning line."

The quartermaster, purple in the face, left us without looking back. I raised my hand to my cap and saluted the Cossacks. A lad with long straight flaxen hair and the handsome face of the Ryazan Cossacks went over to my little trunk and tossed it out at the gate. Then he turned his back on me and with remarkable skill emitted a series of shameful noises.

"To your guns—number double-zero!" an older Cossack shouted at him, and burst out laughing. "Running fire!"

His guileless art exhausted, the lad made off. Then, crawling over the ground, I began to gather together the manuscript and tattered garments that had fallen out of the trunk. I gathered them up and carried them to the other end of the yard. Near the hut, on a brick stove, stood a cauldron in which pork was cooking. The steam that rose from it was like the far-off smoke of home in the village, and it mingled hunger with desperate loneliness in my head. Then I covered my little broken trunk with hay, turning it into a pillow, and lay down on the ground to read in *Pravda* Lenin's speech at the Second Congress of the Comintern. The sun fell upon me from behind the toothed hillocks, the Cossacks trod on my feet, the lad made fun of me untiringly, the beloved lines came toward me along a thorny path and could not reach me. Then I put aside the paper and went out to the landlady, who was spinning on the porch.

"Landlady," I said, "I've got to eat."

The old woman raised to me the diffused whites of her purblind eyes and lowered them again.

"Comrade," she said, after a pause, "what with all this going on, I want to go and hang myself."

"Christ!" I muttered, and pushed the old woman in the chest with my fist. "You don't suppose I'm going to go into explanations with you, do you?"

And turning around I saw somebody's sword lying within reach. A severe-looking goose was waddling about the yard, inoffensively preening its feathers, I overtook it and pressed it to the ground. Its head cracked beneath my boot, cracked and emptied itself. The white neck lay stretched out in the dung, the wings twitched.

"Christ!" I said, digging into the goose with my sword. "Go and cook it for me, landlady."

Her blind eyes and glasses glistening, the old woman picked up the slaughtered bird, wrapped it in her apron, and started to bear it off toward the kitchen.

"Comrade," she said to me, after a while, "I want to go and hang myself." And she closed the door behind her.

The Cossacks in the yard were already sitting around their cauldron. They sat motionless, stiff as heathen priests at a sacrifice, and had not looked at the goose.

"The lad's all right," one of them said, winking and scooping up the cabbage soup with his spoon.

The Cossacks commenced their supper with all the elegance and restraint of peasants who respect one another. And I wiped the sword with sand, went out at the gate, and came in again, depressed. Already the moon hung above the yard like a cheap earring.

"Hey, you," suddenly said Surovkov, an older Cossack. "Sit down and feed with us till your goose is done."

He produced a spare spoon from his boot and handed it to me. We supped up the cabbage soup they had made, and ate the pork.

"What's in the newspaper?" asked the flaxen-haired lad, making room for me.

"Lenin writes in the paper," I said, pulling out *Pravda*. "Lenin writes that there's a shortage of everything."

And loudly, like a triumphant man hard of hearing, I read Lenin's speech out to the Cossacks.

Evening wrapped about me the quickening moisture of its twilight sheets; evening laid a mother's hand upon my burning forehead. I read on and rejoiced, spying out exultingly the secret curve of Lenin's straight line.

"Truth tickles everyone's nostrils," said Surovkov, when I had come to the end. "The question is, how's it to be pulled from the heap. But he goes and strikes at it straight off like a hen pecking at a grain!"

This remark about Lenin was made by Surovkov, platoon commander of the Staff Squadron; after which we lay down to sleep in the hayloft. We slept, all six of us, beneath a wooden roof that let in the stars, warming one another, our legs intermingled. I dreamed: and in my dreams saw women. But my heart, stained with bloodshed, grated and brimmed over.

Alice Munro

Since 1968, the Canadian author Alice Munro has published seven acclaimed collections of short stories and one novel. Her first collection, Dance of the Happy Shades, *received the 1969 Governor General's Award, Canada's premier literary prize. Her stories appear regularly in* The New Yorker, *and have won multiple Best American Short Stories and O. Henry Prize citations. Munro briefly attended the University of Western Ontario from 1949 to 1951, and served there as the Writer-In-Residence from 1974 to 1975. In*

*1976 she moved to Clinton, Ontario, a few miles from her childhood home of
Wingham. "Prue" first appeared in the New Yorker in 1981, and can be
found in the collection The Moons of Jupiter (1983).*

Prue

Prue used to live with Gordon. This was after Gordon left his wife
and before he went back to her—a year and four months in all.
Some time later, he and his wife were divorced. After that came a
period of indecision, of living together off and on; then the wife
went away to New Zealand, most likely for good.

Prue did not go back to Vancouver Island, where Gordon had
met her when she was working as a dining-room hostess in a resort
hotel. She got a job in Toronto, working in a plant shop. She had
many friends in Toronto by that time, most of them Gordon's
friends and his wife's friends. They liked Prue and were ready to
feel sorry for her, but she laughed them out of it. She is very likable.
She has what eastern Canadians call an English accent, though she
was born in Canada—in Duncan, on Vancouver Island. This accent
helps her to say the most cynical things in a winning and light-
hearted way. She presents her life in anecdotes, and though it is
the point of most of her anecdotes that hopes are dashed, dreams
ridiculed, things never turn out as expected, everything is altered
in a bizarre way and there is no explanation ever, people always
feel cheered up after listening to her; they say of her that it is a relief to meet somebody who doesn't take herself too seriously, who
is so unintense, and civilized, and never makes any real demands
or complaints.

The only thing she complains about readily is her name. Prue is
a schoolgirl, she says, and Prudence is an old virgin; the parents
who gave her that name must have been too shortsighted even to
take account of puberty. What if she had grown a great bosom, she
says, or developed a sultry look? Or was the name itself a guaran-
tee that she wouldn't? In her late forties now, slight and fair, attending to customers with a dutiful vivacity, giving pleasure to
dinner guests, she might not be far from what those parents had in
mind: bright and thoughtful, a cheerful spectator. It is hard to
grant her maturity, maternity, real troubles.

Her grownup children, the products of an early Vancouver
Island marriage she calls a cosmic disaster, come to see her, and

instead of wanting money, like other people's children, they bring presents, try to do her accounts, arrange to have her house insulated. She is delighted with their presents, listens to their advice, and, like a flighty daughter, neglects to answer their letters.

Her children hope she is not staying on in Toronto because of Gordon. Everybody hopes that. She would laugh at the idea. She gives parties and goes to parties; she goes out sometimes with other men. Her attitude toward sex is very comforting to those of her friends who get into terrible states of passion and jealousy, and feel cut loose from their moorings. She seems to regard sex as a wholesome, slightly silly indulgence, like dancing and nice dinners—something that shouldn't interfere with people's being kind and cheerful to each other.

Now that his wife is gone for good, Gordon comes to see Prue occasionally, and sometimes asks her out for dinner. They may not go to a restaurant; they may go to his house. Gordon is a good cook. When Prue or his wife lived with him he couldn't cook at all, but as soon as he put his mind to it he became—he says truthfully—better than either of them.

Recently he and Prue were having dinner at his house. He had made chicken Kiev, and crème brûlée for dessert. Like most new, serious cooks, he talked about food.

Gordon is rich, by Prue's—and most people's—standards. He is a neurologist. His house is new, built on a hillside north of the city, where there used to be picturesque, unprofitable farms. Now there are one-of-a-kind, architect-designed, very expensive houses on half-acre lots. Prue, describing Gordon's house, will say, "Do you know there are four bathrooms? So that if four people want to have baths at the same time there's no problem. It seems a bit much, but it's very nice, really, and you'd never have to go through the hall."

Gordon's house has a raised dining area—a sort of platform, surrounded by a conversation pit, a music pit, and a bank of heavy greenery under sloping glass. You can't see the entrance area from the dining area, but there are no intervening walls, so that from one area you hear something of what is going on in the other.

During dinner the doorbell rang. Gordon excused himself and went down the steps. Prue heard a female voice. The person it belonged to was still outside, so she could not hear the words. She heard Gordon's voice, pitched low, cautioning. The door didn't close—it seemed the person had not been invited in—but the voices went on, muted and angry. Suddenly there was a cry from Gordon, and he appeared halfway up the steps, waving his arms.

"The crème brûlée," he said. "Could you?" He ran back down as Prue got up and went into the kitchen to save the dessert. When she returned he was climbing the stairs more slowly, looking both agitated and tired.

"A friend," he said gloomily. "Was it all right?"

Prue realized he was speaking of the crème brûlée, and she said yes, it was perfect, she had got it just in time. He thanked her but did not cheer up. It seemed it was not the dessert he was troubled over but whatever had happened at the door. To take his mind off it, Prue started asking him professional questions about the plants.

"I don't know a thing about them," he said. "You know that."

"I thought you might have picked it up. Like the cooking."

"She takes care of them."

"Mrs. Carr?" said Prue, naming his housekeeper.

"Who did you think?"

Prue blushed. She hated to be thought suspicious.

"The problem is that I think I would like to marry you," said Gordon, with no noticeable lightening of his spirits. Gordon is a large man, with heavy features. He likes to wear thick clothing, bulky sweaters. His blue eyes are often bloodshot, and their expression indicates that there is a helpless, baffled soul squirming around inside this doughty fortress.

"What a problem," said Prue lightly, though she knew Gordon well enough to know that it was.

The doorbell rang again, rang twice, three times, before Gordon could get to it. This time there was a crash, as of something flung and landing hard. The door slammed and Gordon was immediately back in view. He staggered on the steps and held his hand to his head, meanwhile making a gesture with the other hand to signify that nothing serious had happened, Prue was to sit down.

"Bloody overnight bag," he said. "She threw it at me."

"Did it hit you?"

"Glancing."

"It made a hard sound for an overnight bag. Were there rocks in it?"

"Oh."

Prue watched him pour himself a drink. "I'd like some coffee, if I might," she said. She went to the kitchen to put the water on, and Gordon followed her.

"I think I'm in love with this person," he said.

"Who is she?"

"You don't know her. She's quite young."

"Oh."

"But I do think I want to marry you, in a few years' time."

"After you get over being in love?"

"Yes."

"Well. I guess nobody knows what can happen in a few years' time."

When Prue tells about this, she says, "I think he was afraid I was going to laugh. He doesn't know why people laugh or throw their overnight bags at him, but he's noticed they do. He's such a proper person, really. The lovely dinner. Then she comes and throws her overnight bag. And it's quite reasonable to think of marrying me in a few years' time, when he gets over being in love. I think he first thought of telling me to sort of put my mind at rest."

She doesn't mention that the next morning she picked up one of Gordon's cufflinks from his dresser. The cufflinks are made of amber and he bought them in Russia, on the holiday he and his wife took when they got back together again. They look like squares of candy, golden, translucent, and this one warms quickly in her hand. She drops it into the pocket of her jacket. Taking one is not a real theft. It could be a reminder, an intimate prank, a piece of nonsense.

She is alone in Gordon's house; he has gone off early, as he always does. The housekeeper does not come till nine. Prue doesn't have to be at the shop until ten; she could make herself breakfast, stay and have coffee with the housekeeper, who is her friend from olden times. But once she has the cufflink in her pocket she doesn't linger. The house seems too bleak a place to spend an extra moment in. It was Prue, actually, who helped choose the building lot. But she's not responsible for approving the plans—the wife was back by that time.

When she gets home she puts the cufflink in an old tobacco tin. The children bought this tobacco tin in a junk shop years ago, and gave it to her for a present. She used to smoke, in those days, and the children were worried about her, so they gave her this tin full of toffees, jelly beans, and gumdrops, with a note saying, "Please get fat instead." That was for her birthday. Now the tin has in it several things besides the cufflink—all small things, not of great value but not worthless, either. A little enamelled dish, a sterling-silver spoon for salt, a crystal fish. These are not sentimental keepsakes. She never looks at them, and often forgets what she has there. They are not booty, they don't have ritualistic significance. She does not take something every time she goes to Gordon's house, or every time she stays over, or to mark what she might call memorable visits. She doesn't do it in a daze and she doesn't seem to be under a compulsion. She just takes something, every now and then, and puts it away in the dark of the old tobacco tin, and more or less forgets about it.

Anton Chekhov

Anton Chekhov was born in the Russian village of Taganrog in 1860. To support his family while studying medicine at Moscow University between 1879 and 1884, Chekhov began publishing short sketches in popular magazines. In 1885 he moved to St. Petersburg, where, assisted by the prominent editor Alexis Suvorin, he began to receive literary recognition for his short fiction. During his lifetime, Chekhov wrote seven major plays, including The Cherry Orchard *(1904),* The Three Sisters *(1901), and* The Seagull *(1896), as well as over four hundred short stories. Chekhov won numerous awards for both his literary achievements and his humanitarian endeavors, including the Pushkin Prize from the Division of Russian Language and Letters of The Academy of Sciences, and the Order of St. Stanislav for his work in the field of education. In the two decades after his death in 1904, his stories were issued in the West in fifteen volumes. "Gusev" first appeared in the United States in* The Witch and Other Stories *(1918).*

Gusev*

I

It is getting dark, and will soon be night.

Gusev, a discharged private soldier, sits up in his bunk.

"I say, Paul Ivanovich," he remarks in a low voice. "A soldier in Suchan told me their ship ran into a great fish on the way out and broke her bottom."

Translated by Ronald Hingley.

The nondescript person whom he addresses, known to everyone in the ship's sick-bay as Paul Ivanovich, acts as if he has not heard, and says nothing.

Once more quietness descends.

Wind plays in the rigging, the screw thuds, waves thrash, bunks creak, but their ears have long been attuned to all that, and they feel as if their surroundings are slumbering silently. It is boring. The three patients—two soldiers and one sailor—who have spent all day playing cards, are already dozing and talking in their sleep.

The sea is growing rough, it seems. Beneath Gusev the bunk slowly rises and falls, as if sighing—once, twice, a third time.

Something clangs on to the floor—a mug must have fallen.

"The wind's broken loose from its chain," says Gusev, listening.

This time Paul Ivanovich coughs.

"First you have a ship hitting a fish," he replies irritably. "Then you have a wind breaking loose from its chain. Is the wind a beast, that it breaks loose, eh?"

"It's how folk talk."

"Then folk are as ignorant as you, they'll say anything. A man needs a head on his shoulders—he needs to use his reason, you senseless creature."

Paul Ivanovich is subject to sea-sickness, and when the sea is rough he is usually bad-tempered, exasperated by the merest trifle. But there is absolutely nothing to be angry about, in Gusev's opinion. What is there so strange or surprising in that fish, even— or in the wind bursting its bonds? Suppose the fish is mountain-sized, and has a hard back like a sturgeon's. Suppose, too, that there are thick stone walls at the world's end, and that fierce winds are chained to those walls. If the winds haven't broken loose, then why do they thrash about like mad over the whole sea, tearing away like dogs? What happens to them in calm weather if they aren't chained up?

For some time Gusev considers mountainous fish and stout, rusty chains. Then he grows bored and thinks of the home country to which he is now returning after five years' service in the Far East. He pictures a large, snow-covered pond. On one side of the pond is the red-brick pottery with its tall chimney and clouds of black smoke, and on the other side is the village. Out of the fifth yard from the end his brother Alexis drives his sledge with his little son Vanka sitting behind him in his felt over-boots together

with his little girl Akulka, also felt-booted. Alexis has been drinking, Vanka is laughing, and Akulka's face cannot be seen because
she is all muffled up.

"He'll get them kids frostbitten if he don't watch out," thinks
Gusev. "O Lord," he whispers, "grant them reason and the sense
to honor their parents, and not be cleverer than their mum and
dad."

"Those boots need new soles," rambles the delirious sailor in his
deep voice. "Yes indeed."

Gusev's thoughts break off. Instead of the pond, a large bull's
head without eyes appears for no reason whatever, while horse and
sledge no longer move ahead, but spin in a cloud of black smoke.
Still, he's glad he's seen the folks at home. His happiness takes his
breath away. It ripples, tingling, over his whole body, quivers in
his fingers.

"We met again, thanks be to God," he rambles, but at once opens
his eyes and tries to find some water in the darkness.

He drinks and lies back, and again the sledge passes—followed
once more by the eyeless bull's head, smoke, clouds.

And so it goes on till daybreak.

II

First a dark blue circle emerges from the blackness—the port-hole.
Then, bit by bit, Gusev can make out the man in the next bunk—
Paul Ivanovich. Paul sleeps sitting up because lying down makes
him choke. His face is grey, his nose is long and sharp, and his eyes
seem huge because he has grown so fearfully thin. His temples are
sunken, his beard is wispy, his hair is long.

From his face you cannot possibly tell what class he belongs to—
is he gentleman, merchant or peasant? His expression and long
hair might be those of a hermit, or of a novice in a monastery, but
when he speaks he doesn't sound like a monk, somehow. Cough-
ing, bad air and disease have worn him down and made breathing
hard for him as he mumbles with his parched lips.

He sees Gusev watching him, and turns to face him.

"I'm beginning to grasp the point," says he. "Yes, now I see it all."

"See what, Paul Ivanovich?"

"I'll tell you. Why aren't you serious cases kept somewhere
quiet, that's what's been puzzling me? Why should you find

yourselves tossing about in a sweltering hot steamship—a place where everything endangers your lives, in other words? But now it's all clear, indeed it is. Your doctors put you on the ship to get rid of you. They're sick of messing around with such cattle. You pay them nothing, you only cause them trouble, and you spoil their statistics by dying. Which makes you cattle. And getting rid of you isn't hard. There are two requisites. First, one must lack all conscience and humanity. Second, one must deceive the steamship line. Of the first requisite the less said the better— we're pastmasters at that. And the second we can always pull off, given a little practice. Five sick men don't stand out in a crowd of four hundred fit soldiers and sailors. So they get you on board, mix you up with the able-bodied, hurriedly count you and find nothing amiss in the confusion. Then, when the ship's already under way, they see paralytics and consumptives in the last stages lying around on deck."

Not understanding Paul Ivanovich, and thinking he was being told off, Gusev spoke in self-defense.

"I lay around on deck because I was so weak. I was mighty chilly when they unloaded us from the barge."

"It's a scandal," Paul Ivanovich goes on. "The worst thing is, they know perfectly well you can't survive this long journey, don't they? And yet they put you here. Now, let's assume you last out till the Indian Ocean. What happens next doesn't bear thinking of. And such is their gratitude for loyal service and a clean record!"

Paul Ivanovich gives an angry look, frowning disdainfully.

"I'd like a go at these people in the newspapers," he pants. "I'd make the fur fly all right!"

The two soldier-patients and the sailor are already awake and at their cards. The sailor half lies in his bunk, while the soldiers sit on the floor near him in the most awkward postures. One soldier has his right arm in a sling, with the hand bandaged up in a regular bundle, so he holds his cards in his right armpit or in the crook of his elbow, playing them with his left hand. The sea is pitching and rolling heavily—impossible to stand up, drink tea or take medicine.

"Were you an officer's servant?" Paul Ivanovich asks Gusev.

"Yes sir, a batman."

"God, God!" says Paul Ivanovich, with a sad shake of his head. "Uproot a man from home, drag him ten thousand miles, give him tuberculosis and—and where does it all lead, I wonder? To making a batman of him for some Captain Kopeykin or Midshipman Dyrka. Very sensible, I must say!"

"It's not hard work, Paul Ivanovich. You get up of a morning, clean the boots, put the samovar on, tidy the room—then there's no more to do all day. The lieutenant spends all day drawing plans, like, and you can say your prayers, read books, go out in the street—whatever you want. God grant everyone such a life."

"Oh, what could be better! The lieutenant draws his 'plans, like,' and you spend your day in the kitchen longing for your home. 'Plans, like!' It's not plans that matter, it's human life. You only have one life, and that should be respected."

"Well, of course, Paul Ivanovich, a bad man never gets off lightly, either at home or in the service. But you live proper and obey orders—and who needs harm you? Our masters are educated gentlemen, they understand. I was never in the regimental lock-up, not in five years I wasn't, and I wasn't struck—now let me see—not more than once."

"What was that for?"

"Fighting. I'm a bit too ready with my fists, Paul Ivanovich. Four Chinamen come in our yard, carrying firewood or something—I don't recall. Well, I'm feeling bored, so I, er, knock 'em about a bit, and make one bastard's nose bleed. The lieutenant sees it through the window. Right furious he is, and he gives me one on the ear."

"You wretched, stupid man," whispers Paul Ivanovich. "You don't understand anything."

Utterly worn out by the pitching and tossing, he closes his eyes. His head keeps falling back, or forward on his chest, and he several times tries to lie flat, but it comes to nothing because the choking stops him.

"Why did you hit those four Chinamen?" he asks a little later.

"Oh, I dunno. They comes in the yard, so I just hits 'em."

They fall silent.

The card players go on playing for a couple of hours with much enthusiasm and cursing, but the pitching and tossing wear even them out, they abandon their cards and lie down. Once more Gusev pictures the large pond, the pottery, the village.

Once more the sledge runs by, and again Vanka laughs, while that silly Akulka has thrown open her fur and stuck out her legs. "Look, everyone," she seems to say, "I have better snow-boots than Vanka. Mine are new."

"Five years old, and still she has no sense," rambles Gusev. "Instead of kicking your legs, why don't you fetch your soldier uncle a drink? I'll give you something nice."

Then Andron, a flint-lock gun slung over his shoulder, brings a hare he has killed, followed by that decrepit old Jew Isaiah, who offers a piece of soap in exchange for the hare. There's a black calf just inside the front door of the hut, Domna is sewing a shirt and crying. Then comes the eyeless bull's head again, the black smoke.

Overhead someone gives a loud shout, and several sailors run past—dragging something bulky over the deck, it seems, or else something has fallen with a crash. Then they run past again.

Has there been an accident? Gusev lifts his head, listening, and sees the two soldiers and the sailor playing cards again. Paul Ivanovich is sitting up, moving his lips. He chokes, he feels too weak to breathe, and he is thirsty, but the water is warm and nasty.

The boat is still pitching.

Suddenly something strange happens to one of the card-playing soldiers.

He calls hearts diamonds, he muddles the score and drops his cards, then he gives a silly, scared smile and looks round at everyone.

"One moment, lads," says he and lies on the floor.

Everyone is aghast. They call him, but he doesn't respond.

"Maybe you feel bad, eh, Stephen?" asks the soldier with his arm in a sling. "Should we call a priest perhaps?"

"Have some water, Stephen," says the sailor. "Come on, mate, you drink this."

"Now, why bang his teeth with the mug?" asks Gusev angrily. "Can't you see, you fool?"

"What is it?"

"What is it?" Gusev mimics him. "He has no breath in him, he's dead. That's what it is. What senseless people, Lord help us!"

III

The ship is no longer heaving, and Paul Ivanovich has cheered up. He is no longer angry, and his expression is boastful, challenging and mocking.

"Yes," he seems about to say, "I'm going to tell you something to make you all split your sides laughing."

The port-hole is open and a soft breeze blows on Paul Ivanovich. Voices are heard, and the plashing of oars.

Just beneath the port-hole someone sets up an unpleasant, shrill droning—a Chinese singing, that must be.

"Yes, we're in the roadstead now," Paul Ivanovich says with a sardonic smile. "Another month or so and we'll be in Russia. Yes indeed, sirs, gentlemen and barrack-room scum. I'll go to Odessa, and then straight on to Kharkov. I have a friend in Kharkov, a literary man. I'll go and see him.

"'Now, old boy,' I'll say, 'you can drop your loathsome plots about female amours and the beauties of nature for the time being, and expose these verminous bipeds. Here are some subjects for you.'"

He ponders for a minute.

"Know how I fooled them, Gusev?" he asks.

"Fooled who, Paul Ivanovich?"

"Why, those people we were talking about. There are only two classes on this boat, see, first and third. And no one's allowed to travel third class except peasants—the riff-raff, in other words. Wear a jacket and look in the least like a gentleman or bourgeois—then you must go first class, if you please! You must fork out your five hundred rubles if it kills you.

"'Now why,' I ask, 'did you make such a rule? Trying to raise the prestige of the Russian intelligentsia, I assume?'

"'Not at all. We don't allow it because no respectable person should travel third—it's very nasty and messy in there.'

"'Oh yes? Grateful for your concern on behalf of respectable persons, I'm sure! But nice or nasty, I haven't got five hundred roubles either way. I've never embezzled public funds, I haven't exploited any natives. I've not done any smuggling—nor have I ever flogged anyone to death. So judge for yourself—have I any right to travel first class, let alone reckon myself a member of the Russian intelligentsia?'

"But logic gets you nowhere with these people, so I'm reduced to deception. I put on a workman's coat and high boots, I assume the facial expression of a drunken brute, and off I go to the agent. 'Gimme one o' them tickets, kind sir!'"

"And what might your station be in life?" asks the sailor.

"The clerical. My father was an honest priest who always told the powers that be the truth to their faces—and no little did he suffer for it."

Paul Ivanovich is tired of speaking. He gasps for breath, but still goes on.

"Yes, I never mince my words, I fear nothing and no one—there's a vast difference between me and you in this respect. You're a blind, benighted, down-trodden lot. You see nothing—and what you do see you don't understand. People tell you the wind's broken loose from its chain—that you're cattle, savages. And you believe them. They punch you on the neck—you kiss their hand. Some animal in a raccoon coat robs you, then tips you fifteen copecks—and, 'Oh, let me kiss your hand, sir,' say you. You're pariahs, you're a pathetic lot, but me—that's another matter. I live a conscious life, and I see everything as an eagle or hawk sees it, soaring above the earth. I understand it all. I am protest incarnate. If I see tyranny, I protest. If I see a canting hypocrite, I protest. If I see swine triumphant, I protest. I can't be put down, no Spanish Inquisition can silence me. No sir. Cut out my tongue and I'll protest in mime. Wall me up in a cellar and I'll shout so loud, I'll be heard a mile off. Or I'll starve myself to death, and leave that extra weight on their black consciences. Kill me—my ghost will still haunt you. 'You're quite insufferable, Paul Ivanovich'—so say all who know me, and I glory in that reputation. I've served three years in the Far East, and I'll be remembered there for a century. I've had rows with everyone. 'Don't come back,' my friends write from European Russia. So I damn well will come back and show them, indeed I will. That's life, the way I see it—that's what I call living."

Not listening, Gusev looks through the port-hole. On limpid water of delicate turquoise hue a boat tosses, bathed in blinding hot sunlight. In it stand naked Chinese, holding up cages of canaries.

"Sing, sing," they shout.

Another boat bangs into the first, and a steam cutter dashes past. Then comes yet another boat with a fat Chinese sitting in it, eating rice with chopsticks. The water heaves lazily, with lazy white gulls gliding above it.

"That greasy one needs a good clout on the neck," thinks Gusev, gazing at the fat Chinese and yawning.

He is dozing, and feels as if all nature is dream-bound too. Time passes swiftly. The day goes by unnoticed, unnoticed too steals on the dark.

No longer at anchor, the ship forges on to some further destination.

IV

Two days pass. Paul Ivanovich no longer sits up. He is lying down with his eyes shut, and his nose seems to have grown sharper.

"Paul Ivanovich!" Gusev shouts. "Hey, Paul Ivanovich!"

Paul Ivanovich opens his eyes and moves his lips.

"Feeling unwell?"

"It's nothing, nothing," gasps Paul Ivanovich in answer. "On the contrary, I feel better, actually. I can lie down now, see? I feel easier."

"Well, thank God for that, Paul Ivanovich."

"Comparing myself with you poor lads, I feel sorry for you. My lungs are all right, this is only a stomach cough. I can endure hell, let alone the Red Sea. I have a critical attitude to my illness and medicines, what's more. But you—you benighted people, you have a rotten time, you really do."

There is no motion and the sea is calm, but it is sweltering hot, like a steam bath. It was hard enough to listen, let alone speak. Gusev hugs his knees, rests his head on them and thinks of his homeland. Heavens, what joy to think about snow and cold in this stifling heat! You're sledging along, when the horses suddenly shy and bolt.

Roads, ditches, gulleys—it's all one to them. Along they hurtle like mad, right down the village, over pond, past pottery, out through open country.

"Hold him!" shout pottery hands and peasants at the top of their voices. "Hold hard!"

But why hold? Let the keen, cold gale lash your face and bite your hands. Those clods of snow kicked up by horses' hooves—let them fall on cap, down collar, on neck and chest. Runners may squeak, traces and swingletrees snap—to hell with them! And what joy when the sledge overturns and you fly full tilt into a snowdrift, face buried in snow—then stand up, white all over, with icicles hanging from your moustache, no cap, no mittens, your belt undone.

People laugh, dogs bark.

Paul Ivanovich half opens one eye and looks at Gusev.

"Did your commanding officer steal, Gusev?" he asks softly.

"Who can tell, Paul Ivanovich? We know nothing, it don't come to our ears."

A long silence follows. Gusev broods, rambles deliriously, keeps drinking water. He finds it hard to speak, hard to listen, and he is afraid of being talked to. One hour passes, then a second, then a third. Evening comes on, then night, but he notices nothing, and still sits dreaming of the frost.

It sounds as if someone has come into the sick-bay, and voices are heard—but five minutes later everything is silent.

"God be with him," says the soldier with his arm in a sling. "May he rest in peace, he was a restless man."

"What?" Gusev asks. "Who?"

"He's dead, they've just carried him up."

"Ah well," mumbles Gusev with a yawn. "May the Kingdom of Heaven be his."

"What do you think, Gusev?" asks the soldier with the sling after a short pause. "Will he go to heaven or not?"

"Who?"

"Paul Ivanovich."

"Yes, he will—he suffered so long. And then he's from the clergy, and priests always have a lot of relations—their prayers will save him."

The soldier with the sling sits on Gusev's bunk.

"You're not long for this world either, Gusev," he says in an undertone. "You'll never get to Russia."

"Did the doctor or his assistant say so?" Gusev asks.

"It's not that anyone said so, it's just obvious—you can always tell when someone's just going to die. You don't eat, you don't drink, and you're so thin—you're a frightful sight. It's consumption, in fact. I don't say this to upset you, but you may want to have the sacrament and the last rites. And if you have any money you'd better give it to the senior officer."

"I never wrote home," sighs Gusev. "They won't even know I'm dead."

"They will," says the sick sailor in a deep voice. "When you're dead an entry will be made in the ship's log, they'll give a note to the Army Commander in Odessa, and he'll send a message to your parish or whatever it is."

This talk makes Gusev uneasy, and a vague urge disturbs him. He drinks water, but that isn't it. He stretches towards the porthole and breathes in the hot, dank air, but that isn't it either. He tries to think of home and frost—and it still isn't right.

He feels in the end that one more minute in the sick-bay will surely choke him to death.

"I'm real bad, mates," says he. "I'm going on deck—help me up, for Christ's sake."

"All right," agrees the soldier with the sling. "You'll never do it on your own, I'll carry you. Hold on to my neck."

Gusev puts his arms round the soldier's neck, while the soldier puts his able arm round Gusev and carries him up. Sailors and discharged soldiers are sleeping all over the place on deck—so many of them that it is hard to pass.

"Get down," the soldier with the sling says quietly. "Follow me slowly, hold on to my shirt."

It is dark. There are no lights on deck or masts, or in the sea around them. Still as a statue on the tip of the bow stands the man on watch, but he too looks as if he is sleeping. Left to its own devices, apparently, the ship seems to be sailing where it lists.

"They're going to throw Paul Ivanovich in the sea now," says the soldier with the sling. "They'll put him in a sack and throw him in."

"Yes. That's the way of it."

"But it's better to lie in the earth at home. At least your mother will come and cry over your grave."

"Very true."

There is a smell of dung and hay. Bullocks with lowered heads are standing by the ship's rail. One, two, three—there are eight of them. There is a small pony too. Gusev puts his hand out to stroke it, but it tosses its head, bares its teeth, and tries to bite his sleeve.

"Blasted thing!" says Gusev angrily.

The two of them, he and the sailor, quietly thread their way to the bows, then stand by the rail and look up and down without a word. Overhead are deep sky, bright stars, peace, quiet—and it is just like being at home in your village. But down below are darkness and disorder. The tall waves roar for no known reason. Whichever wave you watch, each is trying to lift itself above the others, crushing them and chasing its neighbour, while on it, with a growling flash of its white mane, pounces a third roller no less wild and hideous.

The sea has no sense, no pity. Were the ship smaller, were it not made of stout iron, the waves would snap it without the slightest compunction and devour all the people, saints and sinners alike. The ship shows the same mindless cruelty. That beaked monster drives on, cutting millions of waves in her path, not fearing darkness, wind, void, solitude. She cares for nothing, and if the ocean had its people this juggernaut would crush them too, saints and sinners alike.

"Where are we now?" Gusev asks.

"I don't know. In the ocean, we must be."

"Can't see land."

"Some hope! We shan't see that for a week, they say."

Silently reflecting, both soldiers watch the white foam with its phosphorescent glint. The first to break silence is Gusev.

"It ain't frightening," says he. "It does give you the creeps a bit, though—like sitting in a dark forest. But if they was to lower a dinghy into the water now, say, and an officer told me to go sixty miles over the sea and fish—I'd go. Or say some good Christian was to fall overboard, I'd go in after him. A German or a China-man I wouldn't save, but I'd go in after a Christian."

"Are you afeared of dying?"

"Aye. It's the old home that worries me. My brother's none too steady, see? He drinks, he beats his wife when he didn't ought to, and he don't look up to his parents. It'll all go to rack and ruin without me, and my father and my old mother will have to beg for their bread, very like. But I can't rightly stand up, mate, and it's so stuffy here. Let's go to bed."

V

Gusev goes back to the sick-bay and gets in his bunk. Some vague urge still disturbs him, but what it is he wants he just can't reckon. His chest feels tight, his head's pounding, and his mouth's so parched, he can hardly move his tongue. He dozes and rambles. Tormented by nightmares, cough and sweltering atmosphere, he falls fast asleep by morning. He dreams that they have just taken the bread out of the oven in his barracks. He has climbed into the stove himself, and is having a steam bath, lashing himself with a birch switch. He sleeps for two days. At noon on the third, two soldiers come down and carry him out of the sick-bay.

They sew him up in sail-cloth and put in two iron bars to weigh him down. Sewn in canvas, he looks like a carrot or radish—broad at the head and narrow at the base.

They carry him on deck before sundown, and place him on a plank. One end of the plank rests on the ship's rail, the other on a box set on a stool. Heads bare, discharged soldiers and crew stand by.

"Blessed is the Lord's name," begins the priest. "As it was in the beginning, is now, and ever shall be."

"Amen," chant three sailors.

Soldiers and crew cross themselves, glancing sideways at the waves. Strange that a man has been sewn into that sail-cloth and will shortly fly into those waves. Could that really happen to any of them?

The priest scatters earth over Gusev and makes an obeisance. *Eternal Memory* is sung.

The officer of the watch tilts one end of the plank. Gusev slides down it, flies off head first, does a somersault in the air and—in he splashes! Foam envelops him, and he seems swathed in lace for a second, but the second passes and he vanishes beneath the waves.

He moves swiftly towards the bottom. Will he reach it? It is said to be three miles down. He sinks eight or nine fathoms, then begins to move more and more slowly, swaying rhythmically as if trying to make up his mind. Caught by a current, he is swept sideways more swiftly than downwards.

Now he meets a shoal of little pilot-fish. Seeing the dark body, the fish stop dead. Suddenly all turn tail at once and vanish. Less than a minute later they again pounce on Gusev like arrows and stitch the water round him with zig-zags.

Then another dark hulk looms—a shark. Ponderous, reluctant and apparently ignoring Gusev, it glides under him and he sinks on to its back. Then it turns belly upwards, basking in the warm, translucent water, and languidly opening its jaw with the two rows of fangs. The pilot-fish are delighted, waiting to see what will happen next. After playing with the body, the shark nonchalantly puts its jaws underneath, cautiously probing with its fangs, and the sail-cloth tears along the body's whole length from head to foot. One iron bar falls out, scares the pilot-fish, hits the shark on the flank and goes swiftly to the bottom.

Overhead, meanwhile, clouds are massing on the sunset side—one like a triumphal arch, another like a lion, a third like a pair of scissors.

From the clouds a broad, green shaft of light breaks through, spanning out to the sky's very center. A little later a violet ray settles alongside, then a gold one by that, and then a pink one.

The sky turns a delicate mauve. Gazing at this sky so glorious and magical, the ocean scowls at first, but soon it too takes on tender, joyous, ardent hues for which human speech hardly has a name.

Eudora Welty

Eudora Welty was born in Jackson, Mississippi, in April 1909. Prior to publishing her first short story in 1936, Welty attended the Mississippi State College for Women, the University of Wisconsin, and the Columbia School of Business, and worked for several radio stations, newspapers, and the Works Progress Administration. Over the course of her writing career, she has published poems, lectures, interviews, photography collections, book reviews, novels, novellas, and several major short story collections. She is the recipient of numerous awards, including the Pulitzer Prize for the novel The Optimist's Daughter *(1972). "Old Mr. Marblehall" appeared in 1938 in the* Southern Review *as "Old Mr. Grenada," and appeared in its current form for the first time in* A Curtain of Green and Other Stories, *published in 1941.*

Old Mr. Marblehall

Old Mr. Marblehall never did anything, never got married until he was sixty. You can see him out taking a walk. Watch and you'll see how preciously old people come to think they are made—the way they walk, like conspirators, bent over a little, filled with protection. They stand long on the corners but more impatiently than anyone, as if they expect traffic to take notice of them, rear up the horses and throw on the brakes, so they can go where they want to go. That's Mr. Marblehall. He has short white bangs, and a bit of snapdragon in his lapel. He walks with a big polished stick, a present. That's what people think of him. Everybody says to his face, "So well preserved!" Behind his back they say cheerfully, "One foot in the grave." He has on his thick, beautiful, glowing coat—tweed, but he looks as gratified as an animal in its own tingling fur. You see, even in summer he wears it, because he is cold all the time. He looks quaintly secretive and prepared for anything, out walking very luxuriously on Catherine Street.

His wife, back at home in the parlor standing up to think, is a large, elongated old woman with electric-looking hair and curly lips. She has spent her life trying to escape from the parlor-like jaws of self-consciousness. Her late marriage has set in upon her nerves like a retriever nosing and puffing through old dead leaves out in the woods. When she walks around the room she looks remote and nebulous, out on the fringe of habitation, and rather as if she must have been cruelly trained—otherwise she couldn't do actual, immediate things, like answering the telephone or putting on a hat. But she has gone further than you'd think: into club work. Surrounded by other more suitably exclaiming women, she belongs to the Daughters of the American Revolution and the United Daughters of the Confederacy, attending teas. Her long, disquieted figure towering in the candlelight of other women's houses looks like something accidental. Any occasion, and she dresses her hair like a unicorn horn. She even sings, and is requested to sing. She even writes some of the songs she sings ("O Trees in the Evening"). She has a voice that dizzies other ladies like an organ note, and amuses men like a halloo down the well. It's full of a hollow wind and echo, winding out through the wavery hope of her mouth. Do people know of her perpetual amazement? Back in safety she wonders, her untidy head trembles in the domestic dark. She remembers how everyone in Natchez will suddenly grow quiet around her. Old Mrs. Marblehall, Mr. Marblehall's wife: she even goes out in the rain, which Southern women despise above everything, in big neat biscuit-colored galoshes, for which she "ordered off." She is only looking around—servile, undelighted, sleepy, expensive, tortured Mrs. Marblehall, pinning her mind with a pin to her husband's diet. She wants to tempt him, she tells him. What would he like best, that he can have?

There is Mr. Marblehall's ancestral home. It's not so wonderfully large—it has only four columns—but you always look toward it, the way you always glance into tunnels and see nothing. The river is after it now, and the little back garden has assuredly crumbled away, but the box maze is there on the edge like a trap, to confound the Mississippi River. Deep in the red wall waits the front door— it weighs such a lot, it is perfectly solid, all one piece, black mahogany. . . . And you see—one of *them* is always going in it. There is a knocker shaped like a gasping fish on the door. You have every reason in the world to imagine the inside is dark, with old things about. There's many a big, deathly-looking tapestry, wrinkling and thin, many a sofa shaped like an S. Brocades as tall as the wicked queens in Italian tales stand gathered before the windows. Everything is draped and hooded and shaded, of course, unaffectionate but close. Such rosy lamps! The only sound would be a breath against the prisms, a stirring of the chandelier. It's like old eyelids, the house with one of its shutters, in careful working order, slowly opening outward. Then the little son softly comes and stares out like a kitten, with button nose and pointed ears and little fuzz of silky hair running along the top of his head.

The son is the worst of all. Mr. and Mrs. Marblehall had a child! When both of them were terribly old, they had this little, amazing, fascinating son. You can see how people are taken aback, how they jerk and throw up their hands every time they so much as think about it. At least, Mr. Marblehall sees them. He thinks Natchez people do nothing themselves, and really, most of them have done or could do the same thing. This son is six years old now. Close up, he has a monkey look, a very penetrating look. He has very sparse Japanese hair, tiny little pearly teeth, long little wilted fingers. Every day he is slowly and expensively dressed and taken to the Catholic school. He looks quietly and maliciously absurd, out walking with old Mr. Marblehall or old Mrs. Marblehall, placing his small booted foot on a little green worm, while they stop and wait on him. Everybody passing by thinks that he looks quite as if he thinks his parents had him just to show they could. You see, it becomes complicated, full of vindictiveness.

But now, as Mr. Marblehall walks as briskly as possible toward the river where there is sun, you have to merge him back into his proper blur, into the little party-giving town he lives in. Why look twice at him? There has been an old Mr. Marblehall in Natchez ever since the first one arrived back in 1818—with a theatrical presentation of Otway's *Venice,* ending with *A Laughable Combat between Two Blind Fiddlers*—an actor! Mr. Marblehall isn't so important. His name is on the list, he is forgiven, but nobody gives a hoot about any old Mr. Marblehall. He could die, for all they care; some people even say, "Oh, is he still alive?" Mr. Marblehall walks and walks, and now and then he is driven in his ancient fringed carriage with the candle burners like empty eyes in front. And yes, he is supposed to travel for his health. But why consider his absence? There isn't any other place besides Natchez, and even if there were, it would hardly be likely to change Mr. Marblehall if it were brought up against him. Big fingers could pick him up off the Esplanade and take him through the air, his old legs still measuredly walking in a dangle, and set him down where he could continue that same old Natchez stroll of his in the East or the West or Kingdom Come. What difference could anything make now about old Mr. Marblehall—so late? A week or two would go by in Natchez and then there would be Mr. Marblehall, walking down Catherine Street again, still exactly in the same degree alive and old.

People naturally get bored. They say, "Well, he waited till he was sixty years old to marry, and what did he want to marry for?" as though what he did were the excuse for their boredom and their lack of concern. Even the thought of his having a stroke right in front of one of the Pilgrimage houses during Pilgrimage Week makes them only sigh, as if to say it's nobody's fault but his own if he wants to be so insultingly and precariously well-preserved. He ought to have a little black boy to follow around after him. Oh, his precious old health, which never had reason to be so inspiring! Mr. Marblehall has a formal, reproachful look as he stands on the corners arranging himself to go out into the traffic to cross the streets. It's as if he's thinking of shaking his stick and saying, "Well, look! I've done it, don't you see?" But really, nobody pays much attention to his look. He is just like other people to them. He could have easily danced with a troupe of angels in Paradise every night, and they wouldn't have guessed. Nobody is likely to find out that he is leading a double life.

The funny thing is he just recently began to lead this double life. He waited until he was sixty years old. Isn't he crazy? Before that, he'd never done anything. He didn't know what to do. Everything was for all the world like his first party. He stood about, and looked in his father's books, and long ago he went to France, but he didn't like it.

Drive out any of these streets in and under the hills and you find yourself lost. You see those scores of little galleried houses nearly alike. See the yellowing China trees at the eaves, the round flower beds in the front yards, like bites in the grass, listen to the screen doors whining, the ice wagons dragging by, the twittering noises of children. Nobody ever looks to see who is living in a house like that. These people come out themselves and sprinkle the hose over the street at this time of day to settle the dust, and after they sit on the porch, they go back into the house, and you hear the radio for the next two hours. It seems to mourn and cry for them. They go to bed early.

Well, old Mr. Marblehall can easily be seen standing beside a row of zinnias growing down the walk in front of that little house, bending over, easy, easy, so as not to strain anything, to stare at the flowers. Of course he planted them! They are covered with brown—each petal is a little heart-shaped pocket of dust. They don't have any smell, you know. It's twilight, all amplified with locusts screaming; nobody could see anything. Just what Mr. Marblehall is bending over the zinnias for is a mystery, any way you look at it. But there he is, quite visible, alive and old, leading his double life.

There's his other wife, standing on the night-stained porch by a potted fern, screaming things to a neighbor. This wife is really worse than the other one. She is more solid, fatter, shorter, and while not so ugly, funnier looking. She looks like funny furniture—an unornamented stair post in one of these little houses, with her small monotonous round stupid head—or sometimes like a woodcut of a Bavarian witch, forefinger pointing, with scratches in the air all around her. But she's so static she scarcely moves, from her thick shoulders down past her cylindered brown dress to her short, stubby house slippers. She stands still and screams to the neighbors.

This wife thinks Mr. Marblehall's name is Mr. Bird. She says, "I declare I told Mr. Bird to go to bed, and look at him! I don't understand him!" All her devotion is combustible and goes up in despair. This wife tells everything she knows. Later, after she tells the neighbors, she will tell Mr. Marblehall. Cymbal-breasted, she fills the house with wifely complaints. She calls, "After I get Mr. Bird to bed, what does he do then? He lies there stretched out with his clothes on and don't have one word to say. Know what he does?"

And she goes on, while her husband bends over the zinnias, to tell what Mr. Marblehall (or Mr. Bird) does in bed. She does tell the truth. He reads *Terror Tales* and *Astonishing Stories.* She can't see anything to them: they scare her to death. These stories are about horrible and fantastic things happening to nude women and scientists. In one of them, when the characters open bureau drawers, they find a woman's leg with a stocking and garter on. Mrs. Bird had to shut the magazine. "The glutinous shadows," these stories say, "the red-eyed, muttering old crone," "the moonlight

on her thigh," "an ancient cult of sun worshippers," "an altar sus-
piciously stained . . ." Mr. Marblehall doesn't feel as terrified as
all that, but he reads on and on. He is killing time. It is richness
without taste, like some holiday food. The clock gets a fruity bursting tick, to get through midnight—then leisurely, leisurely on.
When time is passing it's like a bug in his ear. And then Mr. Bird—
he doesn't even want a shade on the light, this wife moans re-
spectably. He reads under a bulb. She can tell you how he goes
straight through a stack of magazines. "He might just as well not
have a family," she always ends, unjustly, and rolls back into the
house as if she had been on a little wheel all this time.

But the worst of them all is the other little boy. Another little
boy just like the first one. He wanders around the bungalow full of
tiny little schemes and jokes. He has lost his front tooth, and in
this way he looks slightly different from Mr. Marblehall's other
little boy—more shocking. Otherwise, you couldn't tell them apart
if you wanted to. They both have that look of cunning little jug-
glers, violently small under some spotlight beam, preoccupied and
silent, amusing themselves. Both of the children will go into sudden fits and tantrums that frighten their mothers and Mr. Marblehall to death. Then they can get anything they want. But this
little boy, the one who's lost the tooth, is the smarter. For a long
time he supposed that his mother was totally solid, down to her
thick separated ankles. But when she stands there on the porch
screaming to the neighbors, she reminds him of those flares that
charm him so, that they leave burning in the street at night—the
dark solid ball, then, tongue-like, the wicked, yellow, continuous,
enslaving blaze on the stem. He knows what his father thinks.

Perhaps one day, while Mr. Marblehall is standing there gently
bent over the zinnias, this little boy is going to write on a fence,
"Papa leads a double life." He finds out things you wouldn't find
out. He is a monkey.

You see, one night he is going to follow Mr. Marblehall (or Mr.
Bird) out of the house. Mr. Marblehall has said as usual that he is
leaving for one of his health trips. He is one of those correct old
gentlemen who are still going to the wells and drinking the waters—exactly like his father, the late old Mr. Marblehall. But why
does he leave on foot? This will occur to the little boy.

So he will follow his father. He will follow him all the way across
town. He will see the shining river come winding around. He will

see the house where Mr. Marblehall turns in at the wrought-iron gate. He will see a big speechless woman come out and lead him in by the heavy door. He will not miss those rosy lamps beyond the many-folded draperies at the windows. He will run around the fountains and around the Japonica trees, past the stone figure of the pigtailed courtier mounted on the goat, down to the back of the house. From there he can look far up at the strange upstairs rooms. In one window the other wife will be standing like a giant, in a long-sleeved gathered nightgown, combing her electric hair and breaking it off each time in the comb. From the next window the other little boy will look out secretly into the night, and see him—or not see him. That would be an interesting thing, a moment of strange telepathies. (Mr. Marblehall can imagine it.) Then in the corner room there will suddenly be turned on the bright, naked light. Aha! Father!

Mr. Marblehall's little boy will easily climb a tree there and peep through the window. There, under a stark shadeless bulb, on a great four-poster with carved griffins, will be Mr. Marblehall, reading *Terror Tales*, stretched out and motionless.

Then everything will come out.

At first, nobody will believe it.

Or maybe the policeman will say, "Stop! How dare you!"

Maybe, better than that, Mr. Marblehall himself will confess his duplicity—how he has led two totally different lives, with completely different families, two sons instead of one. What an astonishing, unbelievable, electrifying confession that would be, and how his two wives would topple over, how his sons would cringe! To say nothing of most men aged sixty-six. So thinks self-consoling Mr. Marblehall.

You will think, what if nothing ever happens? What if there is no climax, even to this amazing life? Suppose old Mr. Marblehall simply remains alive, getting older by the minute, shuttling, still secretly, back and forth?

Nobody cares. Not an inhabitant of Natchez, Mississippi, cares if he is deceived by old Mr. Marblehall. Neither does anyone care that Mr. Marblehall has finally caught on, he thinks, to what people are supposed to do. This is it: they endure something inwardly—for a time secretly; they establish a past, a memory; thus they store up life. He has done this; most remarkably, he has even multiplied his life by deception; and plunging deeper and deeper he speculates upon some glorious finish, a great explosion of revelations . . . the future.

But he still has to kill time, and get through the clocking nights. Otherwise he dreams that he is a great blazing butterfly stitching up a net; which doesn't make sense.

Old Mr. Marblehall! He may have years ahead yet in which to wake up bolt upright in the bed under the naked bulb, his heart thumping, his old eyes watering and wild, imagining that if people knew about his double life, they'd die.

3

AXIOMS AND ALTERNATIVES

You'll never be a poet until you realize that everything I say today and this quarter is wrong. It may be right for me, but it is wrong for you. Every moment I am, without wanting or trying to, telling you to write like me.

—*Richard Hugo,* The Triggering Town

Just as the field of physics (or chemistry, or mathematics) is founded upon a set of natural laws, the field of creative writing is founded upon a set of "axioms" that, in theory at least, make fair stories good and good stories better. Unlike the scientific fields, however, where axioms are carefully codified and supported by laboratory tests, the axioms of creative writing are flexible and subject to numerous exceptions. When a phenomenon defies the law of gravity, physicists must scramble to find a new law that explains the exception; but when a work of fiction defies a law of creative writing, and an author makes a great story in spite of defying our expectations of what makes a great story, that exception only proves that "great writing is larger than any set of rules," which is, ironically, one of the rules of creative writing.

The axioms of fiction are a loose set of guidelines, not ironclad rules. They are rarely written down in any one place; instead, they are passed along like folklore, bits and snatches of advice that any individual who cares about storytelling invariably finds in disparate places: the letters of a favorite author, a lecture delivered by a creative writing teacher, a private conversation with a young writer. In theory, the axioms of fiction represent the gathered and winnowed experience of a thousand years of authors and a hundred years of creative writing teachers. But they represent prejudices as well, specific biases that speak for our time and our place. They are designed to create competent writers, but not excellent ones. As Richard Hugo suggests, you can't be a writer until you learn how to forget what you have been taught. But you have to learn first; you have to have something to rise above in order to rise.

AVOID CLICHES

A cliche is any description, dialogue, article of language, plot turn, or character that has been used so frequently that it is worn out. What it means to be "worn out" varies from reader to reader (for some, for instance, the phrase "worn out" is a cliche): one reader might find an adorable tow-headed six-year-old boy who says "yuck" to be a touching character, while another reader might object to yet another adorable child, the word "adorable" being used to describe him, the fact that he is tow-headed, or the exclamation "yuck" being used at all. In general, however, a cliche is an element of a story that any community of readers recognizes as being overly familiar, or clearly borrowed from other fictions.

Cliches, in many ways, are underrated. The purpose of art and writing, after all, is to express something important that other people will recognize from their own experience. This definition is tantalizingly close to that of a cliche, which is also something readers recognize from their own experience, but are unhappy to see again. Whether or not we like it, there is a considerable overlap between the real world and the world of cliche, and what one person thinks is cliched is exactly what another person will find realistic or memorable. For instance, you may want to avoid the forms of popular romances—Cinderella stories with dashing heroes, women in distress, and happy endings. And yet, popular romances have sold over one billion copies worldwide because there is an enormous audience that prefers a reading experience they know they enjoy over original and unknown reading experiences. Indeed, cliches become cliches because they provide useful ways of communicating important and recognizable facts about the world. Just because they are overused does not mean that they have ceased being effective; it just means they have ceased being effective for some readers.

While these arguments may be justification for writing well-worn prose, however (and even then, on the condition that it moves some readership), they are not excuses for not trying to write something newer and stronger. Two of the central goals of most creative writing instruction, no matter how formal or informal, are to nurture original forms of expression and to encourage respect for language. Learning to avoid cliches is an invaluable lesson in learning how to care about language on a word-by-word, sentence-by-sentence level. An unconsciously used cliche is a signpost, telling you that you have drawn from standardized, accessible sources of inspiration. It is a reminder that you did not work hard enough, possessed limited verbal resources, or pursued the safest, best traveled paths of expression at times when the emotional content of the story somehow became risky, or when inspiration ran low.

Cliches can be transformed and renewed, however. Throughout Grace Paley's "The Pale Pink Roast," her characters speak consistently in verbal cliches to one another:

> "We're really nuts about each other."
> "She was great, a lifesaver."
> "Live it up."
> "Going, going, gone."
> "What's really cooking?"

And yet, Paley's own third-person narration is so consciously inventive that it would be easier to accuse the author of working too hard at word selection, not too little: note, for instance, the adjective and verb choices in a sentence such as "He kicked aside the disappointed acorns and endowed a grand admiring grin to two young girls." In this context, the use of cliches in the dialogue seems like a deliberate artistic choice; Paley's characters speak in borrowed language, but the consistency and vitality of that borrowed language makes it more inventive than the original from which it was derived.

When John Cheever's narrator in "The Death of Justina" uses cliches in his mock advertising copy, he twists them into slightly distorted forms that expose their banality:

> Are you growing old? . . . Are you falling out of love with your image in the looking glass? Does your face in the morning seem rucked and

seamed with alcoholic and sexual excesses and does the rest of you appear to be a grayish-pink lump. . . .

Like Paley, Cheever's use of cliches—his ability to twist them just slightly—reflects control of language. In Cheever's case, however, the use of cliche is linked to the emotional and thematic content of the story. "The Death of Justina" is a story about the tension between conformity and individuality, between staying sane and having a nervous breakdown. Would "The Death of Justina" be as powerful if the narrator was not having trouble distinguishing between real experience and cliched, imagined experience?

> I seemed to hear the jinglebells of the sleigh that would carry me to Grandmother's house although in fact Grandmother spent the last years of her life working as a hostess on an ocean liner and was lost in the tragic sinking of the S.S. *Lorelei* and I was responding to a memory that I had not experienced.

The fact that the narrator shuffles between cliches and invention illustrates how deeply his conflict affects him; but the fact that he can ultimately distinguish between the two is a sign that he has not yet entirely surrendered, either to the nervous breakdown or to his boss in the advertising agency.

In other words, while learning to avoid cliches is an important aspect of learning how to care about language, learning how to *manage* cliches might prove to be a better strategy. There are two situations when using cliches of character, plot, or language is acceptable, even preferable: when you can present familiar themes or characters with enough conviction or innovation to make them seem new again; or, as Paley and Cheever show, when you can use them in the context of other writing strategies that bend the cliches into new forms. To be able to distinguish between cliched and real experience, Cheever seems to be telling us, is sanity; as a writer, to be able to choose between the two is power.

Writing Strategies

1. Select one of your own stories. Find three elements in that story (a character, a piece of dialogue, a plot turn) that appear to have been borrowed from, or based upon, television programming. Even if you believe you have created a completely original piece of

writing, locate three elements that might conceivably overlap with television programming.

Rewrite those three elements, using material that you are completely certain has been taken from your life, or from your imagination.

2. Select a cliche that, despite its status as a cliche, you nevertheless believe to be true: "Love conquers all," "It takes one to know one."

   a. Write a short-short story (two pages) that illustrates the truth of the cliche, without ever specifically mentioning it.
   b. Write a story that disproves the cliche.

3. Describe in exact detail a person from your life whom you have not seen recently. Having written this description, review it carefully for verbal cliches ("She had hair like spun silk") and cliches of character.

4. Make a list of characters you know to be "cliche characters": the cop two weeks short of retirement; the beer-drinking, hard-cussing truck driver; the crinkly faced, sage grandma. (It does not matter whether or not they exist in real life; what matters is that they exist in frequent depictions on television, in movies, and in books.)

Select one of these characters, and make him or her the focus of a short story. But take deliberate pains to make sure that the character possesses one personality trait that completely undermines the remainder of the cliche: the grandma is sage and sweet, but believes that Elvis is not dead; the truck driver drinks and swears but also conceals the fact that he has a Masters' degree in English literature; the cop is not worried about surviving his last two weeks on the force, but secretly debates whether or not to tell his younger partner that he is gay.

SHOW, DON'T TELL

As the writer and teacher Ron McFarland observes, "the advice to 'show' rather than 'tell' qualifies as universal." Usually, "Show, don't tell" means, don't spell out what can be portrayed using description, dialogue, or action. Don't write, "He was angry"; create a character who acts angry, looks angry, or speaks angry dialogue. More generally, however, readers say "Show, don't tell" when a story feels flat and shallow or seems to lack ambiguity or mystery. At these times, the advice "Show, don't tell" also means tell *more*, provide concrete details: the frayed edges of someone's shirt or the way someone's voice cracks.

When you are told to show, not tell, you are expected to make two revisions: first, to remove the kind of broad clinical adjectives that psychologists might use to describe their patients ("angry," "happy," "nervous"); and second, to replace those adjectives with concrete details that appeal to the reader's senses. An example of how "Show, don't tell" is supposed to work can be found in Flannery O'Connor's "A Good Man Is Hard to Find":

> The grandmother offered to hold the baby and the children's mother passed him over the front seat to her. She set him on her knee and bounced him and told him about the things they were passing. She rolled her eyes and screwed up her mouth and stuck her leathery thin face into his smooth bland one. Occasionally he gave her a faraway smile. . . .

If O'Connor were telling, not showing, she might have written, "The grandmother, who is a pretty sad case, spent a great deal of time entertaining her grandchild, who really wasn't interested in her. This was particularly pathetic, because everybody knows that babies usually adore their grandparents." Instead, O'Connor conveys this information through a variety of devices. First, her description possesses the pace and timing of a well-told joke: the grandmother spends several sentences trying to entertain the boy, which conveys the sense of considerable labor; he spends one short sentence barely acknowledging her existence. Second, O'Connor's word choice clearly editorializes: the grandmother's rolling eyes, screwed-up mouth, and leathery thin face "stuck" into the baby's face give her little dignity, and also convey the sense that her efforts to entertain the baby are particularly forced and charmless. Similarly, he does not merely smile at her; his smile is "faraway," and even occasional, which conveys in two different ways that, in his opinion at least, she is not a lovable woman. Lastly, by not drawing comparisons to how other babies act around other grandmothers, O'Connor allows us to make that comparison for ourselves.

An example of how "Show, don't tell" is *not* supposed to work is provided by Milan Kundera's "The Hitchhiking Game":

This role was a complete contradiction of the young man's habitually solicitous approach to the girl. True, before he had met her, he had
in fact behaved roughly rather than gently toward women. But he had
never resembled a heartless tough guy, because he had never demonstrated either a particularly strong will or ruthlessness. However, if
he did not resemble such a man, nonetheless he had *longed* to at one
time. Of course it was a quite naive desire, but there it was. Childish
desires withstand all the snares of the adult mind and often survive
into ripe old age. And this childish desire quickly took advantage of
the opportunity to embody itself in the proffered role.

In this passage, Kundera utilizes no concrete detail or dialogue. He
makes no attempt to show us what the young man is thinking by
showing relevant actions. His vocabulary is abstract, and would fit
a psychology text: "And this childish desire quickly took advantage
of the opportunity to embody itself in the proffered role." The passage is not short, and even seems preachy: "Childish desires withstand all the snares of the adult mind and often survive into ripe
old age." In every way, Kundera appears to be telling, not showing.
But what if this passage is not Kundera preaching to us, but showing us the young man thinking to himself? Then Kundera can be
praised for the precision and depth with which he depicts the psychological details of a particularly powerful romantic crossroads.

The more you look at "Show, don't tell," the more it requires
clarification. On the axiomatic level, it is incorrect: as Kundera's
"The Hitchhiking Game" illustrates, it is possible to write a story
that "tells" in every sentence, but ultimately "shows" something of
real value. On the linguistic level, it is vague: when Scott Bradfield
writes that light is "gentle and imminent like snow," or when
Jeanette Winterson describes a town "stolen from the valleys," are
they showing or are they telling? On a pragmatic level, it is misleading: "Show, don't tell" assumes that you can make a character
or scene radiate with inner life by mechanically appending new
information. If you are not interested in a character, however, no
amount of extra added detail—"her eyes were brown," "her hair
was blonde," "her shoes were old"—will bring that character to
life. If you unenthusiastically create in a second draft a conversation between two characters that was paraphrased in a first draft,
it is likely that the new dialogue will seem lifeless and forced.
When you consider "Show, don't tell," consider the quality of the
concrete details that will make up the "show."

Writing Strategies

1. Using a story you have already written, select a moment in which you have described a character's state of mind in a short, straightforward fashion: "She was angry," "He was sad."

Replace that sentence with a longer sentence or a paragraph in which you describe the character engaged in some specific activity that makes it relatively clear that "she is angry" or "he is sad." Do not select some activity that too plainly telegraphs the emotion involved: she should not stamp her foot or turn red, and he should not cry or sigh.

2. Using a story you have already written, select an instance where you have placed a short, straightforward physical description of a person, setting, or object: "He was tall and good-looking" or "Her coat was red," for example.

Write an entire paragraph in which you describe that person, setting, or object. Consider the possibility that your paragraph-long description can have narrative flow all its own, that it can become a history of the object, a lengthy comparison to something, a poetic aside. If needed, select a person, setting, or object from your life, and use that memory as inspiration.

3. Take a scene in a story you have already written and reduce it to a one-sentence summary written in the voice of the story (first person, second person, or third person). Place it in the story, and cut the scene itself. Which way reads better?

Do the opposite, with a scene that you have described in a short summary ("One day, they got married"). Turn it into a one- to two-page scene that describes the action in concrete detail. Place it in the story in the proper place, and cut the summary that was there previously. Which way reads better?

WRITE WHAT YOU KNOW

The next semester the writing professor is obsessed with writing from personal experience. You must write what you know, what has happened to you.

—Lorrie Moore, "How to Become a Writer"

Eudora Welty wrote about the residents of a small Southern town; so did William Faulkner. Not coincidentally, both authors lived in small Southern towns. John Updike, who grew up precocious and observant in the Eastern Pennsylvania town of Shillington, has written several novels and short stories portraying the lives of people coming of age or growing old in Eastern Pennsylvania towns. Alice Munro, who was born, raised, and lives in Ontario, sets most of her fiction in Ontario in the present day. F. Scott Fitzgerald wove aspects of his personality and his upbringing into *several* characters in his classic novel *The Great Gatsby* (1925), including the narrator and Gatsby himself. It is impossible to list all the small visual scenes, lines of dialogue, or characters that were drawn from some author's own life and appear in stories or novels that are otherwise thoroughly fictional. Similarly, it is impossible to tell what portions of stories that seem based in fact are actually fictitious— which of Welty's many characters, for instance, were based on individuals she imagined. But what cannot be questioned is that fiction writers, in every culture and in every age, draw substantially upon their real lives for the stuff of their stories.

"Write what you know" asks you also to draw upon your personal experience for the materials of fiction. In theory, by writing from experience you will be more confident and have more to say: the writer who has lived through a family divorce, for instance, will be able to write with authority and authenticity from the point of view of a child watching his or her parents break up; the writer who has happily married parents will be able to describe the inner workings of a sustained marriage. "Write what you know" also operates on a second level: it reminds you that what you found interesting in your real life might be interesting in print as well. A memorable relative might become the basis for a character. A character trait from that memorable relative might become the inspiration for a new character, or the turning point of a plot. The house of the memorable relative might turn up as the house in a story which otherwise has no characters that resemble the memorable relative. Or maybe that character had a lamp shaped like a rooster, that you always thought would look good in a story. A lamp like that would go a long way to describe the personality of the character who owns it.

While few writers deliberately and mechanically select elements of their real experiences to draw into their fictions, it is absolutely crucial to respect the workings of your own memory, and to remember that the people and events that your memory saves for its own secret reasons are often the sources of the best stories. In "Fires," Raymond Carver describes how small moments become transformed into fiction:

> I was in the middle of writing a short story when my telephone rang. I answered it. On the other end of the line was the voice of a man who was obviously a black man, someone asking for a party named Nelson. It was a wrong number and I said so and hung up. I went back to my short story. But pretty soon I found myself writing a black character into my story, a somewhat sinister character whose name was Nelson. At that moment the story took a different turn. But happily it was, I see now, and somehow knew at the time, the right turn for the story.

Carver's example also provides a larger commentary about how memory works in general, and how it works in making fiction. As Carver observes, "I don't have the kind of memory that can bring entire conversations back to the present . . . nor can I recall the furnishings of any room I've ever spent time in." Like Carver, most of us can remember only "little things . . . somebody saying something in a particular way; somebody's wild, or low, nervous laughter; a landscape. . . ." It was Carver's choice not to force his memory to perform tricks it was not capable of doing. Rather, he developed a fluid, trusting relationship with his memory and with real life; he trusted the siftings and sortings of memory that made "little things" stand out, and he let accidents like a wrong number become gifts from the muse. "Write what you know," in this context, is a reminder to build a working relationship with your memory, and to trust that the same strange gift that made someone's "low, nervous laughter" significant to you might make it significant to your reader as well.

At the same time, "write what you know" is treacherous advice for several reasons. As Toni Bambara observes, "It does no good to write autobiographical fiction" because

> the minute the book hits the stand here comes your mama screamin how could you and sighin death where is thy sting and she snatches you up out your bed to grill you about what was going down back there in Brooklyn. . . .

For these reasons Bambara decides to write "straight-up fiction . . . cause I value my family and friends, and mostly cause I lie a lot anyway." While writing about real people may unblock your writer's block and make a better story, it often displeases the people whose lives you have borrowed from for your purposes. While they might feel honored, they might also feel diminished, used, or distorted in a funhouse mirror. Family members, for instance, will likely feel a mix of pride and discomfort at finding themselves in your stories. These are small lessons, which have little to do with the art of fiction; but it is still worth remembering that when you bring your real life into your stories, your real life (and the people who reside there) will often resist.

On an artistic level, "write what you know" is treacherous advice because it diminishes your ability to edit yourself properly. While events that seemed striking to the author will often seem striking to the reader, sometimes those same events fall flat. One of the most revealing moments in the development of a writer is when a reader reports that a certain character or plot turn seems false or uninvolving, and the writer wants to answer: how can it be false? It *really happened* to me. This is, of course, no answer: a story has to be judged by its own standards. While there are writers who can artlessly describe their own experiences and move their readers, most writers really *want* to bring to bear the power of their imaginations on that raw material. Fiction writing can be about selecting experiences from real life, molding them, playing with language, and emerging with altered forms of lived experiences that tell a new kind of truth. The fact that a story is "believable" or "authentic" often has nothing to do with whether or not it adheres to actual experience, and the fact that a story is "interesting" or "involving" has little to do with whether or not it is based on events that the author found interesting or involving.

Lastly, "write what you know" is treacherous advice because it implies an equal and opposite piece of advice: don't write about what you don't know. In general, aspiring writers are told to "write what you know" because many suffer from a group of similar writing flaws—vagueness, overambition when choosing subject matter, and lack of concrete detail—and "write what you know" is a solid catch-all cure for these maladies. But what happens to writers who find themselves pulled toward situations, emotional states, and characters with which they have no real experience? As Bambara notes, she doesn't write about her own life because "I lie a lot anyway," and she seems content with that circumstance. When carried to its extreme, "write what you know" means that the writer who does not have divorced parents cannot write about a divorce, and the writer from a broken home cannot describe a happy family. "Write what you know" might discourage you from following the natural leaps of your imagination to new but fertile places; worse still, it might discourage you from developing empathetic bonds with individuals and emotions that have been previously foreign, an acquired skill that has value far beyond the pursuit of creative writing.

Yukio Mishima's "Patriotism" shows how "Write what you know" and "Write what you don't know" can work side by side. Readers can conjecture that Mishima possessed a strong personal understanding of the Japanese concepts of honor and loyalty that compel his major characters; we can similarly guess about Mishima's experience regarding spiritual and romantic love. But it is not possible that Mishima knew what it felt like to commit ritual suicide prior to writing "Patriotism," which did not prevent him from writing several emotional passages from the point of view of the dying lieutenant: "It was a sensation of utter chaos. . . . It struck him as incredible that, amidst this terrible agony, things which could be seen could still be seen, and existing things existed still." In the context of the story, however, these passages are no less plausible than those that preceded them. Given Mishima's long-time fascination with ritual suicide—he himself committed *seppuku* in 1970—it is likely that the strength of his desire to imagine a thing he *did not know* is what makes the closing scenes of "Patriotism" especially intense and memorable.

Overall, in between the advice to "Write what you know" and "Write what you don't know" exists considerable freedom. Washington Irving, in "The Author's Account of Himself" that prefaces his famous *Sketch Book of Geoffrey Crayon, Gentleman* (1819), tried to explain to his readers why America was giving him (or Geoffrey Crayon, his literary alter ego) writer's block, while Europe set his imagination in motion. America, he wrote, was a blank space that offered the artist nothing to contemplate. Europe, for the most part, had an aged and rigid society that offered the author no freedom to express an individual vision. But Europe also had ruins, he wrote, and ghosts, and these were perfect. The incompleteness of the ruin and the evanescence of the ghost left room for his imagination to fill in the parts that were missing, or shrouded in mystery. For Irving, the ruins of Europe were a perfect metaphor for what the author should seek from real-life material: bits and pieces of information that provided inspiration, provoked thought, supplied the perfect visual image or character for a particular scene, but that did not force the author to stick to a journalistic account of things that had already taken place. For Irving, "Write what you know" meant using the real world, and not letting it use you.

Writing Strategies

1. Create a fictional character who lives a version of something you would consider a dream come true. However, like the genie who grants the literal wish, but not the *spirit* of the wish, do not give this character the complete fantasy; instead, provide the fantasy with a twist. For example, give the character a house in the Bahamas, but make him or her the tennis instructor there, or the cook, not the owner.

Write a story about, or from the point of view of, this person.

2. Uncover and develop a memory from your own life, a moment that did not seem significant when it happened but has stayed in your memory ever since.

    a. Write it down, as precisely as you can recall it, in specific detail. If possible (or desirable), write down briefly why you think the scene has stayed in your mind.

    b. Make the scene from (a) the first scene in a story. Make it the last scene in a story.

3. Make an exact (or as close as you can get) transcription of a conversation you had yesterday, and one you had one year ago. Begin a story with the actual conversation from one year ago, but continue in a fictional direction after the conversation ends.

AVOID POLITICS

The advice to "avoid politics" asks you to avoid overt ideological statements. You are being asked not to lecture, or write a story where the political point is so dominant that the potentially complex aspects of human behavior are sacrificed to that point. How, then, do we explain the success of a story like Yukio Mishima's "Patriotism," which, from the moment Mishima writes that the couple "lived beneath the solemn protection of the gods," seems designed to illustrate Mishima's traditionalist beliefs about Japanese honor and spirituality? The two main characters, after all, possess few traits that would differentiate them from any other model citizens of Mishima's dream-Japan; and when Mishima writes that the couple lived "encased in an impenetrable armor of Beauty and Truth," and that the lieutenant was the "essence of young death," it becomes increasingly clear that Mishima wants this couple to represent virtue and to inspire others. And although he deliberately portrayed them as types, not individuals, they are still able to move the reader.

The advice "Avoid politics" should be accepted cautiously. In politics, politicians and voters address important issues, and attempt to assess their true significance; in fiction, writers and readers pursue similar ambitions, but with different language, different emphasis, and often different issues. Shelley once referred to poets as the "unacknowledged legislators of the world," by which he meant that great artists, like great politicians, change the way that people view the world and seek solutions to its problems. Many critics claim that every story has a political message embedded within its contents; other critics claim that the turbulent state of the modern world virtually obliges authors to use their talents to advocate change and social awareness.

The argument over whether politics should be avoided or confronted in fiction is one that changes from country to country, age to age, reader to reader. Still, what cannot be questioned is that many of the most successful novels of the last twenty years, works like Gabriel García Márquez' *One Hundred Years of Solitude,* Don DeLillo's *White Noise,* or Toni Morrison's *Beloved,* all possess strong political visions. But they also possess innovative descriptive language and dialogue, memorable characters, and a strong sense of history and how political movements change the inner lives of real individuals. What these books teach is not to avoid politics, but to accept politics as part of the writing process, on the condition that any political statement be an integrated part of the world of characters, events, and settings that each individual story creates.

Your chief concern, then, is not whether politics belongs in a story, but where and how it belongs. In essence, American readers and writers have an unspoken understanding about politics and fiction: if it becomes *clear* and *obvious* that an author's political agenda is dictating plot or character, and plot and character are not compelling on their own, then the author has broken the unspoken contract. If, for instance, an author writes a story about abortion and depicts everyone on one side of the issue as angels and everyone on the other side of the issue as ogres, then many readers will reject that story as propaganda, and criticize the author for simplifying the complex human possibilities of the issue. The Israeli author Amos Oz, who comes from a country where political fiction is both popular and accepted, offers the following guideline for writing about political issues: never write about any issue when you are comfortably certain that your position is the correct one. For Oz, political fiction brings to life the drama of political issues, and explores the effects of that drama on everyday life. An author who writes a story with a specific political position will tend to reduce the potential complexities of the story to that lowest common denominator, but an author who is exploring the limits of a political position will instead likely be searching and expansive.

In other cases, however, an author succeeds with political material not because of the complexity of the treatment, but because of the empathy. Flaubert designed Emma Bovary to represent an entire class of nineteenth-century French women, but he wrote *Madame Bovary* with such sympathy for the main character (commenting in private that *he* was Madame Bovary) that Emma never feels to the reader like a symbol. Mishima succeeds for different reasons. In "Patriotism," he writes from the exact place where political beliefs bear all the passion of love: "So far from seeing any inconsistency or conflict between the urges of his flesh and the sincerity of his patriotism, the lieutenant was even able to regard the two as parts of the same thing." Rather than dividing romantic love and political beliefs into two separate realms, Mishima joins them, and describes the place where the political and personal meet.

For most writers, politics enter a story by accident. Frequently, even inevitably, a "political" issue is also a personal one. Abortion, homelessness, economic distress, and racism, for instance, all happen to people. But no one should believe that a story is a quality story just because it concerns a topic that the country's national political debate has deemed "important." And no one should avoid writing about a topic because it might be considered political.

Writing Strategies

1. Select a political issue that has received heavy media attention and has been deemed important: gang violence, drugs, divorce, birth control, AIDS, the national debt.

   a. Write from the point of view of a character who is personally involved in that issue, but do not specifically mention the issue.

   b. Do (a), but mention the "issue" in the first sentence, and as frequently as you want afterward.

2. Write from the point of view of someone famous, but do not identify the person and do not include obvious hints as to the person's identity. Rather, try to create a voice and a personality that you believe describes the way this renowned person looks at small things: waking up, mowing the lawn, eating a steak.

USE CONCRETE, SENSORY DETAIL

One of the goals of fiction is to provide enough information about the physical appearance of every character and setting to allow the reader to form clear mental pictures of the story's events. In using concrete, sensory detail—specific physical details described in terms that appeal to one of the five senses—you provide the small brush strokes that will allow readers to complete those clear mental pictures. Each of those inner photographs, in turn, serves to create an imaginary world that is accessible to your readers, and which invites them to fill in the missing details for themselves.

Despite its seeming simplicity, however, the advice "Use concrete, sensory detail" must be taken in context of the larger purposes of a story. Your goal should not be to install concrete, sensory details at regular intervals—one sensory detail for every minor character, two for every major character, and one for every change of setting, as well as regular weather reports. Rather, your goal should be to understand the role of concrete details in stories where they work well. The details in any one story are not detached from the other elements that make up a story. They draw attention to (or away from) certain characters, they slow down (or speed up) the pace of the language, and they often establish a specific level of rapport between you and your reader.

In most cases, the amount of concrete detail depends upon the significance of the person or object being described. Some writers, for instance, introduce each major character with a short biographical or physical description, as Joseph Conrad does in "Heart of Darkness":

> When near the buildings I met a white man, in such an unexpected elegance of get-up that in the first moment I took him for a sort of vision. I saw a high starched collar, white cuffs, a light alpaca jacket, snowy trousers, a clear necktie, and varnished boots. No hat. Hair parted, brushed, oiled, under a green-lined parasol held in a big white hand. He was amazing, and had a penholder behind his ear. . . .

In this case, the physical description also establishes something about the character of the individual, and Conrad's narrator is not shy about violating the rule of "Show, don't tell" to explain to us what the man's appearance implies about his personality:

> I respected the fellow. . . . His appearance was certainly that of a hairdresser's dummy; but in the great demoralization of the land he kept up his appearance. That's backbone. His starched collars and got-up shirtfronts were achievements of character. . . .

Conrad shows how concrete, sensory detail is *supposed* to function in a story: he supplies a full and detailed portrait that possesses the clarity of a photograph. But he does not do it idly, or automatically. He does it because this individual's physical appearance reveals his character and reveals the character of civilized men in the wild, and because that issue is one of the central themes of the novella. If the description itself is tangential to the narrative, and the story has to stop to contain this portrait, it stops out of respect for the value of the image, and not out of respect for the theory that more sensory detail automatically makes a better story.

In addition, the decision to describe certain characters, objects, or actions in a given story also implies an equal and opposite decision not to describe other characters, objects, and actions. If you describe one story element with a lengthy description, that choice naturally draws the reader's attention to that element, and makes it the focus of the story. In "Prue," Alice Munro provides strong sensory detail about a cufflink that Prue steals from Gordon:

> The cufflinks are made of amber and he bought them in Russia, on the holiday he and his wife took when they got back together again.

They look like squares of candy, golden, translucent, and this one warms quickly in her hand.

In the classic manner, Munro's description even appeals to more than one sense. And yet, it is important to note that Munro does not devote this kind of attention to every piece of bric-a-brac in "Prue"; in fact, the reader has less sense of what Gordon looks like than his cufflinks. It is only because the cufflink is important to Prue, because it arrests her attention, that Munro chooses to arrest our attention by providing a detailed image in a story otherwise noteworthy for its brevity and rapid pacing.

While learning to write vivid, clear description is a worthwhile goal, vivid, clear description is not a universal antidote to every story's problems. Description, at all times, has a subjective component, and the ways in which an author distorts or omits details is an important aspect of fiction. There are kinds of "detail" that are not concrete, but that can be extremely effective. Writers often convey images of great impact with one inventive metaphor. For instance, when the narrator of John Cheever's "The Death of Justina" observes that the customers at a crowded supermarket were "wearing such an assortment of clothing that it looked as if they had dressed hurriedly in a burning building," or when the narrator of Jeanette Winterson's *Oranges Are Not the Only Fruit* describes her town as "a huddled place," they communicate volumes about their states of mind and the ambience of their surroundings without actually providing much concrete detail.

Frequently, odd, associative descriptions can be far more evocative than ones that are composed with journalistic clarity. In this description of light falling across a car at night, Scott Bradfield, author of *The History of Luminous Motion*, creates an image that conveys power precisely because it is dreamlike:

> In those days I thought light was layered and textured like leaves in a tree. It moved and ruffled through the car. It felt gentle and imminent like snow.

Any reader might legitimately ask if light falling "gentle and imminent like snow" is an image of physical precision, or a murky, yet poetic metaphor for how light made the narrator feel. What this passage shows, rather, is that the idiosyncrasies of a narrator's descriptions can be intrinsic to the narrator, and come from the same source that makes the rest of the story work. The narrative voice—that of a young boy who speaks like a Ph.D. in metaphysics—provides the most memorable aspect of the novel. To ask Bradfield to make his narrator "use concrete, sensory detail" is the moral equivalent of telling him to make the boy stop running around California with his mother and go to school; it is good practical advice, but it will make a duller story if he abides by it.

In most cases, however, writers use all the resources available to them, intermingling concrete detail with metaphor and subjectivity with journalistic clarity, in conjunction with the other elements of the story. Eudora Welty, in "Old Mr. Marblehall," utilizes a wide repertoire of descriptive techniques. She selects unlikely metaphors that make concrete details striking: Mrs. Marblehall's galoshes are not merely "big, neat galoshes," but "big, neat, biscuit-colored galoshes." She describes characters by providing several concrete details that only loosely sketch their physical appearances, but yield insight into their personalities:

> That's Mr. Marblehall. He has short white bangs, and a bit of snapdragon in his lapel. He walks with a big polished stick. . . .

Similarly, if she feels that she can best describe a character's physical appearance through the use of an elongated metaphor that supplies little physical detail, Welty will do so:

> She looks like funny furniture—an unornamented stair post in one of these little houses, with her small monotonous round stupid head—or sometimes like the woodcut of a Bavarian witch, forefinger pointing, with scratches in the air all around her. But she's so static she scarcely moves. . . .

In "A Good Man Is Hard to Find," Flannery O'Connor also shows how an author can use a broad range of descriptive techniques and styles, but in unity with the other elements of the story:

> She wheeled around then and faced the children's mother, a young woman in slacks, whose face was as broad and innocent as a cabbage and was tied around with a green headkerchief that had two points on top like a rabbit's ears.

In this case, O'Connor does not provide complete detail about the mother; rather she provides one memorable physical detail, the green headkerchief, with one less memorable physical detail, the slacks. In addition to these details, however, O'Connor constructs two unlikely but arrestingly comical metaphors to describe the mother's appearance: the face "as broad and innocent as a cabbage" and the "rabbit's ears." The brevity of the description of the mother's appearance befits her role in the story, which is peripheral; O'Connor's description ensures that we will remember one or two things about her, but not dwell upon her. But then O'Connor's physical description of the mother is enriched by the metaphors, which emphasize the mother's innocence and compare her to things harvested, slaughtered, and devoured. At first, these metaphors might seem random, simply chosen for their expressive value; by the end of the story, however, the reader realizes that the metaphors have conveyed a great deal about the mother's character and her fate.

Overall, good concrete details can provide a forceful and memorable picture of an individual character, event, or setting, or they can provide just enough information to jump start the reader's imagination. They don't have to do both, however, and sometimes they don't have to do either. While many successful works of fiction provide concrete details in a journalistic style, many others provide dream visions of reality, or even no physical descriptions at all. As Milan Kundera has said, "the reader's imagination automatically completes the writer's." It is the writer's responsibility to provide a compelling invitation to the reader to want to fill in the blanks, but that invitation can be offered only by a work of fiction that possesses artistic and psychological strengths of its own. In response to the observation, "You say almost nothing about the physical appearance of your characters," Kundera described his experience of reading Kafka for the first time:

> I first read *The Castle* when I was fourteen years old. At that same period I admired an ice hockey player who lived near us. I imagined K. as looking like him. I still see him that way today.

When asked whether one of his own characters was "dark or fair," Kundera answered, "Choose for yourself!"

Writing Strategies

1. Select a character from a story in this book, a character that has not been physically described in any great detail. Describe this character's clothing and physical appearance based upon what you know of his or her personality.

2. Select a character from one of your own stories, a character that has not been physically described in any great detail. Repeat the first strategy for this character.

Reread your story with this new material inserted in the appropriate places. Does it enhance or improve the story, or slow it down?

3. Make a list of the objects in one of your own stories that could be described in concrete, sensory detail: rooms, furniture, clothing, characters. Make a second list of the amount of energy you have expended to describe these objects: the number of lines, phrases, adjectives.

Does this amount seem appropriate to you? Can you find objects on the list that might benefit from being well described? Are there objects on the list that receive thorough descriptions, but that aren't sufficiently important to the story or your reader to justify the attention?

4. Select a person, setting, or object from your real life that has one or two overriding traits: an ugly baby, a disheveled room, an intimidating person. Write a one-paragraph description, using concrete details of appearance and/or behavior to "argue" in favor of that initial, overriding impression. Your description can have narrative flow and feel to it; it can be playful or dramatic, but it must be vivid.

AVOID THE BIG ISSUES

From an early age, we are told in school that the best fiction deals with important events, universal emotions, and unforgettable characters: as John Cheever's narrator in "The Death of Justina" notes, "It seems to me that if you're going to write fiction you should write about mountain climbing and tempests at sea." However, it is usually not until you begin to write your own stories that a second truth emerges: it is difficult to write well about these things. "Avoid the big issues" is advice that overlaps with "Write what you know," "Show, don't tell," and "Avoid politics." All of these axioms are designed to lead you in the direction of topics that you can write about with more familiarity, authority, and concrete detail. When you are told to "Avoid the big issues," however, you are also being told that you have bitten off more than you can chew. You don't have the control, confidence, or talent to write about large and complex emotional issues.

This can be extremely difficult advice to hear. First, it is difficult to unlearn a lifetime's training: you are told that great fiction deals with death, love, and revolution, but no one has told you how few writers get it right the first time out. Secondly, while "Avoid the big issues" seems like a fairly straightforward piece of advice, it can also sound insulting: it can sound like you are being told that you don't understand complex emotional issues, when you are simply being told that what you cannot control is your ability to write about them with authority and confidence.

In essence, writers who are being told to "avoid the big issues" are being told that they don't yet know what is important—in fiction. Part of the problem arises from confusion over what makes a topic "important." Every individual carries an "official" mental register of important topics: death is important, we know, and love is important, and car crashes are serious, and divorce is unhappy but not necessarily tragic. This register is "official" because it includes those human events that we know we are expected to be affected by. It includes political issues as well: while most people do nothing about homelessness on a daily basis, for instance, we still understand that when someone talks about the homeless at a dinner party, we do not behave callously or make jokes; we nod solemnly and make solemn remarks.

This register can be a real hazard. Writer's block is a common problem for authors on any level, but more experienced writers have developed personal solutions; for a developing writer, it is both easy and natural, consciously or unconsciously, to appeal to these topics for sure-fire winners. More important, because the mere mention of some of these topics in daily conversation brings an instant response, it is easy to believe that a similar result will occur in fiction writing: if a character in your story dies, for instance, your readers will respond by being instantly moved.

A second problem occurs because the standards for what is compelling in fiction are different than the standards for what is compelling in real life. Death is affecting in real life because someone has actually died. A car crash is a serious experience in real life for obvious reasons. Death in fiction is not automatically affecting because it is clear to your reader that no one has really died. And a car crash in a short story can be tremendously uninvolving.

In fact, death in fiction is always a pale shadow of the real thing, and that is true of strong fiction as well as weak. But weak fiction uses the death of a character to compensate for a story that is going nowhere, or a story that has no ending, or a story that never had a subject. Strong fiction does not "use" death at all, but illustrates what loss is about, what mourning is like, or what it is like to die.

In essence, "Avoid the big issues" is advice that asks you to change focus: if "Write what you know" asks you to point your mental camera in the direction of scenes with which you are familiar, "Avoid the big issues" asks you to use your telephoto lens. "Avoid the big issues" asks you to make three alterations in the process by which you write fiction.

The first is to appreciate that complex human issues require and deserve in-depth treatment. You probably cannot write a great short story about the death of a remarkable person in three pages (though people have done it): the size of the canvas and the scale of the topic do not match.

The second alteration asks you to rethink the way you use charged events in your fiction. No charged event should exist for its own sake, or exist without some conscious attempt to explore the emotional ramifications. If you compose a first draft thinking that it is sufficient to end a story with a car crash, you should work on later drafts knowing that the car crash can only be the starting point for an exploration of the events that led up to the car crash, or the aftermath of the crash. In either case, however, you should recognize that it is far better to write three complicated and convincing pages about why a man sitting on a park bench feels sad than three vague and uninteresting pages about a car crash that kills a busload of people we haven't met.

The third alteration asks you to rethink what makes a topic "important," and therefore worthy of fiction. You should break free of "official" important topics and recognize that every individual also carries an "unofficial" register of important topics, charged with peculiar and personal emotions. Sometimes these topics overlap with the "official" ones, but sometimes they do not.

In practice, these changes require trial and error. "Avoid the big issues" is bad advice if it tells you to always write about small things, and better advice if it tells you to write a strong story about something small rather than a weak story about something big. But few writers advance to writing strong stories about large issues by writing raftloads of perfect stories about minor topics first. A perfect, small story is one kind of literary triumph; a large, complicated, often flawed (but always emotionally involving) story is another. The only way to write good stories about big issues is to write bad stories about big issues first.

A young writer composes a three-page story in which a seventeen-year-old driver, a little drunk and racing to make her parent's curfew, accidentally kills a couple in a car crash. In the first draft, the story ends with a policeman telling the young woman that the couple in the other car is dead; his tone is emotionless and her response is not recorded, so it is assumed that the author felt that the fact that the accident killed a couple about whom the reader knows nothing would have emotional impact. In a second draft, the author ends the story with the driver's dawning comprehension that this is the beginning of a long nightmare for her. In the third draft, the story ends with her parents shouting at her in the street, not consoling her at all. She shouts back, but when combined with the changes from the second draft, it becomes clear that she feels horribly guilty; the third draft makes it clear that she is alone. In a fourth draft, the author switches the story into first person, and makes the young woman extremely sympathetic; she is no villain. In the fifth draft, the author adjusts the narrator's pre-accident musings, and makes the driver's feelings toward her parents slightly (but only slightly) more angry: now the parents emerge as characters, and their outburst at the end seems harrowing. The reader begins to feel a sense that the driver is not the only one to blame, but that she will be the only one to take the blame. She is the victim. The murdered couple is forgotten; we don't even know their names.

Writing Strategies

1. Write a short-short (two pages) story that is unquestionably about one of life's most significant events: a death, a wedding, a car crash. The event should be presented to the reader in the very first sentence, or shortly after. There should be no attempt at plot closure; you instead should think of this story as an opportunity to dig deeply into the subject and explore—but not necessarily produce—a polished, well-rounded story structure in a limited space.

2. Using the material from the first strategy, "telescope" the story and focus on, or invent, a peripheral character for whom the event is a minor incident: the organist at the funeral, a bored guest at the wedding. Write a story from this person's point of view, making the major incident of the first story into a minor incident in this one. The same characters and incidents may occur in this second story, but should be background to whatever concerns this character.

3. Select a story of your own, in which something officially "important" happens (if possible, select a story in which this event occurs at the end, and provides narrative closure to your story). Rewrite the important event so that it does not provide closure, or so that it is not *completely* finished: a car crash with survivors, a wedding where the pastor fails to arrive, a diagnosis of cancer that proves to be treatable.

LIKABLE CHARACTERS

On one level, it's hard to disagree with "likable characters." Certainly, one of the functions of good fiction is to make the reader's world a better place, either by providing a pleasurable reading experience, or by providing an emotional or spiritual reward that will stay with the reader afterward. In this context, any story that possesses warmth, good nature, and empathetic characters is bound to provide at least a pleasurable reading experience, and may also create a feeling of intimacy that will involve the reader more deeply in other aspects of the story. While critics have argued that the purpose of art is to enlighten, disturb, and even shock readers, readers have in turn argued that their real lives are already disturbed and complex, and that the best thing a work of fiction can do is provide sustenance.

For these reasons, the pressure to make characters "likable" can be enormous: just as individuals learn to recognize and emphasize those personality traits that make people like them, writers over time intuitively learn which of their stylistic traits please readers, and they learn to emphasize those traits over less successful ones. There is a fine line, however, between the point at which this kind of long-term adaptation is productive, and the point at which you are simply attempting to satisfy what you think other people want. While warmth in fiction and likable characters are worthy goals for certain stories, even many stories, there still exists a point where you might start to feel like a warmth and likability factory.

For many readers, a character is likable for the same reasons that a real-life individual is likable: because he or she possesses a keen sense of humor, a generous spirit, or charisma. Sometimes, fictional characters are likable for different reasons than real-life individuals. The act of reading a novel or short story differs from the act of befriending somebody: the same personality traits that would make someone a wearying companion over the course of years might nevertheless possess the exact level of intensity to maintain a short story or novel. Humbert Humbert, the fictional narrator of Vladimir Nabokov's *Lolita,* possesses a sympathetic and self-deprecating voice that allows the reader to downplay his personality flaws; it would be impossible to forgive a real-life Humbert, however, for his notorious actions regarding a preadolescent girl. Similarly, while F. Scott Fitzgerald makes it easy to appreciate Jay Gatsby's virtues, he also makes sure that we understand the naivete and shallowness that feed his protagonist's grand ambitions.

At the same time, there are numerous examples of successful and even "likable" stories and novels that feature uncharismatic main characters. Many of Flannery O'Connor's short stories, for instance, depict inward, self-important men and women who seem to deserve a slap from the hand of God; the spiritual uplift of O'Connor's stories derives from the compassion and ferocity with which she inexorably delivers those blows on behalf of the Maker. In the case of "A Good Man Is Hard to Find," the grandmother is one such character; she is portrayed by O'Connor with such dazzlingly coruscating wit that the reader actually sympathizes with, even delights in, the judgment that a psychotic killer passes upon her in the story's legendary closing lines of dialogue.

In the story "Dundun," Denis Johnson offers a deeper challenge to the idea of "likability" in character portrayal. The main characters are all heroin addicts, so deeply enmeshed within their addictions that they can neither register concern for one another nor respond properly to an emergency. No one in the story does *anything* remotely likable: the narrator tells us that he is happy to take the injured McInnes to the hospital because "People would talk about it, and I hoped I would be liked"; Dundun makes McInnes promise not to tell anyone who shot him; even McInnes seems self-absorbed and petulant in his dying throes. And yet, the narrator's candor—his inability or unwillingness to rationalize what is taking place—makes him a strangely trustworthy and intimate voice. And when he finally chooses to justify Dundun's violent behavior, beginning with the line, "Will you believe me when I tell you there was kindness in his heart," the reader is truly startled; Johnson has extended a credible invitation to understand, if not exactly sympathize with, a character who has done nothing in the entire story to deserve sympathy. In this manner, "Dundun" defies the rule of "likability" and succeeds instead in making the lives of individuals lost within drug addiction accessible to those who are not.

What these examples prove is that a story can be "likable" without necessarily containing likable characters and happy endings. It is absolutely true that many readers turn away from stories that make them uncomfortable, or reach negative or complex conclusions about human beings. But the worst reaction you can have is to be intimidated by the pressure to make your characters happy and friendly (and this pressure, it is important to emphasize, often comes from within). While readers as a group may prefer a warm story to a cold one, most readers would still prefer a story written with passion and depth to a story that lacks these qualities. Most readers would prefer stories about people with whom they can identify, and will pay the price of listening to bad news about themselves if the story has compensating strengths, or if the bad news is particularly important. When warmth is dishonest, though—when it is your reflex to tack on happy endings and reduce the complexities of human behavior to the range of greeting-card emotions—it often leaves you disconnected from the source of your strengths.

In other words, the fact that "warmth" is a popular human emotion does not mean that it should be a straitjacket: you may find that your true gifts lie in vicious (but decadently funny) gossip, one-dimensional (but deeply allegorical) protagonists, tragic (but moving) endings, or irredeemable (but complex) villains. It is simply possible that the most likable characters are those characters who have been rendered with the most complexity and sympathy, regardless of whether or not their actual personality traits are indeed likable. Heathcliff, Captain Ahab, Jay Gatsby, Shylock, Sister Carrie, Bartleby, Holden Caulfield, Humbert Humbert, and the Wife of Bath are the characters we remember, and they dominate the stories we remember. But you wouldn't exactly say they would make good dinner companions or pleasant next-door neighbors.

Writing Strategies

1. Select an individual from your own memory, a person whom you remember with affection or clarity, despite your awareness that this person was not necessarily a "good" person in the traditional sense. In one page, describe this person and attempt to explain what makes this person remain vividly or fondly in your memory.

Write a story focusing on a fictionalized version of this person. Describe the interaction of this person with someone who is intellectually or emotionally drawn to him or her.

2. Create a character who is clearly not likable, but not clearly villainous—someone who is merely selfish, shallow, vain, or careless. This character may also come from your memory. Write a story where this character receives a comeuppance for this behavior, then write a story where the character receives a reward.

3. Select a character from one of your own stories. Detach this character from the story and write a separate short-short story (two pages) where this character can be seen interacting in a new setting with different people.

Write this new story in such a way that the character's behavior in this new setting reveals personality traits that were not visible in the first story, but are nevertheless plausible.

4. Select a character from one of your stories, a character that you clearly believe to be likable. Write a story that places this character in a different setting, clearly *struggling* with some kind of impulse that is distinctly not likable, or at least would suggest levels of complexity that were not visible in the original story.

PRACTICE ECONOMY: DON'T WASTE A WORD

In 1842 Edgar Allan Poe, reviewing Nathaniel Hawthorne's *Twice-Told Tales*, wrote a paragraph about short-story writing that became the most often quoted axiom in the history of fiction-writing instruction. First, Poe told his readers that every short story should have a single "effect"; he also told his readers that this "effect" should be determined before the author set a word to paper. Then he told his readers that if his [the short-story writer's] very initial sentence tend not the out-bringing of this effect, then he has failed in his first step. In the whole composition, there should be no word written, of which the tendency, direct, or indirect, is not to the one pre-established design.

While modern readers have never agreed on what Poe meant by a "single effect"—some have felt that he was referring to mood or tone, while others have felt he was describing unity of plot, where every scene must somehow be relevant—few have disputed the second half of his advice. Every word, every sentence, every scene, Poe felt, should be *necessary*. Poe's model author had two choices: to begin composition with such a precise idea that no unnecessary word could possibly be written; or, having written a sloppy but potentially valuable story, to return to the text over and over, cutting, cutting, and cutting some more, until the story was lean and focused.

In the twentieth century, this has become one of the guiding rules of short-storytelling. Writers began to think that the novel was a place where you could afford to be sloppy, but that the short story required absolute discipline. William Faulkner, when asked whether the novel was easier to write than the short story, replied, "Yes sir. You can be more careless, you can put more trash in it and be excused for it."

Truman Capote, similarly, said that whatever "discipline" he had developed as a writer he owed to the short-story form. In part, this kind of thinking was a natural response to the way that short stories were published, in contrast to the way that novels were published: short stories were released in magazines, in which editors constantly fretted over column space; novels were released in bound volumes, in which length was not a significant financial concern for the publisher. Similarly, short stories, because they were shorter, fit better into anthologies and fifty-minute classroom periods, and so became the genre of choice for English courses. By the second half of the twentieth century, however, most writers had forgotten that "Don't waste a word" was originally what editors told writers and teachers told students, but writers rarely told themselves and readers rarely told writers. Rather, practicing "economy" became an artistic goal in itself.

Practicing economy has many strong points. First, Poe's advice is sound advice: a story is worth admiring when it does not waste its reader's time but moves swiftly from one scene to the next, and when every scene contributes to a single narrative cause. The short story, after all, is a small object; most readers will swallow one whole in an hour. In that situation, a short story that tries to focus on several different issues or emotional states will likely diffuse and dilute its effects. For this reason, you might want to stay away from overpopulated stories: try to limit the number of characters, the number of plot elements, the number of settings, even the number of descriptive adjectives, and remember at all times that the reader's ability to remember story details is finite and should be respected.

Second, practicing economy is useful because it develops authorial control. In itself, authorial control is a powerful literary device: readers are more likely to continue reading a story when they believe that you know what you are doing, and they are more willing to pursue (or follow) a tangent or slow stretch when you have already proven that a story's flaws will be offset by its strengths. Ultimately, the advice to practice economy resembles similar advice that most individuals attempt to practice in real life: don't bore your readers by making them sift through material they don't need to hear. In conversation, a speaker can sense the signs of boredom in a listener, or the listener can interrupt the speaker, redirect the conversation, or end it. In a written story, however, readers are captive: they can stop reading the story, but they cannot change it. For this reason, you have a doubled responsibility during revision stages to act the part of listener—in effect, reading the story to yourself and deleting scenes, events, plot devices, characters, or descriptions when that internal listener shows signs of impatience.

Third, practicing economy is useful because it teaches the importance of language. Deleting a scene that does not belong in a story is comparatively easy work: the scene provides no new or important information concerning the plot, it does not reveal anything new about the characters that might deepen or enhance the pleasure of reading about them, or it does not in itself entertain the reader. Editing individual words and sentences, however, can be more difficult, because it is a demanding task to edit the smallest units of language in a story while keeping one eye focused on the story's larger vision. Language, like plot, communicates its own quiet message, which may or may not match the more overt messages that a story is sending; and just as a story that has a peerless plot but weak characters nevertheless captivates its readers, a story where words are chosen with care and precision can be a powerful reading experience even when characters, plot, and setting have not been chosen with much care. By practicing economy—line by line, word by word—you can learn how the smallest units of language function as a larger unit, altering the tone, pace, and focus of a story, creating new possibilities for characters and their actions, and allowing (or disallowing) multiple interpretations of major plot events.

While the advice to "practice economy" should be one of the most significant principles of a writer's education, it should never be the dominant principle. Economy should not be practiced at the expense of inspiration. In the ideal situation, you learn to write spirited, loose, sloppy first drafts that take chances, break rules, and follow intuitions; in second and later drafts, you become a tough editor, who evaluates coolly what should be saved, what should be cut, and what should be expanded. The injunction to practice economy, however, can seep into your mind during the first draft; you begin to edit yourself too early, trimming scenes, descriptions, and plot turns before they have a chance to fully unfold and develop potentially inspired forms. While practicing economy is an essential writer's skill, especially during the revision process, it can inhibit your confidence and creativity if practiced too early or too often.

Similarly, much confusion can arise concerning exactly what it means to "practice economy." Creative writing teachers in the first half of the century were unequivocal about what this advice meant: don't waste a word, they told their students; draw a line from the beginning of the story to the end and never deviate. But what does it mean, exactly, to "waste" or "not waste" a word? Consider this excerpt from Mary Robison's "Seizing Control":

> We spent time with the menu reading aloud what side stuff came with the "Wedding Pancake," or with the "Great American French Toast." Willy wanted a Sliced Turkey Dinner Platter, but Terrence said, "Don't get that. It's frozen. I mean frozen when served, as you're eating and trying to chew." The waitress approached, pad in hand. She wore a carnation pink dress for a uniform. We fidgeted in irrelevant ways, as if finding more comfortable spots on the booth seat. But we didn't whisper our orders. We acted important about our need for food.

What would be the proper way to practice economy in this passage? Robison's wording, at first glance, seems strikingly economical: the sentences are brief, adjective-free, almost clipped. But is the passage even *necessary* to the story? Robison could have written: "We went to the International House of Pancakes," and nothing else. Similarly, why does she write that the children read aloud the side dishes for both the "Wedding Pancake" and the "Great American French Toast"? Would not one do? Why does she not tell us what the side dishes were? Why does she tell us the color of the waitress' uniform? Why does she not tell us anything else about the waitress? If Robison's goal were to give her reader the leanest, swiftest description possible, she could have considered countless deletions; inversely, she could have considered countless additions. But Robison's goal seems more complex: it is the child narrator, after all, who is telling the story, dictating the kind and degree of details. And as the narrator observes, the moment is important to the characters: it provides an intuitive signpost marking that the "seizing control" is taking place. That might not make the scene "necessary," but that does make it meaningful.

In this passage from "A Good Man Is Hard to Find," Flannery O'Connor shows how economy can create narrative focus:

> The children's mother still had on slacks and still had her head tied up in a green kerchief, but the grandmother had on a navy blue straw sailor hat with a bunch of white violets on the brim and a navy blue dress with a small white dot in the print. Her collars and cuffs were white organdy trimmed with lace and at her neckline she had pinned a purple spray of cloth violets containing a sachet. In case of an accident, anyone seeing her dead on the highway would know at once that she was a lady.

O'Connor has taken her time with this description because it is both entertaining to read (it too has the structure of a well-told joke, with the sentence "In case of an accident, anyone seeing her dead on the highway would know at once that she was a lady" as the punchline), and because the grandmother's pretensions are an important aspect of the story. If O'Connor had described every character and object in "A Good Man Is Hard to Find" with this kind of specificity, then you might begin to feel like the story was too slow and lacked focus. But because O'Connor devotes this kind of space and wordage only to the important characters in the story (note, for instance, that the description of the mother's clothing is terse, and is included strictly to provide contrast to the grandmother's), she focuses your attention where she wants it to be focused. Economy, in other words, might always be a writerly virtue, but it is a writerly virtue that must be defined differently for every story. While there are abstract advantages to be gained from learning how to carefully edit every line and every sentence of a story, that does not necessarily mean that every word that appears to be unnecessary should be deleted: while Poe said that undue length was a major story flaw, he also said that undue parsimony was to avoided as well. Robison's and O'Connor's examples, rather, suggest that "economy" is a broad and flexible goal, and that it refers to the overall impression a story leaves with its reader.

The passages by O'Connor and Robison raise questions about what makes a description or a character valuable to a story; but frequently, the advice to practice economy is meant to keep the writer alert to unnecessary scenes. The early sections of Milan Kundera's "The Hitchhiking Game" occur during a car trip that takes the young couple to the hotel where the climactic scenes will occur. Every detour or stop could be construed as Kundera slowing down the plot: the question remains as to whether or not those slowdowns are warranted by the story's conclusion. When the two characters stop at the gas station, for instance, you might wonder why that stop is necessary; it is only afterward, when you realize that the stop provided the opportunity for the man and woman to separate and assume their new identities as "hitchhiker" and "driver," that the gas station stop seems justified. But what about this detour?

> The young man had never been here before and it took him a while to orient himself. Several times he stopped the car and asked the passersby directions to the hotel. Several streets had been dug up, so that the drive to the hotel, even though it was quite close by (as all those who had been asked asserted), necessitated so many detours and roundabout routes that it was almost a quarter of an hour before they finally stopped in front of it. . . .

In essence, Kundera slows down the story fifteen minutes, or one paragraph in reading time, while his characters ask directions to their (and our) destination. An astute reader might justifiably ask: Why? Why not just bring them there straightaway? From the moment you begin to consider closely the role of economy in the stories you read and write, you will find that these kind of questions occur in uneconomical abundance.

Economy means, first and foremost, that you should not bore your readers or make them conscious that they are reading a story that is too slow for its own good. More importantly, economy means, give your reader something of value for the time he or she took to read your story. If your story is too long or has boring patches, it will scarcely matter if you have managed to create one or two unforgettable characters, an evocative and memorable setting, or an innovative plot turn.

Ultimately, the advice to practice economy is advice that every writer needs, as long as it is offered with a second piece of advice: don't be afraid to take risks. While the emphasis on economy and efficiency tells writers that stories should function like machines, and finds beauty in machine values when they are well executed in narrative forms, American art has always had a flip side: a crude, energetic, diverse heritage of novels, stories, movies, and music that defies narrative standards, breaks the bounds of good taste, and often stumbles while trying to say three things at once. Who can deny that *Moby-Dick* is hundreds of pages too long, and has tortured thousands of readers with its descriptions of the whale's every nook and cranny? Who can deny that Frank Capra's Depression-era motion pictures (*It's a Wonderful Life, Mr. Smith Goes to Washington*) are awash in lazy sentimentalism and artificial happy endings? Often, the flaws of a work of art are too enmeshed with its strengths to be simply and neatly excised, and often they are essential elements that contribute to the ragged but undeniable grandeur of the finished piece. When you practice economy, you say what needs to be said within a set of narrative standards that everyone intuitively understands and accepts; but sooner or later, and often more than once, *everyone* has an artistic vision that is too large to fit into a well-crafted, economical story.

Writing Strategies

1. Select a story from this book. Read it aloud, alone, or with friends and peers. As you read, are there sentences that you cannot speak without pausing or interrupting? Are there passages

that clearly slow you down? Mark these places. Do you believe that altering these passages would improve the story?

Do the same for one of your own stories.

2. Select one of your own stories. Rewrite the story to make it consciously economical: delete descriptions, shorten sentences, remove adjectives, but protect the integrity of the plot. When characters speak, rewrite their dialogue so that they say the same thing in as few words as possible. Do this exercise ruthlessly, regardless of whether or not you believe that these deletions improve the story.

Reread the story. Which details would you return to the story? Which would you remove permanently?

3. Write a short-short story in which you are consciously economical: few or no descriptions, action sparsely described, dialogue with few or no dialogue tags.

Reread and then rewrite this story, making a conscious decision to add certain details: two or three short descriptions, a few extra adjectives, an added speech.

4. Select one of your own stories. At some point in this story, create a tangent or digression: a new character, a lengthy philosophical digression, a long description.

Reread the story. Does this new material improve the story? Can you change the plot of the story to absorb the material, to make it somehow essential to the story's conclusion?

Milan Kundera

Milan Kundera was born in Brno, Czechoslovakia, in 1929. He is the author of six novels, including the international best-sellers The Book of Laughter and Forgetting *(1980) and* The Unbearable Lightness of Being *(1984), as well as criticism, poetry, plays, and short-story collections. Kundera was educated at the Film Faculty of the Prague Academy of Music and Dramatic Arts, and began teaching cinematography there in 1952. He published his first collection of poetry in 1953, and his first fiction in 1963. In addition to gaining literary recognition in his own country, Kundera served as a leading cultural figure, serving on the Central Committee of the Writer's Union. After the Soviet army invaded Czechoslovakia in 1968, however, he fell from favor, and immigrated to France in*

1975, where he accepted an offer to teach at the University of Renne. "The Hitchhiking Game" appears in Laughable Loves, *a collection first published in English in 1974.*

The Hitchhiking Game*

I

The needle on the gas gauge suddenly dipped toward empty and the young driver of the sports car declared that it was maddening how much gas the car ate up. "See that we don't run out of gas again," protested the girl (about twenty-two), and reminded the driver of several places where this had already happened to them. The young man replied that he wasn't worried, because whatever he went through with her had the charm of adventure for him. The girl objected; whenever they had run out of gas on the highway it had, she said, always been an adventure only for her. The young man had hidden and she had had to make ill use of her charms by thumbing a ride and letting herself be driven to the nearest gas station, then thumbing a ride back with a can of gas. The young man asked the girl whether the drivers who had given her a ride had been unpleasant, since she spoke as if her task had been a hardship. She replied (with awkward flirtatiousness) that sometimes they had been *very* pleasant but that it hadn't done her any good as she had been burdened with the can and had had to leave them before she could get anything going. "Pig," said the young man. The girl protested that she wasn't a pig, but that he really was. God knows how many girls stopped him on the highway, when he was driving the car alone! Still driving, the young man put his arm around the girl's shoulders and kissed her gently on the forehead. He knew that she loved him and that she was jealous. Jealousy isn't a pleasant quality, but if it isn't overdone (and if it's combined with modesty), apart from inconvenience there's even something touching about it. At least that's what the young man thought. Because he was only twenty-eight, it seemed to him that he was old and knew everything that a man could know about

---

Translated by Suzanne Rappaport.

women. In the girl sitting beside him he valued precisely what, until now, he had met with least in women: purity.

The needle was already on empty, when to the right the young man caught sight of a sign, announcing that the station was a quarter of a mile ahead. The girl hardly had time to say how relieved she was before the young man was signaling left and driving into a space in front of the pumps. However, he had to stop a little way off, because beside the pumps was a huge gasoline truck with a large metal tank and a bulky hose, which was refilling the pumps. "We'll have to wait," said the young man to the girl and got out of the car. "How long will it take?" he shouted to the man in overalls. "Only a moment," replied the attendant, and the young man said, "I've heard that one before." He wanted to go back and sit in the car, but he saw that the girl had gotten out the other side. "I'll take a little walk in the meantime," she said. "Where to?" the young man asked on purpose, wanting to see the girl's embarrassment. He had known her for a year now but she would still get shy in front of him. He enjoyed her moments of shyness, partly because they distinguished her from the women he'd met before, partly because he was aware of the law of universal transience, which made even his girl's shyness a precious thing to him.

II

The girl really didn't like it when during the trip (the young man would drive for several hours without stopping) she had to ask him to stop for a moment somewhere near a clump of trees. She always got angry when, with feigned surprise, he asked her why he should stop. She knew that her shyness was ridiculous and old-fashioned. Many times at work she had noticed that they laughed at her on account of it and deliberately provoked her. She always got shy in advance at the thought of how she was going to get shy. She often longed to feel free and easy about her body, the way most of the women around her did. She had even invented a special course in self-persuasion: she would repeat to herself that at birth every human being received one out of the millions of available bodies, as one would receive an allotted room out of the millions of rooms in an enormous hotel. Consequently, the body was fortuitous and impersonal, it was only a ready-made, borrowed thing. She would repeat this to herself in different ways, but she could never manage to feel it. This mind-body dualism was alien to her. She was too much one with her body; that is why she always felt such anxiety about it.

She experienced this same anxiety even in her relations with the young man, whom she had known for a year and with whom she was happy, perhaps because he never separated her body from her soul and she could live with him *wholly*. In this unity there was happiness, but right behind the happiness lurked suspicion, and the girl was full of that. For instance, it often occurred to her that the other women (those who weren't anxious) were more attractive and more seductive and that the young man, who did not conceal the fact that he knew this kind of woman well, would someday leave her for a woman like that. (True, the young man declared that he'd had enough of them to last his whole life, but she knew that he was still much younger than he thought.) She wanted him to be completely hers and she to be completely his, but it often seemed to her that the more she tried to give him everything, the more she denied him something: the very thing that a light and superficial love or a flirtation gives to a person. It worried her that she was not able to combine seriousness with light-heartedness.

But now she wasn't worrying and any such thoughts were far from her mind. She felt good. It was the first day of their vacation (of their two-week vacation, about which she had been dreaming for a whole year), the sky was blue (the whole year she had been worrying about whether the sky would really be blue), and he was beside her. At his, "Where to?" she blushed, and left the car without a word. She walked around the gas station, which was situated beside the highway in total isolation, surrounded by fields. About a hundred yards away (in the direction in which they were traveling), a wood began. She set off for it, vanished behind a little bush, and gave herself up to her mood. (In solitude it was possible for her to get the greatest enjoyment from the presence of the man she loved. If his presence had been continuous, it would have kept on disappearing. Only when alone was she able to *hold on* to it.)

When she came out of the wood onto the highway, the gas station was visible. The large gasoline truck was already pulling out and the sports car moved forward toward the red turret of the pump. The girl walked on along the highway and only at times looked back to see if the sports car was coming. At last she caught sight of it. She stopped and began to wave at it like a hitchhiker waving at a stranger's car. The sports car slowed down and stopped close to the girl. The young man leaned toward the window, rolled it down, smiled, and asked, "Where are you headed, miss?" "Are you going to Bystritsa?" asked the girl, smiling flirtatiously at him. "Yes, please get in," said the young man, opening the door. The girl got in and the car took off.

III

The young man was always glad when his girlfriend was gay. This didn't happen too often; she had a quite tiresome job in an unpleasant environment, many hours of overtime without compensatory leisure and at home, a sick mother. So she often felt tired. She didn't have either particularly good nerves or self-confidence and easily fell into a state of anxiety and fear. For this reason he welcomed every manifestation of her gaiety with the tender solicitude of a foster parent. He smiled at her and said: "I'm lucky today. I've been driving for five years, but I've never given a ride to such a pretty hitchhiker."

The girl was grateful to the young man for every bit of flattery; she wanted to linger for a moment in its warmth and so she said, "You're very good at lying."

"Do I look like a liar?"

"You look like you enjoy lying to women," said the girl, and into her words there crept unawares a touch of the old anxiety, because she really did believe that her young man enjoyed lying to women.

The girl's jealousy often irritated the young man, but this time he could easily overlook it for, after all, her words didn't apply to him but to the unknown driver. And so he just casually inquired, "Does it bother you?"

"If I were going with you, then it would bother me," said the girl and her words contained a subtle, instructive message for the young man; but the end of her sentence applied only to the unknown driver, "but I don't know you, so it doesn't bother me."

"Things about her own man always bother a woman more than things about a stranger" (this was now the young man's subtle, instructive message to the girl), "so seeing that we are strangers, we could get on well together."

The girl purposely didn't want to understand the implied meaning of his message, so she now addressed the unknown driver exclusively:

"What does it matter, since we'll part company in a little while?"

"Why?" asked the young man.

"Well, I'm getting out at Bystritsa."

"And what if I get out with you?"

At those words the girl looked up at him and found that he looked exactly as she imagined him in her most agonizing hours of jealousy. She was alarmed at how he was flattering her and flirting with her (an unknown hitchhiker), and *how becoming it was to him.* Therefore she responded with defiant provocativeness, "What would *you* do with me, I wonder?"

"I wouldn't have to think too hard about what to do with such a beautiful woman," said the young man gallantly and at this moment he was once again speaking far more to his own girl than to the figure of the hitchhiker.

But this flattering sentence made the girl feel as if she had caught him at something, as if she had wheedled a confession out of him with a fraudulent trick. She felt toward him a brief flash of intense hatred and said, "Aren't you rather too sure of yourself?"

The young man looked at the girl. Her defiant face appeared to him to be completely convulsed. He felt sorry for her and longed for her usual, familiar expression (which he used to call childish and simple). He leaned toward her, put his arm around her shoulders, and softly spoke the name with which he usually addressed her and with which he now wanted to stop the game.

But the girl released herself and said: "You're going a bit too fast!"

At this rebuff the young man said: "Excuse me, miss," and looked silently in front of him at the highway.

IV

The girl's pitiful jealousy, however, left her as quickly as it had come over her. After all, she was sensible and knew perfectly well that all this was merely a game. Now it even struck her as a little ridiculous that she had repulsed her man out of a jealous rage. It wouldn't be pleasant for her if he found out why she had done it. Fortunately women have the miraculous ability to change the meaning of their actions after the event. Using this ability, she decided that she had repulsed him not out of anger but so that she could go on with the game, which, with its whimsicality, so well suited the first day of their vacation.

So again she was the hitchhiker, who had just repulsed the over-enterprising driver, but only so as to slow down his conquest and make it more exciting. She half turned toward the young man and said caressingly:

"I didn't mean to offend you, mister!"

"Excuse me, I won't touch you again," said the young man.

He was furious with the girl for not listening to him and refusing to be herself when that was what he wanted. And since the girl insisted on continuing in her role, he transferred his anger to the unknown hitchhiker whom she was portraying. And all at once he discovered the character of his own part: he stopped making the gallant remarks with which he had wanted to flatter his girl in a roundabout way, and began to play the tough guy who treats women to the coarser aspects of his masculinity: willfulness, sarcasm, self-assurance.

This role was a complete contradiction of the young man's habitually solicitous approach to the girl. True, before he had met her, he had in fact behaved roughly rather than gently toward women. But he had never resembled a heartless tough guy, because he had never demonstrated either a particularly strong will or ruthlessness. However, if he did not resemble such a man, nonetheless he had *longed* to at one time. Of course it was a quite naive desire, but there it was. Childish desires withstand all the snares of the adult mind and often survive into ripe old age. And this childish desire quickly took advantage of the opportunity to embody itself in the proffered role.

The young man's sarcastic reserve suited the girl very well—it freed her from herself. For she herself was, above all, the epitome of jealousy. The moment she stopped seeing the gallantly seductive young man beside her and saw only his inaccessible face, her jealousy subsided. The girl could forget herself and give herself up to her role.

Her role? What was her role? It was a role out of trashy literature. The hitchhiker stopped the car not to get a ride, but to seduce the man who was driving the car. She was an artful seductress, cleverly knowing how to use her charms. The girl slipped into this silly, romantic part with an ease that astonished her and held her spellbound.

V

There was nothing the young man missed in his life more than light-heartedness. The main road of his life was drawn with implacable precision. His job didn't use up merely eight hours a day, it also infiltrated the remaining time with the compulsory boredom of meetings and home study, and, by means of the attentiveness of his countless male and female colleagues, it infiltrated the wretchedly little time he had left for his private life as well. This private life never remained secret and sometimes even became the subject of gossip and public discussion. Even two weeks' vacation didn't give him a feeling of liberation and adventure; the gray shadow of precise planning lay even here. The scarcity of summer accommodations in our country compelled him to book a room in the Tatras six months in advance, and since for that he needed a recommendation from his office, its omnipresent brain thus did not cease knowing about him even for an instant.

He had become reconciled to all this, yet all the same from time to time the terrible thought of the straight road would overcome him—a road along which he was being pursued, where he was visible to everyone, and from which he could not turn aside. At this moment that thought returned to him. Through an odd and brief conjunction of ideas the figurative road became identified with the real highway along which he was driving—and this led him suddenly to do a crazy thing.

"Where did you say you wanted to go?" he asked the girl.

"To Banska Bystritsa," she replied.

"And what are you going to do there?"

"I have a date there."

"Who with?"

"With a certain gentleman."

The car was just coming to a large crossroads. The driver slowed down so he could read the road signs, then turned off to the right.

"What will happen if you don't arrive for that date?"

"It would be your fault and you would have to take care of me."

"You obviously didn't notice that I turned off in the direction of Nove Zamky."

"Is that true? You've gone crazy!"

"Don't be afraid, I'll take care of you," said the young man.

So they drove and chatted thus—the driver and the hitchhiker who did not know each other.

The game all at once went into a higher gear. The sports car was moving away not only from the imaginary goal of Banska Bystritsa, but also from the real goal, toward which it had been heading in the morning: the Tatras and the room that had been booked. Fiction was suddenly making an assault upon real life. The young man was moving away from himself and from the implacable straight road, from which he had never strayed until now.

"But you said you were going to the Low Tatras!" The girl was surprised.

"I am going, miss, wherever I feel like going. I'm a free man and I do what I want and what it pleases me to do."

VI

When they drove into Nove Zamky it was already getting dark.

The young man had never been here before and it took him a while to orient himself. Several times he stopped the car and asked the passersby directions to the hotel. Several streets had been dug up, so that the drive to the hotel, even though it was quite close by (as all those who had been asked asserted), necessitated so many detours and roundabout routes that it was almost a quarter of an hour before they finally stopped in front of it. The hotel looked unprepossessing, but it was the only one in town and the young man didn't feel like driving on. So he said to the girl, "Wait here," and got out of the car.

Out of the car he was, of course, himself again. And it was upsetting for him to find himself in the evening somewhere completely different from his intended destination—the more so because no one had forced him to do it and as a matter of fact he hadn't even really wanted to. He blamed himself for this piece of folly, but then became reconciled to it. The room in the Tatras could wait until tomorrow and it wouldn't do any harm if they celebrated the first day of their vacation with something unexpected.

He walked through the restaurant—smoky, noisy, and crowded—and asked for the reception desk. They sent him to the back of the lobby near the staircase, where behind a glass panel a superannuated blonde was sitting beneath a board full of keys. With difficulty, he obtained the key to the only room left.

The girl, when she found herself alone, also threw off her role. She didn't feel ill-humored, though, at finding herself in an unexpected town. She was so devoted to the young man that she never had doubts about anything he did, and confidently entrusted every moment of her life to him. On the other hand the idea once again popped into her mind that perhaps—just as she was now doing—other women had waited for her man in his car, those women whom he met on business trips. But surprisingly enough this idea didn't upset her at all now. In fact, she smiled at the thought of how nice it was that today she was this other woman, this irresponsible, indecent other woman, one of those women of whom she was so jealous. It seemed to her that she was cutting them all out, that she had learned how to use their weapons; how to give the young man what until now she had not known how to give him: light-heartedness, shamelessness, and dissoluteness. A curious feeling of satisfaction filled her, because she alone had the ability to be all women and in this way (she alone) could completely captivate her lover and hold his interest.

The young man opened the car door and led the girl into the restaurant. Amid the din, the dirt, and the smoke he found a single, unoccupied table in a corner.

VII

"So how are you going to take care of me now?" asked the girl provocatively.

"What would you like for an aperitif?"

The girl wasn't too fond of alcohol, still she drank a little wine and liked vermouth fairly well. Now, however, she purposely said: "Vodka."

"Fine," said the young man. "I hope you won't get drunk on me."

"And if I do?" said the girl.

The young man did not reply but called over a waiter and ordered two vodkas and two steak dinners. In a moment the waiter brought a tray with two small glasses and placed it in front of them.

The man raised his glass, "To you!"

"Can't you think of a wittier toast?"

Something was beginning to irritate him about the girl's game. Now sitting face to face with her, he realized that it wasn't just the *words* which were turning her into a stranger, but that her *whole persona* had changed, the movements of her body and her facial expression, and that she unpalatably and faithfully resembled that type of woman whom he knew so well and for whom he felt some aversion.

And so (holding his glass in his raised hand), he corrected his toast: "O.K., then I won't drink to you, but to your kind, in which are combined so successfully the better qualities of the animal and the worse aspects of the human being."

"By 'kind' do you mean all women?" asked the girl.

"No, I mean only those who are like you."

"Anyway it doesn't seem very witty to me to compare a woman with an animal."

"O.K.," the young man was still holding his glass aloft, "then I won't drink to your kind, but to your soul. Agreed? To your soul, which lights up when it descends from your head into your belly, and which goes out when it rises back up to your head."

The girl raised her glass. "O.K., to my soul, which descends into my belly."

"I'll correct myself once more," said the young man. "To your belly, into which your soul descends."

"To my belly," said the girl, and her belly (now that they had named it specifically), as it were, responded to the call; she felt every inch of it.

Then the waiter brought their steaks and the young man ordered them another vodka and some water (this time they drank to the girl's breasts), and the conversation continued in this peculiar, frivolous tone. It irritated the young man more and more how *well able* the girl was to become the lascivious miss. If she was able to do it so well, he thought, it meant that she really *was* like that. After all, no alien soul had entered into her from somewhere in space. What she was acting now was she herself; perhaps it was the part of her being which had formerly been locked up and which the pretext of the game had let out of its cage. Perhaps the girl supposed that by means of the game she was *disowning* herself, but wasn't it the other way around? Wasn't she becoming herself only through the game? Wasn't she freeing herself through the game? No, opposite him was not sitting a strange woman in his girl's body; it was his girl, herself, no one else. He looked at her and felt growing aversion toward her.

However, it was not only aversion. The more the girl withdrew from him *psychically*, the more he longed for her *physically*. The alien quality of her soul drew attention to her body, yes, as a matter of fact it turned her body into a body for *him* as if until now it had existed for the young man hidden within clouds of compassion, tenderness, concern, love, and emotion, as if it had been lost in these clouds (yes, as if this body had been lost!). It seemed to the young man that today he was seeing his girl's body for the first time.

After her third vodka and soda the girl got up and said flirtatiously, "Excuse me."

The young man said, "May I ask you where you are going, miss?"

"To piss, if you'll permit me," said the girl and walked off between the tables back toward the plush screen.

VIII

She was pleased with the way she had astounded the young man with this word, which—in spite of all its innocence—he had never heard from her. Nothing seemed to her truer to the character of the woman she was playing than this flirtatious emphasis placed on the word in question. Yes, she was pleased, she was in the best of moods. The game captivated her. It allowed her to feel what she had not felt till now: a *feeling of happy-go-lucky irresponsibility*.

She, who was always uneasy in advance about her every next step, suddenly felt completely relaxed. The alien life in which she had become involved was a life without shame, without biographical specifications, without past or future, without obligations. It was a life that was extraordinarily free. The girl, as a hitchhiker, could do anything, *everything was permitted her*. She could say, do, and feel whatever she liked.

She walked through the room and was aware that people were watching her from all the tables. It was a new sensation, one she didn't recognize: *indecent joy caused by her body*. Until now she had never been able to get rid of the fourteen-year-old girl within herself who was ashamed of her breasts and had the disagreeable feeling that she was indecent, because they stuck out from her body and were visible. Even though she was proud of being pretty and having a good figure, this feeling of pride was always immediately curtailed by shame. She rightly suspected that feminine beauty functioned above all as sexual provocation and she found this distasteful. She longed for her body to relate only to the man she loved. When men stared at her breasts in the street it seemed to her that they were invading a piece of her most secret privacy which should belong only to herself and her lover. But now she was the hitchhiker, the woman without a destiny. In this role she was relieved of the tender bonds of her love and began to be intensely aware of her body. And her body became more aroused the more alien the eyes watching it.

She was walking past the last table when an intoxicated man, wanting to show off his worldliness, addressed her in French: "*Combien, mademoiselle?*"

The girl understood. She thrust out her breasts and fully experienced every movement of her hips, then disappeared behind the screen.

IX

It was a curious game. This curiousness was evidenced, for example, in the fact that the young man, even though he himself was playing the unknown driver remarkably well, did not for a moment stop seeing his girl in the hitchhiker. And it was precisely this that was tormenting. He saw his girl seducing a strange man, and had the bitter privilege of being present, of seeing at close quarters how she looked and of hearing what she said when she was cheating on him (when she had cheated on him, when she would cheat on him). He had the paradoxical honor of being himself the pretext of her unfaithfulness.

This was all the worse because he worshipped rather than loved her. It had always seemed to him that her inward nature was *real* only within the bounds of fidelity and purity, and that beyond these bounds it simply didn't exist. Beyond these bounds she would cease to be herself, as water ceases to be water beyond the boiling point. When he now saw her crossing this horrifying boundary with nonchalant elegance, he was filled with anger.

The girl came back from the rest room and complained: "A guy over there asked me: *Combien, mademoiselle?*"

"You shouldn't be surprised," said the young man, "after all, you look like a whore."

"Do you know that it doesn't bother me in the least?"

"Then you should go with the gentleman!"

"But I have you."

"You can go with him after me. Go and work out something with him."

"I don't find him attractive."

"But in principle you have nothing against it, having several men in one night?"

"Why not, if they're good-looking."

"Do you prefer them one after the other or at the same time?"

"Either way," said the girl.

The conversation was proceeding to still greater extremes of rudeness; it shocked the girl slightly but she couldn't protest. Even in a game there lurks a lack of freedom; even a game is a trap for the players. If this had not been a game and they had really been two strangers, the hitchhiker could long ago have taken offense and left. But there's no escape from a game. A team cannot flee from the playing field before the end of the match, chess pieces cannot desert the chessboard: the boundaries of the playing field are fixed. The girl knew that she had to accept whatever form the game might take, just because it was a game. She knew that the more extreme the game became, the more it would be a game and the more obediently she would have to play it. And it was futile to evoke good sense and warn her dazed soul that she must keep her distance from the game and not take it seriously. Just because it was only a game her soul was not afraid, did not oppose the game, and narcotically sank deeper into it.

The young man called the waiter and paid. Then he got up and said to the girl, "We're going."

"Where to?" The girl feigned surprise.

"Don't ask, just come on," said the young man.

"What sort of way is that to talk to me?"

"The way I talk to whores," said the young man.

X

They went up the badly lit staircase. On the landing below the second floor a group of intoxicated men was standing near the rest room. The young man caught hold of the girl from behind so that he was holding her breast with his hand. The men by the rest room saw this and began to call out. The girl wanted to break away, but the young man yelled at her: "Keep still!" The men greeted this with general ribaldry and addressed several dirty remarks to the girl. The young man and the girl reached the second floor. He opened the door of their room and switched on the light.

It was a narrow room with two beds, a small table, a chair, and a washbasin. The young man locked the door and turned to the girl. She was standing facing him in a defiant pose with insolent sensuality in her eyes. He looked at her and tried to discover behind her lascivious expression the familiar features which he loved tenderly. It was as if he were looking at two images through the same lens, at two images superimposed one upon the other with the one showing through the other. These two images showing through each other were telling him that *everything* was in the girl, that her soul was terrifyingly amorphous, that it held faithfulness and unfaithfulness, treachery and innocence, flirtatiousness and chastity. This disorderly jumble seemed disgusting to him, like the variety to be found in a pile of garbage. Both images continued to show through each other and the young man understood that the girl differed only on the surface from other women, but deep down was the same as they: full of all possible thoughts, feelings, and vices, which justified all his secret misgivings and fits of jealousy. The impression that certain outlines delineated her as an individual was only a delusion to which the other person, the one who was looking, was subject—namely himself. It seemed to him that the girl he loved was a creation of his desire, his thoughts, and his faith and that the *real* girl now standing in front of him was hopelessly alien, hopelessly *ambiguous*. He hated her.

"What are you waiting for? Strip," he said.

The girl flirtatiously bent her head and said, "Is it necessary?"

The tone in which she said this seemed to him very familiar; it seemed to him that once long ago some other woman had said this to him, only he no longer knew which one. He longed to humiliate her. Not the hitchhiker, but his own girl. The game merged with life. The game of humiliating the hitchhiker became only a pretext for humiliating his girl. The young man had forgotten that he was playing a game. He simply hated the woman standing in front of him. He stared at her and took a fifty-crown bill from his wallet. He offered it to the girl. "Is that enough?"

The girl took the fifty crowns and said: "You don't think I'm worth much."

The young man said: "You aren't worth more."

The girl nestled up against the young man. "You can't get around me like that! You must try a different approach, you must work a little!"

She put her arms around him and moved her mouth toward his. He put his fingers on her mouth and gently pushed her away. He said: "I only kiss women I love."

"And you don't love me?"

"No."

"Whom do you love?"

"What's that got to do with you? Strip!"

XI

She had never undressed like this before. The shyness, the feeling of inner panic, the dizziness, all that she had always felt when undressing in front of the young man (and she couldn't hide in the darkness), all this was gone. She was standing in front of him self-confident, insolent, bathed in light, and astonished at where she had all of a sudden discovered the gestures, heretofore unknown to her, of a slow, provocative striptease. She took in his glances, slipping off each piece of clothing with a caressing movement and enjoying each individual stage of this exposure.

But then suddenly she was standing in front of him completely naked and at this moment it flashed through her head that now the whole game would end, that, since she had stripped off her clothes, she had also stripped away her dissimulation, and that being naked meant that she was now herself and the young man ought to come up to her now and make a gesture with which he would wipe out everything and after which would follow only their most intimate love-making. So she stood naked in front of the young man and at this moment stopped playing the game. She felt embarrassed and on her face appeared the smile, which really belonged to her—a shy and confused smile.

But the young man didn't come to her and didn't end the game. He didn't notice the familiar smile. He saw before him only the beautiful, alien body of his own girl, whom he hated. Hatred cleansed his sensuality of any sentimental coating. She wanted to come to him, but he said: "Stay where you are, I want to have a good look at you." Now he longed only to treat her like a whore. But the young man had never had a whore and the ideas he had about them came from literature and hearsay. So he turned to these ideas and the first thing he recalled was the image of a woman in black underwear (and black stockings) dancing on the shiny top of a piano. In the little hotel room there was no piano, there was only a small table covered with a linen cloth leaning against the wall. He ordered the girl to climb up on it. The girl made a pleading gesture, but the young man said, "You've been paid."

When she saw the look of unshakable obsession in the young man's eyes, she tried to go on with the game, even though she no longer could and no longer knew how. With tears in her eyes she climbed onto the table. The top was scarcely three feet square and one leg was a little bit shorter than the others so that standing on it the girl felt unsteady.

But the young man was pleased with the naked figure, now towering above him, and the girl's shy insecurity merely inflamed his imperiousness. He wanted to see her body in all positions and from all sides, as he imagined other men had seen it and would see it. He was vulgar and lascivious. He used words that she had never heard from him in her life. She wanted to refuse, she wanted to be released from the game. She called him by his first name, but he immediately yelled at her that she had no right to address him so intimately. And so eventually in confusion and on the verge of tears, she obeyed, and bent forward and squatted according to the young man's wishes, saluted, and then wiggled her hips as she did the Twist for him. During a slightly more violent movement, when the cloth slipped beneath her feet and she nearly fell, the young man caught her and dragged her to the bed.

He had intercourse with her. She was glad that at least now finally the unfortunate game would end and they would again be the two people they had been before and would love each other. She wanted to press her mouth against his. But the young man pushed her head away and repeated that he only kissed women he loved. She burst into loud sobs. But she wasn't even allowed to cry, because the young man's furious passion gradually won over her body, which then silenced the complaint of her soul. On the bed there were soon two bodies in perfect harmony, two sensual bodies, alien to each other. This was exactly what the girl had most dreaded all her life and had scrupulously avoided till now: lovemaking without emotion or love. She knew that she had crossed the forbidden boundary, but she proceeded across it without objections and as a full participant—only somewhere, far off in a corner of her consciousness, did she feel horror at the thought that she had never known such pleasure, never so much pleasure as at this moment—beyond the boundary.

XII

Then it was all over. The young man got up off the girl and, reaching out for the long cord hanging over the bed, switched off the light. He didn't want to see the girl's face. He knew that the game was over, but didn't feel like returning to their customary relationship. He feared this return. He lay beside the girl in the dark in such a way that their bodies would not touch.

After a moment he heard her sobbing quietly. The girl's hand diffidently, childishly touched his. It touched, withdrew, then touched again, and then a pleading, sobbing voice broke the silence, calling him by his name and saying, "I am me, I am me. . . ."

The young man was silent, he didn't move, and he was aware of the sad emptiness of the girl's assertion, in which the unknown was defined in terms of the same unknown quantity.

And the girl soon passed from sobbing to loud crying and went on endlessly repeating this pitiful tautology: "I am me, I am me, I am me. . . ."

The young man began to call compassion to his aid (he had to call it from afar, because it was nowhere near at hand), so as to be able to calm the girl. There were still thirteen days' vacation before them.

Yukio Mishima

Yukio Mishima was born in Tokyo in 1925, the son of a senior government official. He received a law degree from Tokyo University in 1947. Mishima published his first short story at the age of sixteen. Overall, he wrote forty

novels, eighteen plays, twenty volumes of short stories, and twenty vol-
umes of essays, including the acclaimed Sun and Steel. *Mishima was nom-*
inated for the Nobel Prize for literature in 1965. "Patriotism" appears in
Death in Midsummer and Other Stories *(1966). Mishima committed*
ritual suicide (seppuku) in 1970.

Patriotism[1]

I

On the twenty-eighth of February, 1936 (on the third day, that is,
of the February 26 incident),[2] Lieutenant Shinji Takeyama of the
Konoe Transport Battalion—profoundly disturbed by the knowledge that his closest colleagues had been with the mutineers from
the beginning, and indignant at the imminent prospect of Imperial troops attacking Imperial troops—took his officer's sword and
ceremonially disemboweled himself in the eight-mat room of his
private residence in the sixth block of Aoba-chō, in Yotsuya Ward.
His wife, Reiko, followed him, stabbing herself to death. The lieutenant's farewell note consisted of one sentence: "Long live the Imperial Forces." His wife's, after apologies for her unfilial conduct
in thus preceding her parents to the grave, concluded: "The day
which, for a soldier's wife, had to come, has come. . . ." The last
moments of this heroic and dedicated couple were such as to make
the gods themselves weep. The lieutenant's age, it should be noted,
was thirty-one, his wife's twenty-three; and it was not half a year
since the celebration of their marriage.

II

Those who saw the bride and bridegroom in the commemorative
photograph—perhaps no less than those actually present at the

---

[1]*Translated by Geoffrey W. Sargent.*
[2]*On February 26, 1936, fourteen hundred soldiers from the Japanese Army's First Di-*
vision mutinied, seizing national government offices, the Tokyo Police headquarters, and
assassinating several major officials, as the culmination of a power struggle between
rival army factions. By February 29, the rebellion was quelled, but the incident led to the
restructuring of the Japanese government into a wartime state, and is considered one of
the major catalysts for Japan's involvement in World War II.

lieutenant's wedding—had exclaimed in wonder at the bearing of this handsome couple. The lieutenant, majestic in military uniform, stood protectively beside his bride, his right hand resting upon his sword, his officer's cap held at his left side. His expression was severe, and his dark brows and wide-gazing eyes well conveyed the clear integrity of youth. For the beauty of the bride in her white over-robe no comparisons were adequate. In the eyes, round beneath soft brows, in the slender, finely shaped nose, and in the full lips, there was both sensuousness and refinement. One hand, emerging shyly from a sleeve of the over-robe, held a fan, and the tips of the fingers, clustering delicately, were like the bud of a moonflower.

After the suicide, people would take out this photograph and examine it, and sadly reflect that too often there was a curse on these seemingly flawless unions. Perhaps it was no more than imagination, but looking at the picture after the tragedy it almost seemed as if the two young people before the gold-lacquered screen were gazing, each with equal clarity, at the deaths which lay before them.

Thanks to the good offices of their go-between, Lieutenant General Ozeki, they had been able to set themselves up in a new home at Aoba-chō in Yotsuya. "New home" is perhaps misleading. It was an old three-room rented house backing onto a small garden. As neither the six- nor the four-and-a-half-mat room downstairs was favored by the sun, they used the upstairs eight-mat room as both bedroom and guest room. There was no maid, so Reiko was left alone to guard the house in her husband's absence.

The honeymoon trip was dispensed with on the grounds that these were times of national emergency.[3] The two of them had spent the first night of their marriage at this house. Before going to bed, Shinji, sitting erect on the floor with his sword laid before him, had bestowed upon his wife a soldierly lecture. A woman who had become the wife of a soldier should know and resolutely accept that her husband's death might come at any moment. It could be tomorrow. It could be the day after. But, no matter when it came—he asked—was she steadfast in her resolve to accept it? Reiko rose to her feet, pulled open a drawer of the cabinet, and took out what was the most prized of her new possessions, the dagger her mother had given her. Returning to her place, she laid the

---

[3] *Japanese forces occupied Manchuria and parts of mainland China.*

dagger without a word on the mat before her, just as her husband had laid his sword. A silent understanding was achieved at once, and the lieutenant never again sought to test his wife's resolve.

In the first few months of her marriage Reiko's beauty grew daily more radiant, shining serene like the moon after rain.

As both were possessed of young, vigorous bodies, their relationship was passionate. Nor was this merely a matter of the night. On more than one occasion, returning home straight from maneuvers, and begrudging even the time it took to remove his mud-splashed uniform, the lieutenant had pushed his wife to the floor almost as soon as he had entered the house. Reiko was equally ardent in her response. For a little more or a little less than a month, from the first night of their marriage Reiko knew happiness, and the lieutenant, seeing this, was happy too.

Reiko's body was white and pure, and her swelling breasts conveyed a firm and chaste refusal; but, upon consent, those breasts were lavish with their intimate, welcoming warmth. Even in bed these two were frighteningly and awesomely serious. In the very midst of wild, intoxicating passions, their hearts were sober and serious.

By day the lieutenant would think of his wife in the brief rest periods between training; and all day long, at home, Reiko would recall the image of her husband. Even when apart, however, they had only to look at the wedding photograph for their happiness to be once more confirmed. Reiko felt not the slightest surprise that a man who had been a complete stranger until a few months ago should now have become the sun about which her whole world revolved.

All these things had a moral basis, and were in accordance with the Education Rescript's[4] injunction that "husband and wife should be harmonious." Not once did Reiko contradict her husband, nor did the lieutenant ever find reason to scold his wife. On the god shelf below the stairway, alongside the tablet from the Great Ise Shrine,[5] were set photographs of their Imperial Majesties, and regularly every morning, before leaving for duty, the lieutenant would

---

[4]*A Confucian-influenced doctrine issued by the Emperor in 1890 and designed to govern all aspects of Japanese moral life.*
[5]*A prominent national shrine and pilgrimage site of the Japanese state-sponsored Shinto religion.*

stand with his wife at this hallowed place and together they would bow their heads low. The offering water was renewed each morning, and the sacred sprig of *sasaki*[6] was always green and fresh. Their lives were lived beneath the solemn protection of the gods and were filled with an intense happiness which set every fiber in their bodies trembling.

III

Although Lord Privy Seal Saitō's[7] house was in their neighborhood, neither of them heard any noise of gunfire on the morning of February 26. It was a bugle, sounding muster in the dim, snowy dawn, when the ten-minute tragedy had already ended, which first disrupted the lieutenant's slumbers. Leaping at once from his bed, and without speaking a word, the lieutenant donned his uniform, buckled on the sword held ready for him by his wife, and hurried swiftly out into the snow-covered streets of the still darkened morning. He did not return until the evening of the twenty-eighth.

Later, from the radio news, Reiko learned the full extent of this sudden eruption of violence. Her life throughout the subsequent two days was lived alone, in complete tranquility, and behind locked doors.

In the lieutenant's face, as he hurried silently out into the snowy morning, Reiko had read the determination to die. If her husband did not return, her own decision was made: she too would die. Quietly she attended to the disposition of her personal possessions. She chose her sets of visiting kimonos as keepsakes for friends of her schooldays, and she wrote a name and address on the stiff paper wrapping in which each was folded. Constantly admonished by her husband never to think of the morrow, Reiko had not even kept a diary and was now denied the pleasure of assiduously rereading her record of the happiness of the past few months and consigning each page to the fire as she did so. Ranged across the top of the radio were a small china dog, a rabbit, a squirrel, a bear, and a fox. There were also a small vase and a water pitcher. These comprised Reiko's one and only collection. But it would

---

[6]*Evergreen tree sacred in Shinto rites.*
[7]*Prominent governmental official killed in February 26 incident.*

hardly do, she imagined, to give such things as keepsakes. Nor again would it be quite proper to ask specifically for them to be included in the coffin. It seemed to Reiko, as these thoughts passed through her mind, that the expressions on the small animals' faces grew even more lost and forlorn.

Reiko took the squirrel in her hand and looked at it. And then, her thoughts turning to a realm far beyond these child-like affections, she gazed up into the distance at the great sunlike principle which her husband embodied. She was ready, and happy, to be hurtled along to her destruction in that gleaming sun chariot—but now, for these few moments of solitude, she allowed herself to luxuriate in this innocent attachment to trifles. The time when she had genuinely loved these things, however, was long past. Now she merely loved the memory of having once loved them, and their place in her heart had been filled by more intense passions, by a more frenzied happiness. . . . For Reiko had never, even to herself, thought of those soaring joys of the flesh as a mere pleasure. The February cold, and the icy touch of the china squirrel, had numbed Reiko's slender fingers; yet, even so, in her lower limbs, beneath the ordered repetition of the pattern which crossed the skirt of her trim *meisen* kimono,[8] she could feel now, as she thought of the lieutenant's powerful arms reaching out toward her, a hot moistness of the flesh which defied the snows.

She was not in the least afraid of the death hovering in her mind. Waiting alone at home, Reiko firmly believed that everything her husband was feeling or thinking now, his anguish and distress, was leading her—just as surely as the power in his flesh—to a welcome death. She felt as if her body could melt away with ease and be transformed to the merest fraction of her husband's thought.

Listening to the frequent announcements on the radio, she heard the names of several of her husband's colleagues mentioned among those of the insurgents. This was news of death. She followed the developments closely, wondering anxiously, as the situation became daily more irrevocable, why no Imperial ordinance was sent down, and watching what had at first been taken as a movement to restore the nation's honor come gradually to be branded with the infamous name of mutiny. There was no communication from the

---

[8] *Kimono intended for casual indoor use.*

regiment. At any moment, it seemed, fighting might commence in the city streets, where the remains of the snow still lay.

Toward sundown on the twenty-eighth Reiko was startled by a furious pounding on the front door. She hurried downstairs. As she pulled with fumbling fingers at the bolt, the shape dimly outlined beyond the frosted-glass panel made no sound, but she knew it was her husband. Reiko had never known the bolt on the sliding door to be so stiff. Still it resisted. The door just would not open.

In a moment, almost before she knew she had succeeded, the lieutenant was standing before her on the cement floor inside the porch, muffled in a khaki greatcoat, his top boots heavy with slush from the street. Closing the door behind him, he returned the bolt once more to its socket. With what significance, Reiko did not understand.

"Welcome home."

Reiko bowed deeply, but her husband made no response. As he had already unfastened his sword and was about to remove his greatcoat, Reiko moved around behind to assist. The coat, which was cold and damp and had lost the odor of horse dung it normally exuded when exposed to the sun, weighed heavily upon her arm. Draping it across a hanger, and cradling the sword and leather belt in her sleeves, she waited while her husband removed his top boots and then followed behind him into the "living room." This was the six-mat room downstairs.

Seen in the clear light from the lamp, her husband's face, covered with a heavy growth of bristle, was almost unrecognizably wasted and thin. The cheeks were hollow, their luster and resilience gone. In his normal good spirits he would have changed into old clothes as soon as he was home and have pressed her to get supper at once, but now he sat before the table still in his uniform, his head drooping dejectedly. Reiko refrained from asking whether she should prepare the supper.

After an interval the lieutenant spoke.

"I knew nothing. They hadn't asked me to join. Perhaps out of consideration, because I was newly married. Kanō, and Homma too, and Yamaguchi."

Reiko recalled momentarily the faces of high-spirited young officers, friends of her husband, who had come to the house occasionally as guests.

"There may be an Imperial ordinance sent down tomorrow. They'll be posted as rebels, I imagine. I shall be in command of a unit with orders to attack them. . . . I can't do it. It's impossible to do a thing like that."

He spoke again.

"They've taken me off guard duty, and I have permission to return home for one night. Tomorrow morning, without question, I must leave to join the attack. I can't do it, Reiko."

Reiko sat erect with lowered eyes. She understood clearly that her husband had spoken of his death. The lieutenant was resolved. Each word, being rooted in death, emerged sharply and with powerful significance against this dark, unmovable background. Although the lieutenant was speaking of his dilemma, already there was no room in his mind for vacillation.

However, there was a clarity, like the clarity of a stream fed from melting snows, in the silence which rested between them. Sitting in his own home after the long two-day ordeal, and looking across at the face of his beautiful wife, the lieutenant was for the first time experiencing true peace of mind. For he had at once known, though she said nothing, that his wife divined the resolve which lay beneath his words.

"Well, then . . ." The lieutenant's eyes opened wide. Despite his exhaustion they were strong and clear, and now for the first time they looked straight into the eyes of his wife. "Tonight I shall cut my stomach."

Reiko did not flinch.

Her round eyes showed tension, as taut as the clang of a bell.

"I am ready," she said. "I ask permission to accompany you."

The lieutenant felt almost mesmerized by the strength in those eyes. His words flowed swiftly and easily, like the utterances of a man in delirium, and it was beyond his understanding how permission in a matter of such weight could be expressed so casually.

"Good. We'll go together. But I want you as a witness, first, for my own suicide. Agreed?"

When this was said a sudden release of abundant happiness welled up in both their hearts. Reiko was deeply affected by the greatness of her husband's trust in her. It was vital for the lieutenant, whatever else might happen, that there should be no irregularity in his death. For that reason there had to be a witness. The fact that he had chosen his wife for this was the first mark of his trust. The second, and even greater mark, was that though he had pledged that they should die together he did not intend to kill his wife first—he had deferred her death to a time when he would no longer be there to verify it. If the lieutenant had been a suspicious husband, he would doubtless, as in the usual suicide pact, have chosen to kill his wife first.

When Reiko said, "I ask permission to accompany you," the lieutenant felt these words to be the final fruit of the education which he had himself given his wife, starting on the first night of their marriage, and which had schooled her, when the moment came, to say what had to be said without a shadow of hesitation. This flattered the lieutenant's opinion of himself as a self-reliant man. He was not so romantic or conceited as to imagine that the words were spoken spontaneously, out of love for her husband.

With happiness welling almost too abundantly in their hearts, they could not help smiling at each other. Reiko felt as if she had returned to her wedding night.

Before her eyes was neither pain nor death. She seemed to see only a free and limitless expanse opening out into vast distances.

"The water is hot. Will you take your bath now?"

"Ah yes, of course."

"And supper . . . ?"

The words were delivered in such level, domestic tones that the lieutenant came near to thinking, for the fraction of a second, that everything had been a hallucination.

"I don't think we'll need supper. But perhaps you could warm some Sake?"[9]

"As you wish."

As Reiko rose and took a *tanzen* gown[10] from the cabinet for after the bath, she purposely directed her husband's attention to the opened drawer. The lieutenant rose, crossed to the cabinet, and looked inside. From the ordered array of paper wrappings he read, one by one, the addresses of the keepsakes. There was no grief in the lieutenant's response to this demonstration of heroic resolve. His heart was filled with tenderness. Like a husband who is proudly shown the childish purchases of a young

---

[9]*Traditional rice wine.*
[10]*Man's padded kimono worn in private during cold weather.*

wife, the lieutenant, overwhelmed by affection, lovingly embraced his wife from behind and implanted a kiss upon her neck.

Reiko felt the roughness of the lieutenant's unshaven skin against her neck. This sensation, more than being just a thing of this world, was for Reiko almost the world itself, but now—with the feeling that it was soon to be lost forever—it had freshness beyond all her experience. Each moment had its own vital strength, and the senses in every corner of her body were reawakened. Accepting her husband's caresses from behind, Reiko raised herself on the tips of her toes, letting the vitality seep through her entire body.

"First the bath, and then, after some Sake . . . lay out the bedding upstairs, will you?"

The lieutenant whispered the words into his wife's ear. Reiko silently nodded.

Flinging off his uniform, the lieutenant went to the bath. To faint background noises of slopping water Reiko tended the charcoal brazier in the living room and began the preparations for warming the sake.

Taking the *tanzen*, a sash, and some underclothes, she went to the bathroom to ask how the water was. In the midst of a coiling cloud of steam the lieutenant was sitting cross-legged on the floor, shaving, and she could dimly discern the rippling movements of the muscles on his damp, powerful back as they responded to the movement of his arms.

There was nothing to suggest a time of any special significance. Reiko, going busily about her tasks, was preparing side dishes from odds and ends in stock. Her hands did not tremble. If anything, she managed even more efficiently and smoothly than usual. From time to time, it is true, there was a strange throbbing deep within her breast. Like distant lightning, it had a moment of sharp intensity and then vanished without trace. Apart from that, nothing was in any way out of the ordinary.

The lieutenant, shaving in the bathroom, felt his warmed body miraculously healed at last of the desperate tiredness of the days of indecision and filled—in spite of the death which lay ahead—with pleasurable anticipation. The sound of his wife going about her work came to him faintly. A healthy physical craving, submerged for two days, reasserted itself.

The lieutenant was confident there had been no impurity in that joy they had experienced when resolving upon death. They had both sensed at that moment—though not, of course, in any clear and conscious way—that those permissible pleasures which they shared in private were once more beneath the protection of Righteousness and Divine Power, and of a complete and unassailable morality. On looking into each other's eyes and discovering there an honorable death, they had felt themselves safe once more behind steel walls which none could destroy, encased in an impenetrable armor of Beauty and Truth. Thus, so far from seeing any inconsistency or conflict between the urges of his flesh and the sincerity of his patriotism, the lieutenant was even able to regard the two as parts of the same thing.

Thrusting his face close to the dark, cracked, misted wall mirror, the lieutenant shaved himself with great care. This would be his death face. There must be no unsightly blemishes. The clean-shaven face gleamed once more with a youthful luster, seeming to brighten the darkness of the mirror. There was a certain elegance, he even felt, in the association of death with this radiantly healthy face.

Just as it looked now, this would become his death face! Already, in fact, it had half departed from the lieutenant's personal possession and had become the bust above a dead soldier's memorial. As an experiment he closed his eyes tight. Everything was wrapped in blackness, and he was no longer a living, seeing creature.

Returning from the bath, the traces of the shave glowing faintly blue beneath his smooth cheeks, he seated himself beside the now well-kindled charcoal brazier. Busy though Reiko was, he noticed, she had found time lightly to touch up her face. Her cheeks were gay and her lips moist. There was no shadow of sadness to be seen. Truly, the lieutenant felt, as he saw this mark of his young wife's passionate nature, he had chosen the wife he ought to have chosen.

As soon as the lieutenant had drained his sake cup he offered it to Reiko. Reiko had never before tasted sake, but she accepted without hesitation and sipped timidly.

"Come here," the lieutenant said.

Reiko moved to her husband's side and was embraced as she leaned backward across his lap. Her breast was in violent commotion, as if sadness, joy, and the potent sake were mingling and reacting within her. The lieutenant looked down into his wife's face. It was the last face he would see in this world, the last face he would see of his wife. The lieutenant scrutinized the face minutely, with the eyes of a traveler bidding farewell to splendid vistas which he will never revisit. It was a face he could not tire of looking at—the features regular yet not cold, the lips lightly closed with a soft strength. The lieutenant kissed those lips, unthinkingly. And suddenly, though there was not the slightest distortion of the face into the unsightliness of sobbing, he noticed that tears were welling slowly from beneath the long lashes of the closed eyes and brimming over into a glistening stream.

When, a little later, the lieutenant urged that they should move to the upstairs bedroom, his wife replied that she would follow after taking a bath. Climbing the stairs alone to the bedroom, where the air was already warmed by the gas heater, the lieutenant lay down on the bedding with arms outstretched and legs apart. Even the time at which he lay waiting for his wife to join him was no later and no earlier than usual.

He folded his hands beneath his head and gazed at the dark boards of the ceiling in the dimness beyond the range of the standard lamp. Was it death he was now waiting for? Or a wild ecstasy of the senses? The two seemed to overlap, almost as if the object of this bodily desire was death itself. But, however that might be, it was certain that never before had the lieutenant tasted such total freedom.

There was the sound of a car outside the window. He could hear the screech of its tires skidding in the snow piled at the side of the street. The sound of its horn re-echoed from nearby walls. . . . Listening to these noises he had the feeling that this house rose like a solitary island in the ocean of a society going as restlessly about its business as ever. All around, vastly and untidily, stretched the country for which he grieved. He was to give his life for it. But would that great country, with which he was prepared to remonstrate to the extent of destroying himself, take the slightest heed of his death? He did not know; and it did not matter. His was a battlefield without glory, a battlefield where none could display deeds of valor: it was the front line of the spirit.

Reiko's footsteps sounded on the stairway. The steep stairs in this old house creaked badly. There were fond memories in that creaking, and many a time, while waiting in bed, the lieutenant had listened to its welcome sound. At the thought that he would hear it no more he listened with intense concentration, striving for every corner of every moment of this precious time to be filled with the sound of those soft footfalls on the creaking stairway. The moments seemed transformed to jewels, sparkling with inner light.

Reiko wore a Nagoya sash about the waist of her *yukata*,[11] but as the lieutenant reached toward it, its redness sobered by the dimness of the light, Reiko's hand moved to his assistance and the sash fell away, slithering swiftly to the floor. As she stood before him, still in her *yukata,* the lieutenant inserted his hands through the side slits beneath each sleeve, intending to embrace her as she was; but at the touch of his finger tips upon the warm naked flesh, and as the armpits closed gently about his hands, his whole body was suddenly aflame.

In a few moments the two lay naked before the glowing gas heater.

Neither spoke the thought, but their hearts, their bodies, and their pounding breasts blazed with the knowledge that this was the very last time. It was as if the words "The Last Time" were spelled out, in invisible brushstrokes, across every inch of their bodies.

The lieutenant drew his wife close and kissed her vehemently. As their tongues explored each other's mouths, reaching out into the smooth, moist interior, they felt as if the still-unknown agonies of death had tempered their senses to the keenness of red-hot steel. The agonies they could not yet feel, the distant pains of death, had refined their awareness of pleasure.

"This is the last time I shall see your body," said the lieutenant. "Let me look at it closely." And, tilting the shade on the lampstand to one side, he directed the rays along the full length of Reiko's outstretched form.

Reiko lay still with her eyes closed. The light from the low lamp clearly revealed the majestic sweep of her white flesh. The lieutenant, not without a touch of egocentricity, rejoiced that he would never see this beauty crumble in death.

At his leisure, the lieutenant allowed the unforgettable spectacle to engrave itself upon his mind. With one hand he fondled the hair, with the other he softly stroked the magnificent face, implanting kisses here and there where his eyes lingered. The quiet coldness of the high, tapering forehead, the closed eyes with their

---

[11]*Thin kimono used in summer or in private.*

long lashes beneath faintly etched brows, the set of the finely shaped nose, the gleam of teeth glimpsed between full, regular lips, the soft cheeks and the small, wise chin . . . these things conjured up in the lieutenant's mind the vision of a truly radiant death face, and again and again he pressed his lips tight against the white throat—where Reiko's own hand was soon to strike— and the throat reddened faintly beneath his kisses. Returning to the mouth he laid his lips against it with the gentlest of pressures, and moved them rhythmically over Reiko's with the light rolling motion of a small boat. If he closed his eyes, the world became a rocking cradle.

Wherever the lieutenant's eyes moved his lips faithfully followed. The high, swelling breasts, surmounted by nipples like the buds of a wild cherry, hardened as the lieutenant's lips closed about them. The arms flowed smoothly downward from each side of the breast, tapering toward the wrists, yet losing nothing of their roundness or symmetry, and at their tips were those delicate fingers which had held the fan at the wedding ceremony. One by one, as the lieutenant kissed them, the fingers withdrew behind their neighbor as if in shame. . . . The natural hollow curving behind the bosom and the stomach carried in its lines a suggestion not only of softness but of resilient strength, and while it gave forewarning of the rich curves spreading outward from here to the hips it had, in itself, an appearance only of restraint and proper discipline. The whiteness and richness of the stomach and hips was like milk brimming in a great bowl, and the sharply shadowed dip of the navel could have been the fresh impress of a raindrop, fallen there that very moment. Where the shadows gathered more thickly, hair clustered, gentle and sensitive, and as the agitation mounted in the now no longer passive body, there hung over this region a scent like the smoldering of fragrant blossoms, growing steadily more pervasive.

At length, in a tremulous voice, Reiko spoke.

"Show me. . . . Let me look too, for the last time."

Never before had he heard from his wife's lips so strong and unequivocal a request. It was as if something which her modesty had wished to keep hidden to the end had suddenly burst its bonds of constraint. The lieutenant obediently lay back and surrendered himself to his wife. Lithely she raised her white, trembling body, and—burning with an innocent desire to return to her husband what he had done for her—placed two white fingers on the lieutenant's eyes, which gazed fixedly up at her, and gently stroked them shut.

Suddenly overwhelmed by tenderness, her cheeks flushed by a dizzying uprush of emotion, Reiko threw her arms about the lieutenant's close-cropped head. The bristly hairs rubbed painfully against her breast, the prominent nose was cold as it dug into her flesh, and his breath was hot. Relaxing her embrace, she gazed down at her husband's masculine face. The severe brows, the closed eyes, the splendid bridge of the nose, the shapely lips drawn firmly together . . . the blue, clean-shaven cheeks reflecting the light and gleaming smoothly. Reiko kissed each of these. She kissed the broad nape of the neck, the strong, erect shoulders, the powerful chest with its twin circles like shields and its russet nipples. In the armpits, deeply shadowed by the ample flesh of the shoulders and chest, a sweet and melancholy odor emanated from the growth of hair, and in the sweetness of this odor was contained, somehow, the essence of young death. The lieutenant's naked skin glowed like a field of barley, and everywhere the muscles showed in sharp relief, converging on the lower abdomen about the small, unassuming navel. Gazing at the youthful, firm stomach, modestly covered by a vigorous growth of hair, Reiko thought of it as it was soon to be, cruelly cut by the sword, and she laid her head upon it, sobbing in pity, and bathed it with kisses.

At the touch of his wife's tears upon his stomach the lieutenant felt ready to endure with courage the cruelest agonies of his suicide.

What ecstasies they experienced after these tender exchanges may well be imagined. The lieutenant raised himself and enfolded his wife in a powerful embrace, her body now limp with exhaustion after her grief and tears. Passionately they held their faces close, rubbing cheek against cheek. Reiko's body was trembling. Their breasts, moist with sweat, were tightly joined, and every inch of the young and beautiful bodies had become so much one with the other that it seemed impossible there should ever again be a separation. Reiko cried out. From the heights they plunged into the abyss, and from the abyss they took wing and soared once more to dizzying heights. The lieutenant panted like the regimental standard-bearer on a route march. . . . As one cycle ended, almost immediately a new wave of passion would be generated, and together—with no trace of fatigue—they would climb again in a single breathless movement to the very summit.

IV

When the lieutenant at last turned away, it was not from weariness. For one thing, he was anxious not to undermine the considerable strength he would need in carrying out his suicide. For another, he would have been sorry to mar the sweetness of these last memories by overindulgence.

Since the lieutenant had clearly desisted, Reiko too, with her usual compliance, followed his example. The two lay naked on their backs, with fingers interlaced, staring fixedly at the dark ceiling. The room was warm from the heater, and even when the sweat had ceased to pour from their bodies they felt no cold. Outside, in the hushed night, the sounds of passing traffic had ceased. Even the noises of the trains and streetcars around Yotsuya station did not penetrate this far. After echoing through the region bounded by the moat, they were lost in the heavily wooded part fronting the broad driveway before Akasaka Palace.[12] It was hard to believe in the tension gripping this whole quarter, where the two factions of the bitterly divided Imperial Army now confronted each other, poised for battle.

Savoring the warmth glowing within themselves, they lay still and recalled the ecstasies they had just known. Each moment of the experience was relived. They remembered the taste of kisses which had never wearied, the touch of naked flesh, episode after episode of dizzying bliss. But already, from the dark boards of the ceiling, the face of death was peering down. These joys had been final, and their bodies would never know them again. Not that joy of this intensity—and the same thought had occurred to them both—was ever likely to be reexperienced, even if they should live on to old age.

The feel of their fingers intertwined—this too would soon be lost. Even the wood-grain patterns they now gazed at on the dark ceiling boards would be taken from them. They could feel death edging in, nearer and nearer. There could be no hesitation now.

---

[12] *A section of the Imperial Palace.*

They must have the courage to reach out to death themselves, and to seize it.

"Well, let's make our preparations," said the lieutenant. The note of determination in the words was unmistakable, but at the same time Reiko had never heard her husband's voice so warm and tender.

After they had risen, a variety of tasks awaited them.

The lieutenant, who had never once before helped with the bedding, now cheerfully slid back the door of the closet, lifted the mattress across the room by himself, and stowed it away inside.

Reiko turned off the gas heater and put away the lamp standard. During the lieutenant's absence she had arranged this room carefully, sweeping and dusting it to a fresh cleanness, and now—if one overlooked the rosewood table drawn into one corner—the eight-mat room gave all the appearance of a reception room ready to welcome an important guest.

"We've seen some drinking here, haven't we? With Kanō and Homma and Noguchi . . ."

"Yes, they were great drinkers, all of them."

"We'll be meeting them before long, in the other world. They'll tease us, I imagine, when they find I've brought you with me."

Descending the stairs, the lieutenant turned to look back into this calm, clean room, now brightly illuminated by the ceiling lamp. There floated across his mind the faces of the young officers who had drunk there, and laughed, and innocently bragged. He had never dreamed then that he would one day cut open his stomach in this room.

In the two rooms downstairs husband and wife busied themselves smoothly and serenely with their respective preparations. The lieutenant went to the toilet, and then to the bathroom to wash. Meanwhile Reiko folded away her husband's padded robe, placed his uniform tunic, his trousers, and a newly cut bleached loincloth in the bathroom, and set out sheets of paper on the living-room table for the farewell notes. Then she removed the lid from the writing box and began rubbing ink from the ink tablet. She had already decided upon the wording of her own note.

Reiko's fingers pressed hard upon the cold gilt letters of the ink tablet, and the water in the shallow well at once darkened, as if a black cloud had spread across it. She stopped thinking that this repeated action, this pressure from her fingers, this rise and fall of faint sound, was all and solely for death. It was a routine domestic task, a simple paring away of time until death should finally stand before her. But somehow, in the increasingly smooth motion of the tablet rubbing on the stone, and in the scent from the thickening ink, there was unspeakable darkness.

Neat in his uniform, which he now wore next to his skin, the lieutenant emerged from the bathroom. Without a word he seated himself at the table, bolt upright, took a brush in his hand, and stared undecidedly at the paper before him.

Reiko took a white silk kimono with her and entered the bathroom. When she reappeared in the living room, clad in the white kimono and with her face lightly made up, the farewell note lay completed on the table beneath the lamp. The thick black brushstrokes said simply:

"Long Live the Imperial Forces—Army Lieutenant Takeyama Shinji."

While Reiko sat opposite him writing her own note, the lieutenant gazed in silence, intensely serious, at the controlled movement of his wife's pale fingers as they manipulated the brush.

With their respective notes in their hands—the lieutenant's sword strapped to his side, Reiko's small dagger thrust into the sash of her white kimono—the two of them stood before the god shelf and silently prayed. Then they put out all the downstairs lights. As he mounted the stairs the lieutenant turned his head and gazed back at the striking, white-clad figure of his wife, climbing behind him, with lowered eyes, from the darkness beneath.

The farewell notes were laid side by side in the alcove of the upstairs room. They wondered whether they ought not to remove the hanging scroll, but since it had been written by their go-between, Lieutenant General Ozeki, and consisted, moreover, of two Chinese characters signifying "Sincerity," they left it where it was. Even if it were to become stained with splashes of blood, they felt that the lieutenant general would understand.

The lieutenant, sitting erect with his back to the alcove, laid his sword on the floor before him.

Reiko sat facing him, a mat's width away. With the rest of her so severely white the touch of rouge on her lips seemed remarkably seductive.

Across the dividing mat they gazed intently into each other's eyes. The lieutenant's sword lay before his knees. Seeing it, Reiko recalled their first night and was overwhelmed with sadness. The lieutenant spoke, in a hoarse voice:

"As I have no second to help me I shall cut deep. It may look unpleasant, but please do not panic. Death of any sort is a fearful thing to watch. You must not be discouraged by what you see. Is that all right?"

"Yes."

Reiko nodded deeply.

Looking at the slender white figure of his wife the lieutenant experienced a bizarre excitement. What he was about to perform was an act in his public capacity as a soldier, something he had never previously shown his wife. It called for a resolution equal to the courage to enter battle; it was a death of no less degree and quality than death in the front line. It was his conduct on the battlefield that he was now to display.

Momentarily the thought led the lieutenant to a strange fantasy. A lonely death on the battlefield, a death beneath the eyes of his beautiful wife . . . in the sensation that he was now to die in these two dimensions, realizing an impossible union of them both, there was sweetness beyond words. This must be the very pinnacle of good fortune, he thought. To have every moment of his death observed by those beautiful eyes—it was like being borne to death on a gentle, fragrant breeze. There was some special favor here. He did not understand precisely what it was, but it was a domain unknown to others: a dispensation granted to no one else had been permitted to himself. In the radiant, bridelike figure of his white-robed wife the lieutenant seemed to see a vision of all those things he had loved and for which he was to lay down his life—the Imperial Household, the Nation, the Army Flag. All these, no less than the wife who sat before him, were presences observing him closely with clear and never-faltering eyes.

Reiko too was gazing intently at her husband, so soon to die, and she thought that never in this world had she seen anything so beautiful. The lieutenant always looked well in uniform, but now, as he contemplated death with severe brows and firmly closed lips, he revealed what was perhaps masculine beauty at its most superb.

"It's time to go," the lieutenant said at last.

Reiko bent her body low to the mat in a deep bow. She could not raise her face. She did not wish to spoil her make-up with tears, but the tears could not be held back.

When at length she looked up she saw hazily through the tears that her husband had wound a white bandage around the blade of his now unsheathed sword, leaving five or six inches of naked steel showing at the point.

Resting the sword in its cloth wrapping on the mat before him, the lieutenant rose from his knees, resettled himself crosslegged, and unfastened the hooks of his uniform collar. His eyes no longer saw his wife. Slowly, one by one, he undid the flat brass buttons. The dusky brown chest was revealed, and then the stomach. He unclasped his belt and undid the buttons of his trousers. The pure whiteness of the thickly coiled loincloth showed itself. The lieutenant pushed the cloth down with both hands, further to ease his stomach, and then reached for the white-bandaged blade of his sword. With his left hand he massaged his abdomen, glancing downward as he did so.

To reassure himself on the sharpness of his sword's cutting edge the lieutenant folded back the left trouser flap, exposing a little of his thigh, and lightly drew the blade across the skin. Blood welled up in the wound at once, and several streaks of red trickled downward, glistening in the strong light.

It was the first time Reiko had ever seen her husband's blood, and she felt a violent throbbing in her chest. She looked at her husband's face. The lieutenant was looking at the blood with calm appraisal. For a moment—though thinking at the same time that it was hollow comfort—Reiko experienced a sense of relief.

The lieutenant's eyes fixed his wife with an intense, hawklike stare. Moving the sword around to his front, he raised himself slightly on his hips and let the upper half of his body lean over the sword point. That he was mustering his whole strength was apparent from the angry tension of the uniform at his shoulders. The lieutenant aimed to strike deep into the left of his stomach. His sharp cry pierced the silence of the room.

Despite the effort he had himself put into the blow, the lieutenant had the impression that someone else had struck the side of his stomach agonizingly with a thick rod of iron. For a second or so his head reeled and he had no idea what had happened. The five or six inches of naked point had vanished completely into his flesh, and the white bandage, gripped in his clenched fist, pressed directly against his stomach.

He returned to consciousness. The blade had certainly pierced the wall of the stomach, he thought. His breathing was difficult, his chest thumped violently, and in some far deep region, which he could hardly believe was a part of himself, a fearful and excruciating pain came welling up as if the ground had split open to disgorge a boiling stream of molten rock. The pain came suddenly nearer, with terrifying speed. The lieutenant bit his lower lip and stifled an instinctive moan.

Was this *seppuku*?[13]—he was thinking. It was a sensation of utter chaos, as if the sky had fallen on his head and the world was reeling drunkenly. His will power and courage, which had seemed so robust before he made the incision, had now dwindled to something like a single hairlike thread of steel, and he was assailed by the uneasy feeling that he must advance along this thread, clinging to it with desperation. His clenched fist had grown moist. Looking down, he saw that both his hand and the cloth about the blade were drenched in blood. His loincloth too was dyed a deep red. It struck him as incredible that, amidst this terrible agony, things which could be seen could still be seen, and existing things existed still.

The moment the lieutenant thrust the sword into his left side and she saw the deathly pallor fall across his face, like an abruptly lowered curtain, Reiko had to struggle to prevent herself from rushing to his side. Whatever happened, she must watch. She must be a witness. That was the duty her husband had laid upon her. Opposite her, a mat's space away, she could clearly see her husband biting his lip to stifle the pain. The pain was there, with absolute certainty, before her eyes. And Reiko had no means of rescuing him from it.

The sweat glistened on her husband's forehead. The lieutenant closed his eyes, and then opened them again, as if experimenting. The eyes had lost their luster, and seemed innocent and empty like the eyes of a small animal.

The agony before Reiko's eyes burned as strong as the summer sun, utterly remote from the grief which seemed to be tearing

---

[13]*Ritual form of military suicide.*

herself apart within. The pain grew steadily in stature, stretching upward. Reiko felt that her husband had already become a man in a separate world, a man whose whole being had been resolved into pain, a prisoner in a cage of pain where no hand could reach out to him. But Reiko felt no pain at all. Her grief was not pain. As she thought about this, Reiko began to feel as if someone had raised a cruel wall of glass high between herself and her husband.

Ever since her marriage her husband's existence had been her own existence, and every breath of his had been a breath drawn by herself. But now, while her husband's existence in pain was a vivid reality, Reiko could find in this grief of hers no certain proof at all of her own existence.

With only his right hand on the sword the lieutenant began to cut sideways across his stomach. But as the blade became entangled with the entrails it was pushed constantly outward by their soft resilience; and the lieutenant realized that it would be necessary, as he cut, to use both hands to keep the point pressed deep into his stomach. He pulled the blade across. It did not cut as easily as he had expected. He directed the strength of his whole body into his right hand and pulled again. There was a cut of three or four inches.

The pain spread slowly outward from the inner depths until the whole stomach reverberated. It was like the wild clanging of a bell. Or like a thousand bells which jangled simultaneously at every breath he breathed and every throb of his pulse, rocking his whole being. The lieutenant could no longer stop himself from moaning. But by now the blade had cut its way through to below the navel, and when he noticed this he felt a sense of satisfaction, and a renewal of courage.

The volume of blood had steadily increased, and now it spurted from the wound as if propelled by the beat of the pulse. The mat before the lieutenant was drenched red with splattered blood, and more blood overflowed onto it from pools which gathered in the folds of the lieutenant's khaki trousers. A spot, like a bird, came flying across to Reiko and settled on the lap of her white silk kimono.

By the time the lieutenant had at last drawn the sword across to the right side of his stomach, the blade was already cutting shallow and had revealed its naked tip, slippery with blood and grease. But, suddenly stricken by a fit of vomiting, the lieutenant cried out hoarsely. The vomiting made the fierce pain fiercer still, and the stomach, which had thus far remained firm and compact, now abruptly heaved, opening wide its wound, and the entrails burst through, as if the wound too were vomiting. Seemingly ignorant of their master's suffering, the entrails gave an impression of robust health and almost disagreeable vitality as they slipped smoothly out and spilled over into the crotch. The lieutenant's head drooped, his shoulders heaved, his eyes opened to narrow slits, and a thin trickle of saliva dribbled from his mouth. The gold markings on his epaulettes caught the light and glinted.

Blood was scattered everywhere. The lieutenant was soaked in it to his knees, and he sat now in a crumpled and listless posture, one hand on the floor. A raw smell filled the room. The lieutenant, his head drooping, retched repeatedly, and the movement showed vividly in his shoulders. The blade of the sword, now pushed back by the entrails and exposed to its tip, was still in the lieutenant's right hand.

It would be difficult to imagine a more heroic sight than that of the lieutenant at this moment, as he mustered his strength and flung back his head. The movement was performed with sudden violence, and the back of his head struck with a sharp crack against the alcove pillar. Reiko had been sitting until now with her face lowered, gazing in fascination at the tide of blood advancing toward her knees, but the sound took her by surprise and she looked up.

The lieutenant's face was not the face of a living man. The eyes were hollow, the skin parched, the once so lustrous cheeks and lips the color of dried mud. The right hand alone was moving. Laboriously gripping the sword, it hovered shakily in the air like the hand of a marionette and strove to direct the point at the base of the lieutenant's throat. Reiko watched her husband make this last, most heart-rending, futile exertion. Glistening with blood and grease, the point was thrust at the throat again and again. And each time it missed its aim. The strength to guide it was no longer there. The straying point struck the collar and the collar badges. Although its hooks had been unfastened, the stiff military collar had closed together again and was protecting the throat.

Reiko could bear the sight no longer. She tried to go to her husband's help, but she could not stand. She moved through the blood on her knees, and her white skirts grew deep red. Moving to the rear of her husband, she helped no more than by loosening the collar. The quivering blade at last contacted the naked flesh of the throat. At that moment Reiko's impression was that she herself had propelled her husband forward; but that was not the case. It was a movement planned by the lieutenant himself, his last exertion of strength. Abruptly he threw his body at the blade, and the blade pierced his neck, emerging at the nape. There was a tremendous spurt of blood and the lieutenant lay still, cold blue-tinged steel protruding from his neck at the back.

V

Slowly, her socks slippery with blood, Reiko descended the stairway. The upstairs room was now completely still.

Switching on the ground-floor lights, she checked the gas jet and the main gas plug and poured water over the smoldering, half-buried charcoal in the brazier. She stood before the upright mirror in the four-and-a-half-mat room and held up her skirts. The bloodstains made it seem as if a bold, vivid pattern was printed across the lower half of her white kimono. When she sat down before the mirror, she was conscious of the dampness and coldness of her husband's blood in the region of her thighs, and she shivered. Then, for a long while, she lingered over her toilet preparations. She applied the rouge generously to her cheeks, and her lips too she painted heavily. This was no longer make-up to please her husband. It was make-up for the world which she would leave behind, and there was a touch of the magnificent and the spectacular in her brushwork. When she rose, the mat before the mirror was wet with blood. Reiko was not concerned about this.

Returning from the toilet, Reiko stood finally on the cement floor of the porchway. When her husband had bolted the door here last night it had been in preparation for death. For a while she stood immersed in the consideration of a simple problem. Should she now leave the bolt drawn? If she were to lock the door, it could be that the neighbors might not notice their suicide for several days. Reiko did not relish the thought of their two corpses putrifying before discovery. After all, it seemed, it would be best to leave it open. . . . She released the bolt, and also drew open the frosted-glass door a fraction. . . . At once a chill wind blew in. There was no sign of anyone in the midnight streets, and stars glittered ice-cold through the trees in the large house opposite.

Leaving the door as it was, Reiko mounted the stairs. She had walked here and there for some time and her socks were no longer slippery. About halfway up, her nostrils were already assailed by a peculiar smell.

The lieutenant was lying on his face in a sea of blood. The point protruding from his neck seemed to have grown even more prominent than before. Reiko walked heedlessly across the blood. Sitting beside the lieutenant's corpse, she stared intently at the face, which lay on one cheek on the mat. The eyes were opened wide, as if the lieutenant's attention had been attracted by something. She raised the head, folding it in her sleeve, wiped the blood from the lips, and bestowed a last kiss.

Then she rose and took from the closet a new white blanket and a waist cord. To prevent any derangement of her skirts, she wrapped the blanket about her waist and bound it there firmly with the cord.

Reiko sat herself on a spot about one foot distant from the lieutenant's body. Drawing the dagger from her sash, she examined its dully gleaming blade intently, and held it to her tongue. The taste of the polished steel was slightly sweet.

Reiko did not linger. When she thought how the pain which had previously opened such a gulf between herself and her dying husband was now to become a part of her own experience, she saw before her only the joy of herself entering a realm her husband had already made his own. In her husband's agonized face there had been something inexplicable which she was seeing for the first time. Now she would solve that riddle. Reiko sensed that at last she too would be able to taste the true bitterness and sweetness of that great moral principle in which her husband believed. What had until now been tasted only faintly through her husband's example she was about to savor directly with her own tongue.

Reiko rested the point of the blade against the base of her throat. She thrust hard. The wound was only shallow. Her head blazed, and her hands shook uncontrollably. She gave the blade a strong pull sideways. A warm substance flooded into her mouth, and everything before her eyes reddened, in a vision of spouting blood. She gathered her strength and plunged the point of the blade deep into her throat.

Denis Johnson

Denis Johnson is the author of four novels and one story collection, as well as two collections of poetry. He was born in 1949 in Munich, Germany, and now lives in Bonners Ferry, Idaho. His first novel, Angels, *received the Sue Kaufman Prize for First Fiction in 1984 from the American Academy and Institute of Arts and Letters. "Dundun" originally appeared in Es-*quire *in 1990 and was reprinted in the collection* Jesus' Son.

Dundun

I went out to the farmhouse where Dundun lived to get some pharmaceutical opium from him, but I was out of luck.

He greeted me as he was coming out into the front yard to go to the pump, wearing new cowboy boots and a leather vest, with his flannel shirt hanging out over his jeans. He was chewing on a piece of gum.

"McInnes isn't feeling too good today. I just shot him."

"You mean killed him?"

"I didn't mean to."

"Is he really dead?"

"No. He's sitting down."

"But he's alive."

"Oh, sure, he's alive. He's sitting down now in the back room."

Dundun went on over to the pump and started working the handle.

I went around the house and in through the back. The room just through the back door smelled of dogs and babies. Beatle stood in the opposite doorway. She watched me come in. Leaning against the wall was Blue, smoking a cigarette and scratching her chin thoughtfully. Jack Hotel was over at an old desk, setting fire to a pipe, the bowl of which was wrapped in tinfoil.

When they saw it was only me, the three of them resumed looking at McInnes, who sat on the couch all alone, with his left hand resting gently on his belly.

"Dundun shot him?" I asked.

"Somebody shot somebody," Hotel said.

Dundun came in behind me carrying some water in a china cup and a bottle of beer and said to McInnes: "Here."

"*I* don't want that," McInnes said.

"Okay. Well, here, then." Dundun offered him the rest of his beer.

"No thanks."

I was worried. "Aren't you taking him to the hospital or anything?"

"Good idea," Beatle said sarcastically.

"We started to," Hotel explained, "but we ran into the corner of the shed out there."

I looked out the side window. This was Tim Bishop's farm. Tim Bishop's Plymouth, I saw, which was a very nice old grey-and-red sedan, had sideswiped the shed and replaced one of the corner posts, so that the post lay on the ground and the car now held up the shed's roof.

"The front windshield is in millions of bits," Hotel said.

"How'd you end up way over there?"

"Everything was completely out of hand," Hotel said.

"Where's Tim, anyway?"

"He's not here," Beatle said.

Hotel passed me the pipe. It was hashish, but it was pretty well burned up already.

"How you doing?" Dundun asked McInnes.

"I can feel it right here. It's just stuck in the muscle."

Dundun said, "It's not bad. The cap didn't explode right, I think."

"It misfired."

"It misfired a little bit, yeah."

Hotel asked me, "Would you take him to the hospital in your car?"

"Okay," I said.

"I'm coming, too," Dundun said.

"Have you got any of the opium left?" I asked him.

"No," he said. "That was a birthday present. I used it all up."

"When's your birthday?" I asked him.

"Today."

"You shouldn't have used it all up before your birthday, then," I told him angrily.

But I was happy about this chance to be of use. I wanted to be the one who saw it through and got McInnes to the doctor without a wreck. People would talk about it, and I hoped I would be liked.

In the car were Dundun, McInnes, and myself.

This was Dundun's twenty-first birthday. I'd met him in the Johnson County facility during the only few days I'd ever spent in jail, around the time of my eighteenth Thanksgiving. I was the older of us by a month or two. As for McInnes, he'd been around forever, and in fact, I, myself, was married to one of his old girlfriends.

We took off as fast as I could go without bouncing the shooting victim around too heavily.

Dundun said, "What about the brakes? You get them working?"

"The emergency brake does. That's enough."

"What about the radio?" Dundun punched the button, and the radio came on making an emission like a meat grinder.

He turned it off and then on, and now it burbled like a machine that polishes stones all night.

"How about you?" I asked McInnes. "Are you comfortable?"

"What do you think?" McInnes said.

It was a long straight road through dry fields as far as a person could see. You'd think the sky didn't have any air in it, and the earth was made of paper. Rather than moving, we were just getting smaller and smaller.

What can be said about those fields? There were blackbirds circling above their own shadows, and beneath them the cows stood around smelling one another's butts. Dundun spat his gum out the window while digging in his shirt pocket for his Winstons. He lit a Winston with a match. That was all there was to say.

"We'll never get off this road," I said.

"What a lousy birthday," Dundun said.

McInnes was white and sick, holding himself tenderly. I'd seen him like that once or twice even when he hadn't been shot. He had a bad case of hepatitis that often gave him a lot of pain.

"Do you promise not to tell them anything?" Dundun was talking to McInnes.

"I don't think he hears you," I said.

"Tell them it was an accident, okay?"

McInnes said nothing for a long moment. Finally he said, "Okay."

"Promise?" Dundun said.

But McInnes said nothing. Because he was dead.

Dundun looked at me with tears in his eyes. "What do you say?"

"What do you mean, what do I say? Do you think I'm here because I know all about this stuff?"

"He's dead."

"All *right*. I *know* he's dead."

"Throw him out of the car."

"Damn right throw him out of the car," I said. "I'm not taking him anywhere now."

For a moment I fell asleep, right while I was driving. I had a dream in which I was trying to tell someone something and they kept interrupting, a dream about frustration.

"I'm glad he's dead," I told Dundun. "He's the one who started everybody calling me Fuckhead."

Dundun said, "Don't let it get you down."

We whizzed along down through the skeleton remnants of Iowa.

"I wouldn't mind working as a hit man," Dundun said.

Glaciers had crushed this region in the time before history. There'd been a drought for years, and a bronze fog of dust stood over the plains. The soybean crop was dead again, and the failed, wilted cornstalks were laid out on the ground like rows of underthings. Most of the farmers didn't even plant anymore. All the false visions had been erased. It felt like the moment before the Savior comes. And the Savior did come, but we had to wait a long time.

Dundun tortured Jack Hotel at the lake outside of Denver. He did this to get information about a stolen item, a stereo belonging to Dundun's girlfriend, or perhaps to his sister. Later, Dundun beat a man almost to death with a tire iron right on the street in Austin, Texas, for which he'll also someday have to answer, but now he is, I think, in the state prison in Colorado.

Will you believe me when I tell you there was kindness in his heart? His left hand didn't know what his right hand was doing. It was only that certain important connections had been burned through. If I opened up your head and ran a hot soldering iron around in your brain, I might turn you into someone like that.

Italo Calvino

During the course of his literary career, Italo Calvino published fifteen volumes of short fiction, three novels, and two collections of essays. Calvino was born in Cuba in 1923, where his parents were employed on a botanical project. Calvino was raised and educated in Italy, and studied agronomy *and English literature at the University of Turin, where he received a de-gree in 1947. During World War II, Calvino served with the Italian Resis-tance. After the war, he pursued a writing career while working as an editor for the Turin publisher Guilio Einaurdi Editore. Calvino lived in Paris for fifteen years before returning to Italy in 1980. "The Distance of the Moon" appeared in this country in* Cosmicomics, *published in 1965. Calvino died in 1985.*

The Distance of the Moon*

At one time, according to Sir George H. Darwin, the Moon was very close to the Earth. Then the tides gradually pushed her far away: the tides that the Moon herself causes in the Earth's waters, where the Earth slowly loses energy.

How well I know!—*old Qfwfq cried,*—the rest of you can't re-member, but I can. We had her on top of us all the time, that enor-mous Moon: when she was full—nights as bright as day, but with a butter-colored light—it looked as if she were going to crush us; when she was new, she rolled around the sky like a black um-brella blown by the wind; and when she was waxing, she came forward with her horns so low she seemed about to stick into the peak of a promontory and get caught there. But the whole busi-ness of the Moon's phases worked in a different way then: be-cause the distances from the Sun were different, and the orbits, and the angle of something or other, I forget what; as for eclipses, with Earth and Moon stuck together the way they were, why, we had eclipses every minute: naturally, those two big monsters managed to put each other in the shade constantly, first one, then the other.

Orbit? Oh, elliptical, of course: for a while it would huddle against us and then it would take flight for a while. The tides, when the Moon swung closer, rose so high nobody could hold them back. There were nights when the Moon was full and very, very low, and the tide was so high that the Moon missed a ducking in the sea by a hair's-breadth; well, let's say a few yards anyway. Climb up on the Moon? Of course we did. All you had to do was row out to it in a boat and, when you were underneath, prop a lad-der against her and scramble up.

---

*Translated by William Weaver.

The spot where the Moon was lowest, as she went by, was off the Zinc Cliffs. We used to go out with those little rowboats they had in those days, round and flat, made of cork. They held quite a few of us: me, Captain Vhd Vhd, his wife, my deaf cousin, and sometimes little Xlthlx—she was twelve or so at that time. On those nights the water was very calm, so silvery it looked like mercury, and the fish in it, violet-colored, unable to resist the Moon's attraction, rose to the surface, all of them, and so did the octopuses and the saffron medusas. There was always a flight of tiny creatures—little crabs, squid, and even some weeds, light and filmy, and coral plants—that broke from the sea and ended up on the Moon, hanging down from that lime-white ceiling, or else they stayed in midair, a phosphorescent swarm we had to drive off, waving banana leaves at them.

This is how we did the job: in the boat we had a ladder: one of us held it, another climbed to the top, and a third, at the oars, rowed until we were right under the Moon; that's why there had to be so many of us (I only mentioned the main ones). The man at the top of the ladder, as the boat approached the Moon, would become scared and start shouting: "Stop! Stop! I'm going to bang my head!" That was the impression you had, seeing her on top of you, immense, and all rough with sharp spikes and jagged, saw-tooth edges. It may be different now, but then the Moon, or rather the bottom, the underbelly of the Moon, the part that passed closest to the Earth and almost scraped it, was covered with a crust of sharp scales. It had come to resemble the belly of a fish, and the smell too, as I recall, if not downright fishy, was faintly similar, like smoked salmon.

In reality, from the top of the ladder, standing erect on the last rung, you could just touch the Moon if you held your arms up. We had taken the measurements carefully (we didn't yet suspect that she was moving away from us); the only thing you had to be very careful about was where you put your hands. I always chose a scale that seemed fast (we climbed up in groups of five or six at a time), then I would cling first with one hand, then with both, and immediately I would feel ladder and boat drifting away from below me, and the motion of the Moon would tear me from the Earth's attraction. Yes, the Moon was so strong that she pulled you up; you realized this the moment you passed from one to the other: you had to swing up abruptly, with a kind of somersault, grabbing the scales, throwing your legs over your head, until your feet were on the Moon's surface. Seen from the Earth, you looked as if you were hanging there with your head down, but for you, it was the normal position, and the only odd thing was that when you raised your eyes you saw the sea above you, glistening, with the boat and the others upside down, hanging like a bunch of grapes from the vine.

My cousin, the Deaf One, showed a special talent for making those leaps. His clumsy hands, as soon as they touched the lunar surface (he was always the first to jump up from the ladder), suddenly became deft and sensitive. They found immediately the spot where he could hoist himself up; in fact just the pressure of his palms seemed enough to make him stick to the satellite's crust. Once I even thought I saw the Moon come toward him, as he held out his hands.

He was just as dexterous in coming back down to Earth, an operation still more difficult. For us, it consisted in jumping, as high as we could, our arms upraised (seen from the Moon, that is, because seen from the Earth it looked more like a dive, or like swimming downwards, arms at our sides), like jumping up from the Earth in other words, only now we were without the ladder, because there was nothing to prop it against on the Moon. But instead of jumping with his arms out, my cousin bent toward the Moon's surface, his head down as if for a somersault, then made a leap, pushing with his hands. From the boat we watched him, erect in the air as if he were supporting the Moon's enormous ball and were tossing it, striking it with his palms; then, when his legs came within reach, we managed to grab his ankles and pull him down on board.

Now, you will ask me what in the world we went up on the Moon for; I'll explain it to you. We went to collect the milk, with a big spoon and a bucket. Moon-milk was very thick, like a kind of cream cheese. It formed in the crevices between one scale and the next, through the fermentation of various bodies and substances of terrestrial origin which had flown up from the prairies and forests and lakes, as the Moon sailed over them. It was composed chiefly of vegetal juices, tadpoles, bitumen, lentils, honey, starch crystals, sturgeon eggs, molds, pollens, gelatinous matter, worms, resins, pepper, mineral salts, combustion residue. You had only to dip the spoon under the scales that covered the Moon's scabby terrain, and you brought it out filled with that precious muck. Not in the pure state, obviously; there was a lot of refuse. In the fermentation (which took place as the Moon passed over the expanses of hot air above the deserts) not all the bodies melted; some remained stuck in it: fingernails and cartilage, bolts, sea horses, nuts and peduncles, shards of crockery, fishhooks, at times even a comb. So this paste, after it was collected, had to be refined, filtered. But that wasn't the difficulty: the hard part was transporting it down to the Earth. This is how we did it: we hurled each spoonful into the air with both hands, using the spoon as a catapult. The cheese flew, and if we had thrown it hard enough, it stuck to the ceiling, I mean the surface of the sea. Once there, it floated, and it was easy enough to pull it into the boat. In this operation, too, my deaf cousin displayed a special gift; he had strength and a good aim; with a single, sharp throw, he could send the cheese straight into a bucket we held up to him from the boat. As for me, I occasionally misfired; the contents of the spoon would fail to overcome the Moon's attraction and they would fall back into my eye.

I still haven't told you everything, about the things my cousin was good at. That job of extracting lunar milk from the Moon's scales was child's play to him: instead of the spoon, at times he had only to thrust his bare hand under the scales, or even one finger. He didn't proceed in any orderly way, but went to isolated places, jumping from one to the other, as if he were playing tricks on the Moon, surprising her, or perhaps tickling her. And wherever he put his hand, the milk spurted out as if from a nanny goat's teats. So the rest of us had only to follow him and collect with our spoons the substance that he was pressing out, first here, then there, but always as if by chance, since the Deaf One's movements seemed to have no clear, practical sense. There were places, for example, that he touched merely for the fun of touching them: gaps between two scales, naked and tender folds of lunar flesh. At times my cousin pressed not only his fingers but—in a carefully gauged leap—his big toe (he climbed onto the Moon barefoot) and this seemed to be the height of amusement for him, if we could judge by the chirping sounds that came from his throat as he went on leaping.

The soil of the Moon was not uniformly scaly, but revealed irregular bare patches of pale, slippery clay. These soft areas inspired the Deaf One to turn somersaults or to fly almost like a bird, as if he wanted to impress his whole body into the Moon's pulp. As he ventured farther in this way, we lost sight of him at one point. On the Moon there were vast areas we had never had any reason or curiosity to explore, and that was where my cousin vanished; I had suspected that all those somersaults and nudges he indulged in before our eyes were only a preparation, a prelude to something secret meant to take place in the hidden zones.

We fell into a special mood on those nights off the Zinc Cliffs: gay, but with a touch of suspense, as if inside our skulls, instead of the brain, we felt a fish, floating, attracted by the Moon. And so we navigated, playing and singing. The Captain's wife played the harp; she had very long arms, silvery as eels on those nights, and armpits as dark and mysterious as sea urchins; and the sound of the harp was sweet and piercing, so sweet and piercing it was almost unbearable, and we were forced to let out long cries, not so much to accompany the music as to protect our hearing from it.

Transparent medusas rose to the sea's surface, throbbed there a moment, then flew off, swaying toward the Moon. Little Xlthlx amused herself by catching them in midair, though it wasn't easy. Once, as she stretched her little arms out to catch one, she jumped up slightly and was also set free. Thin as she was, she was an ounce or two short of the weight necessary for the Earth's gravity to over-come the Moon's attraction and bring her back: so she flew up among the medusas, suspended over the sea. She took fright, cried, then laughed and started playing, catching shellfish and minnows as they flew, sticking some into her mouth and chewing them. We rowed hard, to keep up with the child: the Moon ran off in her el-lipse, dragging that swarm of marine fauna through the sky, and a train of long, entwined seaweeds and Xlthlx hanging there in the midst. Her two wispy braids seemed to be flying on their own, outstretched toward the Moon; but all the while she kept wrig-gling and kicking at the air, as if she wanted to fight that influ-ence, and her socks—she had lost her shoes in the flight—slipped off her feet and swayed, attracted by the Earth's force. On the lad-der, we tried to grab them.

The idea of eating the little animals in the air had been a good one; the more weight Xlthlx gained, the more she sank toward the Earth; in fact, since among those hovering bodies hers was the largest, mollusks and seaweeds and plankton began to gravitate about her, and soon the child was covered with siliceous little shells, chitinous carapaces, and fibers of sea plants. And the farther she vanished into that tangle, the more she was freed of the Moon's influence, until she grazed the surface of the water and sank into the sea.

We rowed quickly, to pull her out and save her: her body had remained magnetized, and we had to work hard to scrape off all the things encrusted on her. Tender corals were wound about her head, and every time we ran the comb through her hair there was a shower of crayfish and sardines; her eyes were sealed shut by limpets clinging to the lids with their suckers; squids' tentacles were coiled around her arms and her neck; and her little dress now seemed woven only of weeds and sponges. We got the worst of it off her, but for weeks afterwards she went on pulling out fins and shells, and her skin, dotted with little diatoms, remained affected forever, looking—to someone who didn't observe her carefully—as if it were faintly dusted with freckles.

This should give you an idea of how the influences of Earth and Moon, practically equal, fought over the space between them. I'll tell you something else: a body that descended to the Earth from the satellite was still charged for a while with lunar force and rejected the attraction of our world. Even I, big and heavy as I was: every time I had been up there, I took a while to get used to the Earth's up and its down, and the others would have to grab my arms and hold me, clinging in a bunch in the swaying boat while I still had my head hanging and my legs stretching up toward the sky.

"Hold on! Hold on to us!" they shouted at me, and in all that groping, sometimes I ended up by seizing one of Mrs. Vhd Vhd's breasts, which were round and firm, and the contact was good and secure and had an attraction as strong as the Moon's or even stronger, especially if I managed, as I plunged down, to put my other arm around her hips, and with this I passed back into our world and fell with a thud into the bottom of the boat, where Captain Vhd Vhd brought me around, throwing a bucket of water in my face.

This is how the story of my love for the Captain's wife began, and my suffering. Because it didn't take me long to realize whom the lady kept looking at insistently: when my cousin's hands clasped the satellite, I watched Mrs. Vhd Vhd, and in her eyes I could read the thoughts that the deaf man's familiarity with the Moon were arousing in her; and when he disappeared in his mysterious lunar explorations, I saw her become restless, as if on pins and needles, and then it was all clear to me, how Mrs. Vhd Vhd was becoming jealous of the Moon and I was jealous of my cousin. Her eyes were made of diamonds, Mrs. Vhd Vhd's; they flared when she looked at the Moon, almost challengingly, as if she were saying: "You shan't have him!" And I felt like an outsider.

The one who least understood all of this was my deaf cousin. When we helped him down, pulling him—as I explained to you—by his legs, Mrs. Vhd Vhd lost all her self-control, doing everything she could to take his weight against her own body, folding her long silvery arms around him; I felt a pang in my heart (the times I clung to her, her body was soft and kind, but not thrust forward, the way it was with my cousin), while he was indifferent, still lost in his lunar bliss.

I looked at the Captain, wondering if he also noticed his wife's behavior; but there was never a trace of any expression on that face of his, eaten by brine, marked with tarry wrinkles. Since the Deaf One was always the last to break away from the Moon, his return was the signal for the boats to move off. Then, with an unusually polite gesture, Vhd Vhd picked up the harp from the bottom of the boat and handed it to his wife. She was obliged to take it and play a few notes. Nothing could separate her more from the Deaf One than the sound of the harp. I took to singing in a low voice that sad song that goes: "Every shiny fish is floating, floating; and every dark fish is at the bottom, at the bottom of the sea . . ." and all the others, except my cousin, echoed my words.

Every month, once the satellite had moved on, the Deaf One returned to his solitary detachment from the things of the world; only the approach of the full Moon aroused him again. That time I had arranged things so it wasn't my turn to go up, I could stay in the boat with the Captain's wife. But then, as soon as my cousin had climbed the ladder, Mrs. Vhd Vhd said: "This time I want to go up there, too!"

This had never happened before; the Captain's wife had never gone up on the Moon. But Vhd Vhd made no objection, in fact he almost pushed her up the ladder bodily, exclaiming: "Go ahead then!," and we all started helping her, and I held her from behind, felt her round and soft on my arms, and to hold her up I began to press my face and the palms of my hands against her, and when I felt her rising into the Moon's sphere I was heartsick at that lost contact, so I started to rush after her, saying: "I'm going to go up for a while, too, to help out!"

I was held back as if in a vise. "You stay here; you have work to do later," the Captain commanded, without raising his voice.

At that moment each one's intentions were already clear. And yet I couldn't figure things out; even now I'm not sure I've interpreted it all correctly. Certainly the Captain's wife had for a long time been cherishing the desire to go off privately with my cousin up there (or at least to prevent him from going off alone with the Moon), but probably she had a still more ambitious plan, one that would have to be carried out in agreement with the Deaf One: she wanted the two of them to hide up there together and stay on the Moon for a month. But perhaps my cousin, deaf as he was, hadn't understood anything of what she had tried to explain to him, or perhaps he hadn't even realized that he was the object of the lady's desires. And the Captain? He wanted nothing better than to be rid of his wife; in fact, as soon as she was confined up there, we saw him give free rein to his inclinations and plunge into vice, and then we understood why he had done nothing to hold her back. But had he known from the beginning that the Moon's orbit was widening?

None of us could have suspected it. The Deaf One perhaps, but only he: in the shadowy way he knew things, he may have had a presentiment that he would be forced to bid the Moon farewell that night. This is why he hid in his secret places and reappeared only when it was time to come back down on board. It was no use for the Captain's wife to try to follow him: we saw her cross the scaly zone various times, length and breadth, then suddenly she stopped, looking at us in the boat, as if about to ask us whether we had seen him.

Surely there was something strange about that night. The sea's surface, instead of being taut as it was during the full Moon, or even arched a bit toward the sky, now seemed limp, sagging, as if the lunar magnet no longer exercised its full power. And the light, too, wasn't the same as the light of other full Moons; the night's shadows seemed somehow to have thickened. Our friends up there must have realized what was happening; in fact, they looked up at us with frightened eyes. And from their mouths and ours, at the same moment, came a cry: "The Moon's going away!"

The cry hadn't died out when my cousin appeared on the Moon, running. He didn't seem frightened, or even amazed: he placed his hands on the terrain, flinging himself into his usual somersault, but this time after he had hurled himself into the air he remained suspended, as little Xlthlx had. He hovered a moment between Moon and Earth, upside down, then laboriously moving his arms, like someone swimming against a current, he headed with unusual slowness toward our planet.

From the Moon the other sailors hastened to follow his example. Nobody gave a thought to getting the Moon-milk that had been collected into the boats, nor did the Captain scold them for this. They had already waited too long, the distance was difficult to cross by now; when they tried to imitate my cousin's leap or his swimming, they remained there groping, suspended in midair. "Cling together! Idiots! Cling together!" the Captain yelled. At this command, the sailors tried to form a group, a mass, to push all together until they reached the zone of the Earth's attraction: all of a sudden a cascade of bodies plunged into the sea with a loud splash.

The boats were now rowing to pick them up. "Wait! The Captain's wife is missing!" I shouted. The Captain's wife had also tried to jump, but she was still floating only a few yards from the Moon, slowly moving her long, silvery arms in the air. I climbed up the ladder, and in a vain attempt to give her something to grasp I held the harp out toward her. "I can't reach her! We have to go after her!" and I started to jump up, brandishing the harp. Above me the enormous lunar disk no longer seemed the same as before: it had become much smaller, it kept contracting, as if my gaze were driving it away, and the emptied sky gaped like an abyss where, at the bottom, the stars had begun multiplying, and the night poured a river of emptiness over me, drowned me in dizziness and alarm.

"I'm afraid," I thought. "I'm too afraid to jump. I'm a coward!" and at that moment I jumped. I swam furiously through the sky, and held the harp out to her, and instead of coming toward me she rolled over and over, showing me first her impassive face and then her backside.

"Hold tight to me!" I shouted, and I was already overtaking her, entwining my limbs with hers. "If we cling together we can go down!" and I was concentrating all my strength on uniting myself more closely with her, and I concentrated my sensations as I enjoyed the fullness of that embrace. I was so absorbed I didn't realize at first that I was, indeed, tearing her from her weightless condition, but was making her fall back on the Moon. Didn't I realize it? Or had that been my intention from the very beginning? Before I could think properly, a cry was already bursting from my throat. "I'll be the one to stay with you for a month!" Or rather, "On you!" I shouted, in my excitement: "On you for a month!" and at that moment our embrace was broken by our fall to the Moon's surface, where we rolled away from each other among those cold scales.

I raised my eyes as I did every time I touched the Moon's crust, sure that I would see above me the native sea like an endless ceiling, and I saw it, yes, I saw it this time, too, but much higher, and much more narrow, bound by its borders of coasts and cliffs and promontories, and how small the boats seemed, and how unfamiliar my friends' faces and how weak their cries! A sound reached me from nearby: Mrs. Vhd Vhd had discovered her harp and was caressing it, sketching out a chord as sad as weeping.

A long month began. The Moon turned slowly around the Earth. On the suspended globe we no longer saw our familiar shore, but the passage of oceans as deep as abysses and deserts of glowing lapilli, and continents of ice, and forests writhing with reptiles, and the rocky walls of mountain chains gashed by swift rivers, and swampy cities, and stone graveyards, and empires of clay and mud. The distance spread a uniform color over everything: the alien perspectives made every image alien; herds of elephants and swarms of locusts ran over the plains, so evenly vast and dense and thickly grown that there was no difference among them.

I should have been happy: as I had dreamed, I was alone with her, that intimacy with the Moon I had so often envied my cousin and with Mrs. Vhd Vhd was now my exclusive prerogative, a month of days and lunar nights stretched uninterrupted before us, the crust of the satellite nourished us with its milk, whose tart flavor was familiar to us, we raised our eyes up, up to the world where we had been born, finally traversed in all its various expanse, explored landscapes no Earth-being had ever seen, or else we contemplated the stars beyond the Moon, big as pieces of fruit, made of light, ripened on the curved branches of the sky, and everything exceeded my most luminous hopes, and yet, and yet, it was, instead, exile.

I thought only of the Earth. It was the Earth that caused each of us to be that someone he was rather than someone else; up there, wrested from the Earth, it was as if I were no longer that I, nor she that She, for me. I was eager to return to the Earth, and I trembled at the fear of having lost it. The fulfillment of my dream of love had lasted only that instant when we had been united, spinning between Earth and Moon; torn from its earthly soil, my love now knew only the heart-rending nostalgia for what it lacked: a where, a surrounding, a before, an after.

This is what I was feeling. But she? As I asked myself, I was torn by my fears. Because if she also thought only of the Earth, this could be a good sign, a sign that she had finally come to understand me, but it could also mean that everything had been useless, that her longings were directed still and only toward my deaf cousin. Instead, she felt nothing. She never raised her eyes to the old planet, she went off, pale, among those wastelands, mumbling dirges and stroking her harp, as if completely identified with her temporary (as I thought) lunar state. Did this mean I had won out over my rival? No; I had lost: a hopeless defeat. Because she had finally realized that my cousin loved only the Moon, and the only thing she wanted now was to become the Moon, to be assimilated into the object of that extrahuman love.

When the Moon had completed its circling of the planet, there we were again over the Zinc Cliffs. I recognized them with dismay: not even in my darkest previsions had I thought the distance would have made them so tiny. In that mud puddle of the sea, my friends had set forth again, without the now useless ladders; but from the boats rose a kind of forest of long poles; everybody was brandishing one, with a harpoon or a grappling hook at the end, perhaps in the hope of scraping off a last bit of Moon-milk or of lending some kind of help to us wretches up there. But it was soon clear that no pole was long enough to reach the Moon; and they dropped back, ridiculously short, humbled, floating on the sea; and in that confusion some of the boats were thrown off balance and overturned. But just then, from another vessel a longer pole, which till then they had dragged along on the water's surface, began to rise: it must have been made of bamboo, of many, many bamboo poles stuck one into the other, and to raise it they had to go slowly because—thin as it was—if they let it sway too much it might break. Therefore, they had to use it with great strength and skill, so that the wholly vertical weight wouldn't rock the boat.

Suddenly it was clear that the tip of that pole would touch the Moon, and we saw it graze, then press against the scaly terrain, rest there a moment, give a kind of little push, or rather a strong push that made it bounce off again, then come back and strike that same spot as if on the rebound, then move away once more. And I recognized, we both—the Captain's wife and I—recognized my cousin: it couldn't have been anyone else, he was playing his last game with the Moon, one of his tricks, with the Moon on the tip of his pole as if he were juggling with her. And we realized that his virtuosity had no purpose, aimed at no practical result, indeed you would have said he was driving the Moon away, that he was helping her departure, that he wanted to show her to her more distant orbit. And this, too, was just like him: he was unable to conceive desires that went against the Moon's nature, the Moon's course and destiny, and if the Moon now tended to go away from him, then he would take delight in this separation just as, till now, he had delighted in the Moon's nearness.

What could Mrs. Vhd Vhd do, in the face of this? It was only at this moment that she proved her passion for the deaf man hadn't been a frivolous whim but an irrevocable vow. If what my cousin now loved was the distant Moon, then she too would remain distant, on the Moon. I sensed this, seeing that she didn't take a step toward the bamboo pole, but simply turned her harp toward the Earth, high in the sky, and plucked the strings. I say I saw her, but to tell the truth I only caught a glimpse of her out of the corner of my eye, because the minute the pole had touched the lunar crust, I had sprung and grasped it, and now, fast as a snake, I was climbing up the bamboo knots, pushing myself along with jerks of my arms and knees, light in the rarefied space, driven by a natural power that ordered me to return to the Earth, oblivious of the motive that had brought me here, or perhaps more aware of it than ever and of its unfortunate outcome; and already my climb up the swaying pole had reached the point where I no longer had to make any effort but could just allow myself to slide, head-first, attracted by the Earth, until in my haste the pole broke into a thousand pieces and I fell into the sea, among the boats.

My return was sweet, my home refound, but my thoughts were filled only with grief at having lost her, and my eyes gazed at the Moon, forever beyond my reach, as I sought her. And I saw her. She was there where I had left her, lying on a beach directly over our heads, and she said nothing. She was the color of the Moon; she held the harp at her side and moved one hand now and then in slow arpeggios. I could distinguish the shape of her bosom, her arms, her thighs, just as I remember them now, just as now, when the Moon has become that flat, remote circle, I still look for her as soon as the first sliver appears in the sky, and the more it waxes, the more clearly I imagine I can see her, her or something of her, but only her, in a hundred, a thousand different vistas, she who makes the Moon the Moon and, whenever she is full, sets the dogs to howling all night long, and me with them.

4

REVISION

In revision, the challenge is to see your story again, to try to see it in a fresh light, and from that light to make it stronger and better. While writers may line edit a story, or change a paragraph here and there, a true revision will take into consideration the entire story. A true revision calls for changes affecting the entire story that will require you to rethink—to resee—your work from the opening sentence to the last word, from the first moment of conflict to the final resolution. Not every story needs a true revision, but you ought to allow yourself the opportunity to consider all of your story's possibilities. Revision requires as much ambition, and yields as much satisfaction, as the creation of a first draft.

SEEING THE WORK ANEW

The first task of the writer is to write the story. The second, equally essential, task is to read it, not only to evaluate the story, but also to be able to reenter the voice of the story. To evaluate the story requires one kind of reading, but to reenter the writing voice of the story requires another kind of reading. Revision reading can occur in a series of steps. It may be useful to allow yourself the luxury of reading your work as if it were something you just wanted to enjoy, rather than fix. Try to feel the experience of reading your work as if you were coming to it for the first time. Let your story surprise you, let it confound you, let it challenge you. Here the essential "seeing" of your story can begin; this reading of your story will allow you to see it anew.

195

If your story has been discussed by a writer's group or a workshop, or if you have shown the story to someone who is interested in your work, you may want to read your audience's comments or recall any of your readers' reactions. Some readers will offer concrete "rewrite suggestions," while others will shy away from what they may consider prescriptive and intrusive commentary. Some readers may just note what they liked and disliked. Some comments might summarize what the story has meant to the particular reader, and you can use these comments to see if your story has had its intended effect. Regardless of the nature of the comments, try to consider them all. The metaphor of the workshop applies here: if the tool the reader is giving you works in helping you see the story, then keep the tool handy. If the tool the reader is providing you does not seem to apply at all to the story, then retain it in your collection—it may apply to a work you've already written, or a work you'll write in the future.

Once you've considered all the comments you've been able to gather, read your story once more. This time read critically, but without taking a pen to the manuscript, keeping in mind the reactions of your readers and your own heightened knowledge of how your work has affected them.

Finally, think about the story. Allow yourself time to let the story simmer; take as much or as little time as you feel comfortable with, depending on your temperament. The most important step is to consider every aspect of your story open to change, fluid, unfinished. Here, too, through readings and reflection, you should be able to accomplish a reentry into the voice in which you have written your story. Once you feel you have reentered the voice, then you can begin to revise.

Writing Strategies

1. Reread one of your stories without making a single mark on it, or pausing to write a single note. What effect does the story have on you? Does it cause an emotional reaction? Are the kinds of reactions that it does cause the kinds of reactions you intended?

2. Take at least a week off from looking at the story from the first strategy, then reread it. How has the passage of time affected your understanding and appreciation of the story?

REVISION STRATEGIES

Approaches to revision are wide-ranging. You can rewrite your story from scratch, without any touchstone whatsoever, or with the old copy in front of you. While both approaches are labor-intensive, they give you the freedom to make as many changes as you want without feeling restricted by the typescript of the previous draft. As you set down each word, you are giving yourself the chance to consider it again. Revisions from scratch are time-consuming, irritating, and rewarding. Such an approach is not for everyone.

Another approach is to "parachute" into your story at what you consider to be its problem points, revising, for example, the introduction of problematic characters and weak plot escalation. You can then revise entirely from the first problem point, or you can continue to revise selectively, leaving large portions of your story unchanged. You still must consider that a revision partway through the story will have an effect on all that has come before it. If a character in a story bought a chainsaw instead of an apple, the reader's whole idea of that character would be revised. The character's remark at the story's outset, that "we are what we buy," would be read entirely differently by the end of the story.

When considering a revision, you might make a list of your story's strengths and a list of your story's weaknesses. Through these lists, a solution to your story's problems may emerge. A weak character may have to be strengthened through more active interaction with other characters or more detailed characterization, or the character may have to be reinvented entirely or even dropped. A particularly strong and interesting character may indicate a need for a change in narrative perspective that would incorporate more of that character's thoughts and actions. A weak or contrived plot movement, under scrutiny, may require drastic surgery or complete omission. This "dialectics of revision" requires that you consider candidly your story's strengths as well as its weaknesses, in order for you to determine revision strategies. The willingness to contemplate profound change can lead to an understanding of a story's essence, its necessary elements. And the ability to recognize your strengths may help you apply those strengths, in one form or another, to help resolve the story's weaknesses. A writer who is strong at describing objects but weak at portraying the interaction of characters, for instance, can look at the language and see if there is a shift in tone or word choice from one section to the next, or if perhaps a shift needs to occur. A writer who finds that the story does not seem as immediate as it should may want to change verb tense the way John Updike did in switching from the past tense to the present tense between drafts in his story "A Sense of Shelter."

Writers revise differently. You can try more radical exercises such as rewriting your story from an entirely different point of view; for example, you can switch from the third person to a first person. The choices you make in such a revision will reveal much about the story. Why have you chosen a particular character's perspective in shifting the story's initial point of view? Do you see the character as a witness to the action, a central figure in the action, or someone who serves in both roles? Does your shift in point of view change the tone of the story, and, if so, how is the meaning of the story affected? The shift in point of view can lead to shifts in story structure, changing which actions are set offstage, outside of the reader's view, and which actions are heightened and dramatized.

You can also try a revision where you alter the characters' destinies by changing the critical plot point: for example, you can change the climactic scene where one character declares love for another to a scene where the love interest doesn't even show up to hear the proclamation. What, for instance, would have occurred if the grandmother in "A Good Man Is Hard to Find" had failed to recognize The Misfit, or had had the sense not to articulate that recognition? What does the change in plot say about the nature of the characters? Has such a change shifted the balance of power between or among the characters? How has it changed the meaning of the story?

Such broad strokes of revision can also change the voice of the narrator. A narrator who seems muted can be instilled with urgency; or a narrator who seems melodramatic can be muted. You can infuse a narrator with greater—or lesser—intelligence. The question of the narrator's intelligence is indivisibly linked to the vision of the story—a narrator's perceived lack of intelligence may signal that the writer is "writing down" to his characters. Any substantial shift in voice has the potential for dramatically altering the nature and the meaning of your story. As with the other changes suggested above, such revision will most likely require rewriting your story from the first word. While changing plot or point of view or voice can seem radical or contrived, it can also free you to see the story's multiple possibilities.

Writing Strategies

1. Take the opening paragraph of one of your stories and try two different revision techniques on it. For example, line edit the paragraph for issues of voice and clarity and movement. Then, take the same paragraph, and put it aside, and try to rewrite it from scratch. How do the line-edit changes differ from the changes you've made by revising from scratch? Did you change point of view as well? Which version do you like better?

2. Reread one of your stories without marking it up, then immediately make a list of its strengths and weaknesses. For strengths, which aspects of the story did you like, and why? For weaknesses, which aspects of the story bothered you, or irritated you, or seemed simply to lack power? Since it will be clear that the weaknesses need to be addressed, what kind of revision strategies can you develop from looking at both strengths and weaknesses?

3. Take the opening paragraph of one of your stories and try rewriting it from a different perspective. How does the change in perspective affect the story, and how does it affect your perception of the story? Do you prefer the new perspective? In changing the perspective, did you actually change the voice of your story, or did you supplant one pronoun (such as "we") for another pronoun (such as "they")? What made you choose the new perspective, as opposed to other potential perspectives? Has the perspective shift changed the role of the narrator, and, if so, has the movement taken the narrator closer to the action of the story or further away from it? Does your shift in point of view change the tone of the story, and, if so, how is the meaning of the story affected?

4. Take a crucial plot development in one of your stories and alter it in order to alter the characters' destinies. What does the change in plot say about the nature of the characters? How has it changed the meaning of the story?

5. Take the opening paragraph of one of your stories and change the voice of it (but not necessarily the perspective) by changing

sentence length and structure, or deleting all adverbs, or instilling it with humor, or supplanting any urgency with irony (or vice versa). How does the shift in voice alter the nature and meaning of your story?

LINE EDITING

Whichever method of revision you choose, a fresh line edit is essential, from start to finish. A paragraph that you've completely changed somewhere in the middle of your story could affect the meaning and music of other paragraphs. Allow yourself a couple more readings of the story: one to see how the story sounds, without taking a pen or typewriter or word processor to it; another to revise actively and aggressively.

Line editing can accomplish any number of objectives: it can vary the music of your story, it can strengthen the language, it can change the tone, it can cut the irony, it can trim abstract description. "I want, for instance," William Gass, author of the story collection *In the Heart of the Heart of the Country,* said in an interview in *The Paris Review,* "a certain word to sound like a bell the whole time the reader is reading certain lines. I want this bong going bong all the bonging time. I'm trying to figure out what device will work—on the page—not only to give the proper instruction to the reader, but make him begin to hear it—dead dead dead dead—the way it's supposed to go. But as soon as you try to note it the page goes crazy and you get a dozen other things you want no part of." Your strategy for line editing depends entirely on the story itself. But line editing does seek to change that which is false to the story, and that which is ineffective. Line editing will also tell you what is strong in the story, and will seek to bring every other sentence up to the standard of that sentence. Ernest Hemingway's famous advice to cut the best line of every page was dedicated, perhaps, to rooting out that which was too "writerly," or too poetic, or merely too perfect to be credible.

Line editing can also ensure that, word by word, language comes from within the story rather than from outside it. If, for example, your story focuses on a young couple struggling to make a living on the nineteenth-century American frontier, a line edit might cut or rewrite anachronistic comparisons such as "the butter churn was the size of a Kenmore dryer," or "he talked in a mechanical manner, as if there were a computer chip in his brain." More often, determining the language that seems outside of your story can be an intricate task, and demands not only that you be loyal to a story's setting and time, but to a character's way of thinking and of perceiving the world around him or her. Why does the narrator of Isaac Babel's "My First Goose" see the moon as "a cheap earring," when at first consideration cheap earrings do not appear to be foremost in his line of thought or in his arena of personal experience? A previous comparison made by the narrator justifies his particular perception of the moon: "His long legs were like girls sheathed to the neck in shining riding boots." There is also the story's penultimate line: "I dreamed, and in my dreams saw women." The earring comparison is fundamentally true to the narrator's character. Being true to your characters and to your story requires more than just plot; it requires that the language of the story be organic to its characters. Line editing checks and ensures that language.

Line editing can be aided by reading the story aloud, either to yourself or to a group of people. Hearing someone else read the story aloud to you can be very helpful—suddenly inflections in dialogue that seemed obvious might be missing. Words and phrases will ring false in a literal way, and this will help your "ear" for writing. In addition, reading aloud can be helpful in overall revision. Reading aloud not only captures the spoken sound of each word, but it demonstrates the actual pacing and energy in fiction. If you read the story to an audience, you ought to be able to feel the rising and waning interest in the room. You might mark these points in the margins as you sense them.

Writing Strategies

1. Read one of your stories for words and phrases that ring false, either because of tone or level of diction or anachronistic quality, and mark each one of them.

2. Read and mark the same story for ineffective or unclear sentences and phrases, and words and clauses that only "approximate" meaning, as Mark Twain says, rather than actually pinpointing the meaning.

3. Read the same story for clunky and awkward word choices, phrases, and sentences that bounce you from the story because of their awkward quality. Mark these instances.

4. Read one of your stories aloud, either to yourself or to a group of people. Mark wherever the story sounds slow or off, or wherever you sense your own attention or your audience's attention waning.

HOW PROSE LOOKS

After you've written a story, you may want to step back and consider the superficial visual effect of what you have composed. In this respect you can almost think of each individual page of your story as a frame that is part of a series of frames that makes up the entire story. If one page were made up of one solid paragraph, that particular page would be a block. If it had several paragraphs, the page would contain several blocks of varying sizes, depending on the length of the individual paragraphs. Lines of dialogue, depending, again, on how long they are, would be lines or blocks within such a frame. An entire page of one-line exchanges between or among characters would create the image of a series of lines.

The point of this exercise is to experience the story from a kind of visual distance, as many readers will before actually reading what has been written. Page after page containing just a continuous block may put off some readers; page after page of lines of dialogue may put off other readers. Variety may attract a lot of readers, but it may be inappropriate to your story.

The form of your fiction also has a more practical effect on the reader. Each paragraph is a particular unit of thought that the reader enters with a set of standard expectations. A longer paragraph is expected to be more complex, and, as such, the reader enters it more slowly, preparing to assimilate the material within the body of the paragraph and approaching its completion with a heightened expectation that the end of the paragraph will carry a substantial reward for this effort. Short paragraphs, depending on just how short, can be assimilated almost as quickly as headlines.

Consider, for example, a longer paragraph and the shorter paragraph that Babel juxtaposes it with in "My First Goose":

His guileless art exhausted, the lad made off. Then, crawling over the ground, I began to gather together the manuscripts and tattered garments that had fallen out of the trunk. I gathered them up and carried them to the other end of the yard. Near the hut, on a brick stove, stood a cauldron in which pork was cooking. The steam that rose from it was like the far-off smoke of home in the village, and it mingled hunger with desperate loneliness in my head. Then I covered my little broken trunk with hay, turning it into a pillow, and lay down on the ground to read in *Pravda* Lenin's speech at the Second Congress of the Comintern. The sun fell upon me from behind the toothed hillocks, the Cossacks trod on my feet, the lad made fun of me untiringly, the beloved lines came toward me along a thorny path and could not reach me. Then I put aside the paper and went out to the landlady, who was spinning on the porch.

"Landlady," I said, "I got to eat."

Here, the speed in reading is varied both by paragraph length and sentence length, and the longest sentence contains the most important thought and comes near the end of the long paragraph, when we are reading at our slowest speed and fully prepared for the revelation contained in "the beloved lines came toward me along a thorny path and could not reach me." The ensuing short paragraph has great dramatic effect—the voice of the narrator has changed—and at the same time spins us back into what's come before, and tells us how the story will proceed. That simple, short paragraph tells us how to read the story around it.

Depending on what you're writing, you may want to consciously manipulate the speed of reading by tinkering with the length of your paragraphs. This kind of revision, however, can be extraordinarily difficult when considering that each paragraph must somehow conform to the perception of the reader that it contains a coherent unit of thought.

Writing Strategies

1. Using a story you have already written, step back and consider the visual effect of what you have composed, thinking of each individual page of your story as a frame that is part of a series of frames that makes up the entire story. Is the visual effect varied or monotonous? Does it need to be broken up, or is the unity intended?

2. Using the same story from the first strategy, step into the story, looking at the length and size of individual paragraphs. Do the long paragraphs and the short paragraphs have their intended effects? Does each paragraph strike you as an organic unit of meaning? Consider breaking up and/or combining paragraphs.

3. Read the story from the previous strategies again, conscious of your reading speed. Where are you reading slower, or faster? Is this effect intended? Manipulate speed by shortening or lengthening paragraphs and sentences.

HOW MANY DRAFTS?

The most important element of revision is that you allow yourself the freedom and the capacity to "see anew" the work you have created, to remain alert and open to the unexploited possibilities of your fiction. The process of revision can take more than one draft. Simply put, revision requires as many drafts as are needed.

Ralph Lombreglia, the short-story writer, rewrites each story twenty times. Stephen Dixon rewrites each page before proceeding to the next. Shirley Jackson wrote "The Lottery" in a morning, and sent it off to *The New Yorker* that same afternoon. Some writers revise in the bathtub, in bed, out by the pool, or with the radio on to take some of the pressure off the process. Other writers require the exact same conditions and environment for revision as they do for first drafts.

Some novel writers are inclined to revise chapter by chapter, not proceeding to the next one until the one they are working on is satisfactory. Other writers try to prolong access to inspiration by creating a first draft in its entirety before considering any revision. Writers revise as differently as they compose, but almost every writer does revise. Again, it's important to experiment with approaches to revision in order to find the one that is most suitable for you. Even then, the actual revision each piece demands depends on the piece itself.

Whichever revision techniques and strategies you choose, the most important consideration is to allow yourself access to the process of discovery that the writing of the first draft inspired in you. While a number of writers are fond of saying how much they loathe revision, a mark of a good writer is to *want* to revise, rather than to dread it. As John Updike says, "Writing and rewriting are a constant search for what it is one is saying."

Writing Strategies

1. Select one of your stories. Consider its history.
    a. When did you first start it? Were you able to write the entire first draft right away, or did the writing take place over a series of days, or weeks, or months?
    b. Did you start revising immediately?
    c. Has anybody besides you read it, and how did it affect your readers?
    d. How many times have you reread your story, and has this rereading occurred over a long or a short period of time? Have you tried putting the story aside for a length of time (a week, a month, or longer), and, if so, what effect did this distance of time have on your reading and reworking of the story?
    e. Have you allowed yourself the opportunity to explore all of the story's possibilities, given the length of time you have spent on writing the story, the length of time you have spent on revising the story, and the overall length of time that has passed between finishing the first draft and finishing the latest revision?

2. Using the same story from the first strategy, consider the physical amount of revision that you have done.
    a. Have you worked line by line on the story, adding and changing and cutting words and sentences?
    b. Have you worked on character and plot, considering the nature of the individual characters and how they interact; adding and changing and deleting lines of dialogue, details, and gestures; and adding and changing and deleting plot points?
    c. How many words or pages have you cut? How many words or pages have you added? How many words or pages have you changed? What fraction are these revisions of the overall length of the first draft of the story?

Sandra Cisneros

Sandra Cisneros was born in December 1954. She was raised in Chicago, attended Loyola University, and received an M.F.A. from the University of Iowa Writer's Workshop in 1978. Cisneros is the author of two books of fiction, The House on Mango Street *(winner of the 1985 Before Columbus Book Award) and* Woman Hollering Creek and Other Stories *(1991), and two collections of poetry,* Bad Boys *(1980) and* My Wicked, Wicked Ways *(1978). "My Lucy Friend Who Smells Like Corn" is excerpted from* Woman Hollering Creek and Other Stories.

My Lucy Friend Who Smells Like Corn

Lucy Anguiano, Texas girl who smells like corn, like Frito Bandito chips, like tortillas, something like that warm smell of *nixtamal* or bread the way her head smells when she's leaning close to you over a paper cut-out doll or on the porch when we are squatting over marbles trading this pretty crystal that leaves a blue star on your hand for that giant cat-eye with a grasshopper green spiral in the center like the juice of bugs on the windshield when you drive to the border, like the yellow blood of butterflies.

Have you ever eated dog food? I have. After crunching like ice, she opens her big mouth to prove it, only a pink tongue rolling around in there like a blind worm, and Janey looking in because she said Show me. But me I like that Lucy, corn smell hair and aqua flip-flops just like mine that we bought at the Kmart for only 79 cents same time.

I'm going to sit in the sun, don't care if it's a million trillion degrees outside, so my skin can get so dark it's blue where it bends like Lucy's. Her whole family like that. Eyes like knife slits. Lucy and her sisters. Norma, Margarita, Ofelia, Herminia, Nancy, Olivia, Cheli, *y la* Amber Sue.

Screen door with no screen. *Bang!* Little black dog biting his fur. Fat couch on the porch. Some of the windows painted blue, some pink, because her daddy got tired that day or forgot. Mama in the kitchen feeding clothes into the wringer washer and clothes rolling out all stiff and twisted and flat like paper. Lucy got her arm stuck once and had to yell Maaa! and her mama had to put the machine in reverse and then her hand rolled back, the finger black and later, her nail fell off. *But did your arm get flat like the clothes? What happened to your arm? Did they have to pump it with air?* No, only the finger, and she didn't cry neither.

Lean across the porch rail and pin the pink sock of the baby Amber Sue on top of Cheli's flowered T-shirt, and the blue jeans of *la* Ofelia over the inside seam of Olivia's blouse, over the flannel nightgown of Margarita so it don't stretch out, and then you take the work shirts of their daddy and hang them upside down like this, and this way all the clothes don't get so wrinkled and take up less space and you don't waste pins. The girls all wear each other's clothes, except Olivia, who is stingy. There ain't no boys here. Only girls and one father who is never home hardly and one mother who says *Ay! I'm real tired* and so many sisters there's no time to count them.

I'm sitting in the sun even though it's the hottest part of the day, the part that makes the streets dizzy, when the heat makes a little hat on the top of your head and bakes the dust and weed grass and sweat up good, all steamy and smelling like sweet corn.

I want to rub heads and sleep in a bed with little sisters, some at the top and some at the feets. I think it would be fun to sleep with sisters you could yell at one at a time or all together, instead of alone on the fold-out chair in the living room.

When I get home Abuelita will say *Didn't I tell you?* and I'll get it because I was supposed to wear this dress again tomorrow. But first I'm going to jump off an old pissy mattress in the Anguiano yard. I'm going to scratch your mosquito bites, Lucy, so they'll itch you, then put Mercurochrome smiley faces on them. We're going to trade shoes and wear them on our hands. We're going to walk over to Janey Ortiz's house and say *We're never ever going to be your friend again forever!* We're going to run home backwards and we're going to run home frontwards, look twice under the house where the rats hide and I'll stick one foot in there because you dared me, sky so blue and heaven inside those white clouds. I'm going to peel a scab from my knee and eat it, sneeze on the cat, give you three M & M's I've been saving for you since yesterday, comb your hair with my fingers and braid it into teeny-tiny braids real pretty. We're going to wave to a lady we don't know on the bus. Hello! I'm going to somersault on the rail of the front porch even though my *chones* show. And cut paper dolls we draw ourselves, and color in their clothes with crayons, my arm around your neck.

And when we look at each other, our arms gummy from an orange Popsicle we split, we could be sisters, right? We could be, you and me waiting for our teeths to fall and money. You laughing something into my ear that tickles, and me going Ha Ha Ha Ha. Her and me, my Lucy friend who smells like corn.

Ida Fink

Ida Fink was born in 1921 in Zbaraz, Poland, and immigrated to Israel in 1957. She has written three radio plays and a novel, Podroz *(1990). Her story collection,* A Scrap of Time *(1985), was awarded the Anne Frank Prize for Literature in 1985 and the Prix Litteraire Wizo in 1990. She is a contributor to* The New Yorker, *as well as literary journals in Europe and Israel. Her writings have been translated into German, Dutch, Spanish, French, and Italian.*

A Scrap of Time*

I want to talk about a certain time not measured in months and years. For so long I have wanted to talk about this time, and not in the way I will talk about it now, not just about this one scrap of time. I wanted to, but I couldn't, I didn't know how. I was afraid, too, that this second time, which is measured in months and years, had buried the other time under a layer of years, that this second time had crushed the first and destroyed it within me. But no. Today, digging around in the ruins of memory, I found it fresh and untouched by forgetfulness. This time was measured not in months but in a word—we no longer said "in the beautiful month of May," but "after the first 'action,' or the second, or right before the third." We had different measures of time, we different ones, always different, always with that mark of difference that moved some of us to pride and others to humility. We, who because of our difference were condemned once again, as we had been before in our history, we were condemned once again during this time

---

*Translated by Madeline Levine and Francine Prose.

measured not in months nor by the rising and setting of the sun, but by a word—"action," a word signifying movement, a word you would use about a novel or a play.

I don't know who used the word first, those who acted or those who were the victims of their action; I don't know who created this technical term, who substituted it for the first term, "round-up"—a word that became devalued (or dignified?) as time passed, as new methods were developed, and "round-up" was distinguished from "action" by the borderline of race. Round-ups were for forced labor.

We called the first action—that scrap of time that I want to talk about—a round-up, although no one was rounding anyone up; on that beautiful, clear morning, each of us made our way, not willingly, to be sure, but under orders, to the marketplace in our little town, a rectangle enclosed by high, crooked buildings—a pharmacy, clothing stores, an ironmonger's shop—and framed by a sidewalk made of big square slabs that time had fractured and broken. I have never again seen such huge slabs. In the middle of the marketplace stood the town hall, and it was right there, in front of the town hall, that we were ordered to form ranks.

I should not have written "we," for I was not standing in the ranks, although, obeying the order that had been posted the previous evening, I had left my house after eating a perfectly normal breakfast, at a table that was set in a normal way, in a room whose doors opened onto a garden veiled in morning mists, dry and golden in the rising sun.

Our transformation was not yet complete; we were still living out of habit in that old time that was measured in months and years, and on that lovely peaceful morning, filled with dry, golden mists, we took the words "conscription of labor" literally, and as mature people tend to read between the lines, our imaginations replaced the word "labor" with "labor camp," one of which, people said, was being built nearby. Apparently those who gave the order were perfectly aware of the poverty of our imaginations; that is why they saved themselves work by issuing a written order. This is how accurately they predicted our responses: after finishing a normal breakfast, at a normally set table, the older members of the family decided to disobey the order because they were afraid of the heavy physical labor, but they did not advise the young to do likewise—the young, who, if their disobedience were discovered, would not be able to plead old age. We were like infants.

This beautiful, clear morning that I am digging out of the ruins of my memory is still fresh; its colors and aromas have not faded: a grainy golden mist with red spheres of apples hanging in it, and the shadows above the river damp with the sharp odor of burdock, and the bright blue dress that I was wearing when I left the house and when I turned around at the gate. It was then, probably at that very moment, that I suddenly progressed, instinctively, from an infantile state to a still naive caution—instinctively, because I wasn't thinking about why I avoided the gate that led to the street and instead set off on a roundabout route, across the orchard, along the riverbank, down a road we called "the back way" because it wound through the outskirts of town. Instinctively, because at that moment I still did not know that I wouldn't stand in the marketplace in front of the town hall. Perhaps I wanted to delay that moment, or perhaps I simply liked the river.

Along the way, I stopped and carefully picked out flat stones, and skipped them across the water; I sat down for a while on the little bridge, beyond which one could see the town, and dangled my legs, looking at my reflection in the water and at the willows that grew on the bank. I was not yet afraid then, nor was my sister. (I forgot to say that my younger sister was with me, and she, too, skipped stones across the water and dangled her legs over the river, which is called the Gniezna—a pitiful little stream, some eight meters wide.) My sister, too, was not yet afraid; it was only when we went further along the street, beyond the bridge, and the view of the marketplace leapt out at us from behind the building on the corner, that we suddenly stopped in our tracks.

There was the square, thick with people as on a market day, only different, because a market-day crowd is colorful and loud, with chickens clucking, geese honking, and people talking and bargaining. This crowd was silent. In a way it resembled a rally—but it was different from that, too. I don't know what it was exactly. I only know that we suddenly stopped and my sister began to tremble, and then I caught the trembling, and she said, "Let's run away," and although no one was chasing us and the morning was still clear and peaceful, we ran back to the little bridge, but we no longer noticed the willows or the reflections of our running figures in the water; we ran for a long time until we were high up the steep slope known as Castle Hill—the ruins of an old castle stood on top of it—and on this hillside, the jewel of our town, we sat down in the bushes, out of breath and still shaking.

From this spot we could see our house and our garden—it was just as it always was, nothing had changed—and we could see our neighbor's house, from which our neighbor had emerged, ready to beat her carpets. We could hear the slap slap of her carpet beater.

We sat there for an hour, maybe two, I don't know, because it was then that time measured in the ordinary way stopped. Then we climbed down the steep slope to the river and returned to our house, where we heard what had happened in the marketplace, and that our cousin David had been taken, and how they took him, and what message he had left for his mother. After they were taken away, he wrote down again what he had asked people to tell her; he threw a note out of the truck and a peasant brought it to her that evening—but that happened later. First we learned that the women had been told to go home, that only the men were ordered to remain standing there, and that the path chosen by our cousin had been the opposite of ours. We had been horrified by the sight of the crowd in the marketplace, while he was drawn towards it by an enormous force, a force as strong as his nerves were weak, so that somehow or other he did violence to his own fate, he himself, himself, himself, and that was what he asked people to tell his mother, and then he wrote it down: "I myself am to blame, forgive me."

We would never have guessed that he belonged to the race of the Impatient Ones, doomed to destruction by their anxiety and their inability to remain still, never—because he was round-faced and chubby, not at all energetic, the sort of person who can't be pulled away from his book, who smiles timidly, girlishly. Only the end of the war brought us the truth about his last hours. The peasant who delivered the note did not dare tell us what he saw, and although other people, too, muttered something about what they had seen, no one dared to believe it, especially since the Germans offered proofs of another truth that each of us grasped at greedily; they measured out doses of it sparingly, with restraint—a perfect cover-up. They went to such trouble, created so many phantoms, that only time, time measured not in months and years, opened our eyes and convinced us.

Our cousin David had left the house later than we did, and when he reached the marketplace it was already known—not by everyone, to be sure, but by the so-called Council, which in time became the *Judenrat*—that the words "conscription for labor" had nothing to do with a labor camp. One friend, a far-sighted older man, ordered the boy to hide just in case, and since it was too late to return home because the streets were blocked off, he led him to his own apartment in one of the houses facing the marketplace. Like us, not comprehending that the boy belonged to the race of the Impatient Ones, who find it difficult to cope with isolation and who act on impulse, he left David in a room that locked from inside. What our cousin experienced, locked up in that room, will remain forever a mystery. Much can be explained by the fact that the room had a view of the marketplace, of that silent crowd, of the faces of friends and relatives, and it may be that finally the isolation of his hiding place seemed to him more unbearable than the great and threatening unknown outside the window—an unknown shared by all who were gathered in the marketplace.

It was probably a thought that came in a flash: not to be alone, to be together with everyone. All that was needed was one movement of his hand.

I think it incorrect to assume that he left the hiding place because he was afraid that they would search the houses. That impatience of the heart, that trembling of the nerves, the burden of isolation, condemned him to extermination together with the first victims of our town.

He stood between a lawyer's apprentice and a student of architecture and to the question, "Profession?" he replied, "Teacher," although he had been a teacher for only a short time and quite by chance. His neighbor on the right also told the truth, but the architecture student lied, declaring himself a carpenter, and this lie saved his life—or, to be more precise, postponed the sentence of death for two years.

Seventy people were loaded into trucks; at the last moment the rabbi was dragged out of his house—he was the seventy-first. On the way to the trucks they marched past the ranks of all those who had not yet managed to inform the interrogators about the work they did. It was then that our cousin said out loud, "Tell my mother that it's my own fault and that I beg her forgiveness." Presumably, he had already stopped believing what all of us still believed later: that they were going to a camp. He had that horrifying clarity of vision that comes just before death.

The peasant who that evening brought us the note that said, "I myself am to blame, forgive me," was somber and didn't look us in the eye. He said he had found the note on the road to Lubianki and that he didn't know anything else about it; we knew that he knew, but we did not want to admit it. He left, but he came back after the war to tell us what he had seen.

A postcard from the rabbi arrived two days later, convincing everyone that those who had been taken away were in a labor camp. A month later, when the lack of any further news began to make us doubt the camp, another postcard arrived, this one written by someone else who had been deported—an accountant, I think. After the postcard scheme came the payment of contributions: the authorities let it be understood that kilos of coffee or tea—or gold— would provide a family with news of their dear ones. As a gesture of compassion they also allowed people to send food parcels to the prisoners, who, it was said, were working in a camp in the Reich. Once again, after the second action, a postcard turned up. It was written in pencil and almost indecipherable. After this postcard, we said, "They're done for." But rumors told a different story alto- gether—of soggy earth in the woods by the village of Lubianki, and of a bloodstained handkerchief that had been found. These rumors came from nowhere; no eyewitnesses stepped forward.

The peasant who had not dared to speak at the time came back after the war and told us everything. It happened just as rumor had it, in a dense, overgrown forest, eight kilometers outside of town, one hour after the trucks left the marketplace. The execu- tion itself did not take long; more time was spent on the prepara- tory digging of the grave.

At the first shots, our chubby, round-faced cousin David, who was always clumsy at gymnastics and sports, climbed a tree and wrapped his arms around the trunk like a child hugging his mother, and that was the way he died.

VOICE

THE STORY SPOKEN ALOUD

Voice is the element of fiction that many readers love to talk about, but few want to define. It combines aspects of tone, style, point of view, character, and language to form a distinctive sound both in the writer's ear and the reader's ear: a sound as if the story were spoken aloud. Hopefully, that sound is the same to both writer and reader; and hopefully that sound will make sense within the context of the story.

A variety of levels of voice exist in virtually every story, and can be delineated among *author's* or *narrator's report* (an author or narrator telling the story), *direct* (a character or narrator speaking out loud in the story), and *interior* (a character in thought). In a third-person story, for instance, there is the voice of the narrator, the voice of each character in dialogue, perhaps the voice of one or more characters in their third-person limited interiors. The third-person voice can come from a perspective and indulge in an inconsistency that allows a complexity of material to emerge. In Alice Munro's "Prue," for example, the narrator appears to be a potential character in the story who never enters the scene, someone who must know Prue in her fictive world. Yet this narrator knows more than is actually possible for a real character to know: "She doesn't mention that the next morning she picked up one of Gordon's cufflinks from his dresser." The narrator is for an instant omniscient. In Yukio Mishima's "Patriotism," once the opening summarizes the crucial facts of the double suicide, the narrative eye faithfully follows the story up to that point, with the exception in section II in which the narrative eye momentarily turns to the future beyond the suicide, as it describes people examining the photo of the doomed couple *after* their suicide.

The voice of the narrator, too, might change in the third-person voice as it seeks to call attention to something—the voice might become muted or erudite, or shrill, or harrowed depending on the event or aspect it is bringing to light. The narrator in Eudora Welty's "Old Mr. Marblehall" allows the speculative interior voice of Mr. Marblehall into the story when he ponders what would happen if his deceit were uncovered. William Kennedy, in his novel *Ironweed,* writes with great sophistication about characters who are essentially street people, to show that the workings of such characters are as complex as the workings of any character imaginable. Consequently, the voice of the narrator *elevates* (rises in complexity of word choice and diction) during third-person interiors.

If the voice comes from a character in the story, then it most likely is written from the first-person point of view. A first-person voice will contain the voices of other characters speaking, either through direct dialogue or summarized dialogue. But the reader and the writer are conscious of the fact that the first person has selected these utterances of other characters, and the consciousness of the first-person voice can tint the utterances of the characters with its own personality. Perhaps this is why Henry James called the first-person voice "the first person barbaric."

Regardless of the voice with which the story is told, it will, like any real voice, vary. A song of one note would not be much of a song; a story in one tone will not have much music. A number of devices exist for varying voice. Flannery O'Connor signals a voice shift with the trigger "as if." It is almost impossible to read a page of O'Connor without stumbling into this construction. In a critical moment of "A Good Man Is Hard to Find," O'Connor's narrator notes: "His face was as familiar to her as if she had known him all her life but she could not recall who he was." O'Connor's use of "as if" is her way of turning the corner that connects what does exist with what does not exist in the world of the character. "As if" allows her to operate on two levels seemingly without the reader noticing it.

In "My First Goose," Isaac Babel uses the drumroll effect of repetition to extend time and thereby heighten the pitch of the story's opening: "Savitsky, Commander of VI Division, rose when he saw me, and I wondered at the beauty of his girl's body. He rose, the purple of his riding breeches and the crimson of his little tilted cap and the decorations stuck on his chest cleaving the hut as a standard cleaves the sky." In the short story, "The Dead," James Joyce uses the effect of inverted word order to heighten the pitch of his ending: "His soul swooned slowly as he heard the snow falling faintly through the universe and faintly falling, like the descent of their last end, upon all the living and the dead."

Ernest Hemingway is renowned for using simple words and phrases that he repeats with a kind of obstinacy to create a distinctive voice: "Nick was happy as he crawled inside the tent. He had not been unhappy all day. This was different though. Now things were done. There had been this to do. Now it was done. It had been a hard trip. He was very tired. That was done. He had made his camp. He was settled. Nothing could touch him. It was a good place to camp. He was there, in the good place. He was in his home where he had made it. Now he was hungry." Forty years later, in a climactic moment of dialogue in "Dundun," Denis Johnson creates distinctive voices and distinctive fiction with the same kind of simple repetition:

> "What do you say?"
> "What do you mean, what do I say?"
> "He's dead."
> "All right. I know he's dead."
> "Throw him out of the car."
> "Damn right throw him out of the car."

Even something as technical as verb tense can have a profound effect on how the reader hears a story. The present tense can signal a spontaneity and immediacy in storytelling, and make the reader feel that the narrator and reader are experiencing the story simultaneously; neither knows what will happen next. Chekhov uses the present tense in "Gusev" to convey urgency and tell a story in a casual style. The past tense signals a narrator who knows how the story ends, and has shaped its events. Mishima's "Patriotism," for example, is deliberately fashioned to enclose the suicides within a sociopolitical context. Most writers use one tense consistently in a story in creating and sustaining a voice, but occasionally, writers choose to vary tense for a specific reason. Cormac McCarthy, in his novel *Blood Meridian*, begins in the present tense and switches, after a few pages, to the past, to dip only occasionally into the present tense for the remainder of the novel. Alice Munro, in "Prue," begins in the past tense and switches, after a few lines, to the present, to return to the past only twice more: in one four-line series and in one extended scene. The shifting of tense can signal an important moment, or the narrator's desire to stop the time of the story, thereby enlarging the scope or depth of the narrative.

Writing Strategies

1. Select at random three long paragraphs from three stories included in this book.

   a. Read the paragraphs aloud and briefly describe each voice, indicating the point of view and the tone.
   b. Consider how each paragraph has achieved its voice. How do elements such as diction level and sentence length contribute to the overall effect?

2. Read your own work aloud. What kind of sound does it make to your ear? What techniques do you use to achieve this sound? Is the voice ironic, sly, nostalgic? Is this effect intended? Does the voice change? If so, how can you describe this change?

3. If possible, make a tape of yourself reading aloud, then listen to it. Note the distinctions between what you heard when you were reading aloud, compared to what you can hear when you are listening to the tape.

YOUR OWN VOICE

There are as many methods of creating a voice as there are voices. Voice is minutely composed of word choice, punctuation, and sentence length and structure. The number of components of voice are as great and as varied as the number of components of fiction, and as such are open to an infinite amount of manipulation and experimentation.

A critical question for any writer is what his or her voice *is*. Have you found it, and is it a worthwhile voice? Perhaps the best answer to these questions is to have someone else read your work aloud while you listen. How does it *sound* to you? Is it interesting, unique, engaging? Does it have the quality of life, of liveliness, to it? Compare it to other stories and novels you've read: how does your voice measure up? Does your voice feel like you, or like somebody you want yourself to be, or to sound like?

The question of voice is different for every author. Although you might have an identifiable voice from story to story, it is quite possible that within the grain of a particular narrative you discover a new voice, not artificially unlike your own, but simply rooted in the new work you are writing.

If, as a writer, you find yourself feeling trapped in a particular voice, there are many choices for escape. You can choose a different point of view, a different style, a different tone, a different type of conflict, a different story. But there are aspects of your own writing which are inalterable, which are particular to you. Your opinions, your artistic vision, your self-perception and the way you perceive the world, your *personality* are all inherently you. The fundamental essences of yourself, as they constitute your voice, can only help to contribute to the originality of your writing.

Some writers contend that each writer's voice is distinct, that no matter what a particular person writes, that person will be recognizable to his or her readers as the writer. Other writers believe that each story has its own voice, filtered, of course, through the voice of the writer, but so finely filtered as to make the writer a relatively soundless presence behind the voice of the narrator. The question of voice is limited to the story you're writing, and, in particular, the tone of that story. Is the story ironic, melancholy, bitter, humorous, or a combination of a half-dozen other moods? The tone creates and continues to work with the mood, and is an intrinsic and inseparable part of voice.

On occasion, a voice can get in the way of telling the story. Fiction written in dialect, with roundabout syntax and agrammatical sentences, challenges its readers on the essential issues of clarity and sense. "I know y'all got no bidness doin nuthin," a story might begin, but that opening will stop some readers from even continuing. While some writers can get away with it, the dialect must be in service of more than just itself—it must somehow reveal a character or a worldview so particularized and unusual that it is worth the trouble of the reader wading through it.

Numerous devices exist to help create voice. You can make dialect choices to make the voice of a story approximate the cultural background of the characters, as Sandra Cisneros does in "My Lucy Friend Who Smells Like Corn," or as Alice Walker does in the novel *The Color Purple*. You can achieve a chorus of voices and have many voices sounding many ways and still have a unified voice. The first person is the easiest way to create a single voice, but it is not as simple as it appears. You can examine the level of a character's consciousness that Joyce chooses to write from in novels such as *Portrait of the Artist as a Young Man* or *Ulysses,* and pick a level of consciousness that you know well and write from that. You can, as Scott Bradfield does in *The History of Luminous Motion,* create a unique voice through a truly unique character. You can, as Mark Twain achieved with Huck Finn, arrive at a once-in-a-literature voice.

Writing Strategies

1. Have someone else read your work aloud while you listen. How does it *sound* to you now? How has this sound changed from when you've read it aloud yourself? Is it engaging? Does it have the quality of life, of liveliness, to it? How would you describe the voice? Read aloud a few paragraphs of stories such as "Old Mr. Marblehall" and "Dundun." How does the voice of your story compare?

2. Choose a different point of view, a different style, a different tone, or a different type of conflict to write from. Now how does your voice sound? Are there qualities that strike you as similar to your previous writing? Make notes on what is similar about your various writing voices. What would you like to be less similar, more distinct from story to story? What is particular to the writing voice that strikes you as essential? What is particular to the writing voice that strikes you as weak or in need of improvement?

3. Try writing about a familiar subject in a voice you've never used before, such as the voice of a historical character, or a child, or a comedian. How is the writing different from other pieces you've done? Is it still recognizable as yours?

FIRST-PERSON VOICE

The first-person point of view is the easiest way to create a single voice, and can contain the most energy and intimacy, but it is also the most difficult to maintain. The first person promises to remain true to the character, to come intrinsically from the character. To stay within a single character for the length of a story is to expose yourself to inconsistencies in voice that can mean inconsistencies in character. Would the character really say that? Would the character really think that? These are questions readers ask when reading the first person. The longer the character remains on stage, the harder you must concentrate to retain the believability of that character.

An allure of writing in a first-person voice is that, by coming from a particular character, you have the opportunity to get inside that character. Consequently, some practitioners of the first-person voice are prone to try to dramatize the consciousness of the first person, to look within the soul of the first-person narrator and talk about what's going on in there. A challenge of the first-person voice is to turn the eye outward, as Isaac Babel does in "My First Goose," rather than inward, and dramatize the state of the first person by dramatizing the world around the first person, not the world within the first person. In "Seizing Control," Mary Robison is writing from a first person so purposefully looking at the world around her that she is practically unidentifiable in the story; no one even utters her name.

Another apparent attraction of the first-person voice is the relentless subjectivity it seems to offer: the narrator creates the world he or she is in by speaking about it. As such, the narrator is the sole authority on that world. The narrator determines the appearances of all the other characters, and decides just which actions to relate and how such actions should be described. An effective first-person voice will create a neutral space, where its carefully portrayed reality will seem objective. A promise of fiction is to create a kind of reality that the reader can share in and experience. While the first-person voice attracts some writers for the endless potential of subjectivity, for the promise that the narrator is the sole creator of the fictive world, for the opportunity for rambling and harangue and interrogation and streams of self-consciousness, a difficult challenge of the first-person voice is to allow as much as possible of a relatively objective reality to emerge. The first-person narrator needs to be visible in neutral light, in some way, for the reader to share in the narrator's experience and to be affected by it.

Ultimately, first person is neither more nor less difficult than third person or second person. It offers you immediate possibilities in creating intimacy, energy, and a distinctive voice. But it also requires that you achieve as much of a total picture as if the piece were written in third person.

The choices writers make in the first person are just as distinctive as the choice among first and second and third person. F. Scott Fitzgerald, in *The Great Gatsby*, selects a first person who is more a witness than a protagonist, just as Mary Robison does in "Seizing Control." Albert Camus, in *The Stranger*, chooses a first person who is the center of the drama and yet is able to present a rather distant perspective on all the action, just as Isaac Babel does in "My First Goose." In all cases, the first person serves to reveal both itself and the other characters in the fictional world. In both Sandra Cisneros' "My Lucy Friend Who Smells Like Corn" and Jamaica Kincaid's "Girl," the first-person voice "allows" another character's voice into the story in brief lines of italics. In several of William Faulkner's novels, such as *As I Lay Dying* and *The Sound and the Fury*, he works with a multiple first-person point of view. The faceting of the various voices creates a compelling richness and allows a greater totality of reality to emerge by creating discrete but overlapping realities as viewed by the different first-person voices.

One way of experimenting with first person is to take a story you've written in the first person and supplant "I" for "you" or "he" or "she." If the story turns around too easily into another point of view, it is worth asking what the first person is accomplishing. On the other hand, if the new point of view leaves you feeling as if the story makes no impression at all, it is worth examining the nature of the reality that the first-person voice has created. This exercise can seem burdensome, and some writers only try it for a paragraph to see how language and tone are working in the story. Other writers, however, like the experiment so much that they are inclined to change the entire story into the new perspective.

Writing Strategies

1. Take a story you've written in the first person and supplant "I" for "you" or "he" or "she." What effect has the change accomplished? Does the story translate too easily into another point of view? How are language and tone working with this shift?

2. Take a story you've written in the first person and rewrite it (or at least the first paragraph of it) in the first person from a different character's point of view. How is the action different? How is the meaning different? How is the voice different?

3. Take a story you've written in the first person and mark all the subjective descriptions and phrases that impart the narrator's opinion or draw conclusions for the reader. If you remove all these phrases from the story, how is the reader's perception of the story changed?

THIRD-PERSON VOICE

A third-person narrative can possess a great variety of voices, all of which can work together so that a unified voice arises. Eudora Welty, in "Old Mr. Marblehall," delivers a judgmental voice that sounds as if the entire town were speaking as one, even to the point that elements of a second-person voice creep in (we're addressed as if we were part of the town). In such pieces as Stanley Elkin's "Criers and Kibbutzers," for example, up to five levels of voice can be delineated in the first paragraph: the author's report, third-person interior thought, first-person interior thought, interior direct discourse, and direct discourse.

> Greenspahn cursed the steering wheel shoved like the hard edge of someone's hand against his stomach. Goddamn lousy cars, he thought. Forty-five hundred dollars and there's not room to breathe. He thought sourly of the smiling salesman who had sold it to him, calling him Jake all the time he had been in the showroom. Lousy *podler*. He slid across the seat, moving carefully as though he carried something fragile, and eased his big body out of the car. Seeing the parking meter, he experienced a dark rage. They don't let you live, he thought. *I'll put your nickels in the meter for you, Mr. Greenspahn,* he mimicked the Irish cop. Two dollars a week for the lousy grubber. Plus the nickels that were supposed to go into the meter. And they talked about the Jews.

He saw the cop across the street writing out a ticket. He went around his car, carefully pulling at the handle of each door, and he started toward his store.

Elkin carefully prepares the reader for the various shifts in voice through forthright tags such as "he thought" and conventional techniques such as the use of italics. Not all writers bother with such preparations, and often particularly complex works like *The Sound and the Fury* and *Ulysses* may feel to their readers as if a special map is required to follow the narrative logic. While there are no set rules in creating voice in the third person, it is helpful to consider how your choices may affect readers. If, for example, you choose to confound the reader with multiple shifts in time and point of view, you also may choose to appeal to the reader with a tone of urgency, a tone that promises that the story is of such essential importance that it is worth the struggle to understand it.

Just as with the first person, the third person is not necessarily as simple as it appears. It is your choice to make the voice as simple or as layered as the story needs it to be. Writers such as Raymond Carver, for example, have worked toward an ultimate simplicity. Consider the opening of "Why Don't You Dance?":

> In the kitchen, he poured another drink and looked at the bedroom suite in his front yard. The mattress was stripped and the candy-striped sheets lay beside two pillows on the chiffonier. Except for that, things looked much the way they had in the bedroom—nightstand and reading lamp on his side of the bed, nightstand and reading lamp on her side.
> His side, her side.
> He considered this as he sipped the whiskey.

Here Carver uses direct statements delivered in a muted, almost flat voice. By retaining emotion without excess, he presents a distillation of a conflicted life.

The voice of Flannery O'Connor's third-person stories resides somewhere between the complicated stylistic choices of Elkin or Welty and the straightforward narration of Carver. The opening paragraph of "Everything That Rises Must Converge," for example, reveals a subtle layering of voices:

> Her doctor had told Julian's mother that she must lose twenty pounds on account of her blood pressure, so on Wednesday nights

Julian had to take her downtown on the bus for a reducing class at the Y. The reducing class was designed for working girls over fifty, who weighed from 165 to 200 pounds. His mother was one of the slimmer ones, but she said ladies did not tell their age or weight. She would not ride the buses by herself at night since they had been integrated, and because the reducing class was one of her few pleasures, necessary for her health, and *free,* she said Julian could at least put himself out to take her, considering all she did for him. Julian did not like to consider all she did for him, but every Wednesday night he braced himself and took her.

While the story begins in Julian's voice with "had to" and "working girls," within this voice is clearly an echo of his mother's voice: "he could at least take her." This cohabitation of the two voices is mirrored in the storyline itself, which artfully portrays an increasingly heroic mother, in spite of the fact that the reader is essentially privy to Julian's justifiably negative thoughts about her.

As is evident from these excerpts, each third-person voice is as distinctive as a first-person voice, and is, in fact, as much a part of character as a first-person voice.

Writing Strategies

1. Take a story you've written in the third person and mark all the different voices. What are they? How do they work separately? How do they fill the story together? Is there opportunity for even more levels of voice? Is there a need for cutting back some of the levels? Are transitions between levels clear, and, if not, is there a good reason for that lack of clarity?

2. Take a story you've written in the third person limited, in which you are not inside the minds of all your characters, and experiment with omitting some characters' interiors and exploring other characters' interiors. How does this experimentation change the meaning and the pacing of the story? How does it change the voice of the story?

3. Take a story you've written in third person and revise it, or at least part of it, to a first-person point of view. Which character did you choose and why? How has the change in voice affected the meaning and the action of the story?

SECOND-PERSON VOICE

Second-person voice is most often used within the context of another voice, where the "you" defines the audience for the narrator's story. In such cases, the audience can be another character in the fiction, or it can be the actual reader of the fiction. Denis Johnson, for example, concludes "Dundun" by directly addressing the reader. The narrator of "Old Mr. Marblehall" addresses the audience throughout the story, implying with such familiarity that the audience is part of the town.

Occasionally, however, second person is used to establish the *you* as the main character of the fiction. Here the you can be the reader becoming a character in the story, as in the case of a story in the form of operating instructions. The you can also be the self of the narrator: the narrator is merely talking to itself, but for some reason has decided not to identify itself as the first person. Why? One reason is to create more intimacy with the reader—to let the reader initially think that the reader is the you. This use of you also can create a profound psychological tension, causing the reader to wonder at the narrator's self-denying state.

Given the ambiguity of determining whether the second person is the reader or the narrator talking to itself, the use of second person, like the use of any voice, has to be sustained by the content of the fiction. For instance, in "How to Become a Writer," Lorrie Moore's choice of second person makes the fiction true to the form of a "how to" guide of instruction, but it also is the best choice given the subject matter. If the story were written in the first person, the piece would seem too self-involved (given that the act of writing is a solitary pursuit and so is primarily involved with the self) and autobiographical. Even if the piece is autobiographical, or even if it is the narrator talking aloud to herself, the use of second person actively involves us in the life of the narrator. If the story were written in the third person, the character would seem too remote.

Whether you write in first person, second person, or third person, voice very much depends not only on you as a writer, but on the characters whom you've created and on the form of the fiction.

Writing Strategies

1. Select a story you've written that contains elements of second person. Is it clear who the second person is? How does the second-person address add to the story?

2. Using the same story from the first strategy, delete all use of the second person. How has this omission changed the story?

3. Take a story you've written in the first person and try changing it to the second person. How has this change affected the story?

Mary Robison

Mary Robison has published five collections of short stories from 1979 to 1991. Robison was born in Washington, D.C., in January, 1949, one of eight children. She received an M.A. from Johns Hopkins in 1977. Her work has appeared frequently in The New Yorker, *and her stories have been awarded inclusion in* The Pushcart Prizes 1983, Best American Short Stories 1982, *and the 1987* O. Henry Prize Stories. *She has held teaching appointments at Bennington College, Harvard University, and most recently, the University of Houston. "Seizing Control" is the opening story from her collection* Believe Them *(1988).*

Seizing Control

We weren't supposed to stay up all night, but Mother was in the hospital having Jules, and Father was at the hospital waiting.

We spent a long time out in this blizzard. We had the floodlights on out behind the house, and our backyard shadows were mammoth. We kicked a maze—each of us making a path that led to a fort like an igloo we piled up at the center of the maze. We built the fort last, but then nobody wanted to get inside. Hazel patted the fort and said, "Victory!"—from a movie she knew or something. We didn't quit and come in until Sarah, the youngest, was whimpering.

Our cuffs and gloves were stiff and had ice balls crusted on them. Our socks were soaked. All of us had snow in our boots— even Terrence, who had boots with buckles. Zippers were stuck with cold. Our ears burned for a long while after, and our hair was dripping wet from melted snow. We put everything we could fit into the clothes dryer and turned it to roll for an hour.

Our neighbors on both sides had been asked to guard us and watch the house (there were five of us kids, not counting Jules), so when it got late and the TV had signed off we put out the lights and had a fire in the fireplace instead. We didn't subscribe to cable, and Providence, where we lived, has no all-night channel on weekends (this was a Friday). Sometimes we could get Channel 5 from Boston, but not that night, not with the blizzard.

Hazel, who was the oldest of us, was happy about the fire but baffled about the television. Hazel was retarded. She'd get the show listings from the *Providence Journal* and underline what she wanted to see. To do this, she must have had some kind of coding system she'd memorized, because of course she couldn't read. This was the first time Hazel had ever been awake when the TV wasn't.

She watched the fireplace, and once when she saw an upshoot of flame she said, "The blue star!" which was what she called a beautiful blue ring that our mother wore. Hazel watched the fire some more and kept quiet enough. She had her texture board with her on her lap. "Smooth . . . grainy . . . soft," she recited, but just to herself, as she felt the different squares.

Terrence got on the telephone and called up a friend of his—Vic, who'd claimed he always stayed up all night. Terrence couldn't get anyone but Vic's very alarmed parents. He didn't give them his name. Terrence was also drinking a bottle of wine cooler—Father's—which wasn't allowed, but the rest of us had shared a can of beer earlier and now we were having coffee that we'd made in the drip machine, neither of which we were allowed to do, either. We figured we were all about even and no one would tell.

Hazel started to get annoying with her texture board. She had torn off the square of wide-wale corduroy, and she kept wanting the rest of us to feel the beads of rubber cement left on the backing. "Touch this," she said over and over to Willy, our other brother.

We took her to bed, to our parents' king-sized bed—which we thought would be all right this once. And Sarah, the baby, was there in bed already. At first Sarah pretended to be asleep while Hazel was undressing. She could undress herself if she stood before a mirror, and she knew to arch her back and work her hands behind to get her bra unhooked. She never wore clothing that looked retarded. In fact, whenever Father said to her, "How come you always look so pretty?" Hazel really would look pretty. She swung her arms when she walked, the same as the rest of us.

Sarah pretended to wake up suddenly. She wanted her cherry Chap Stick—her lips were so dry, she complained. Terrence must have heard Sarah—we were downstairs—because she was being so insistent. He called, "You left it out in the yard! You had it outside with you. You left it." Sarah believed Terrence, because his voice had authority. He was very attuned to voices, and he knew how to use his though he was only seventeen. He'd say to Hazel, "Don't sound like you're six years old. You're not six." Or if someone said just what was expected and predictable Terrence would ask, "Why should I listen when you're only making noise?"

Sarah wanted us to retrieve her Chap Stick. But the blizzard was still on, and nobody was going back out there, however sorry for her we felt. Most of the time when Sarah was outside, she'd kept her wool muffler over her mouth to protect it. Willy had to wrap it around her, under the hood of her parka, so it was just right. She had baby skin and the cold got to her.

Late in the night, Hazel punched Sarah in the face when they were supposed to be sleeping. Probably they were asleep, and Hazel was probably having a dream. Terrence was interested in dreams and wrote about his in a dream journal he kept. Sometimes he'd ask us questions about ours, or he'd talk to Mother and Father about the meaning of dreams. But he didn't ask Hazel if she was dreaming when she swung and socked Sarah.

We all talked at once: "I can't find a coat. . . . Wear mine. . . . Un unh, I *hate* that coat. . . . This is wet! . . . Go look in the dryer. . . . Get a blanket—get two! . . . No one will see you except maybe the doctor. . . . It makes virtually no *difference* what you're wearing or how you look. . . . Another towel for her nose! . . . Let's just get out of here."

Terrence warmed up the old Granada out on the street, where Father parked it because the driveway was snowed over. We left Hazel alone in our parents' bed, and we carried Sarah. We put her in the back, and then two of us got on either side of her. Sarah was covered up with a blanket and also Father's old topcoat.

The snow blew around in the headlights. No one else was out, and we urged Terrence to run the red lights. He said he couldn't af-ford to—his license was only a learner's permit. He also had a fake license from one of his friends, but the fake said Terrence was twenty-six, which wasn't believable. We begged him to put on some speed. We said that with a hurt person aboard, the police might even give us an escort through the storm. Terrence said, "Well, I checked her out and she's not that hurt, unfortunately."

A man walking his brown poodle loomed up beside us for a moment. The poodle was jumping around in the deep snow, loving it.

"Dog," Sarah said through her towel bandage. She was wide awake.

After the emergency room, we left Sarah on the car seat. She was out cold from the shot, even though the doctor said it was just to relax her. Her nose was nowhere near broken.

We'd driven awhile and then we hustled into an all-night pancake place, there off Thayer Street. Inside it was steamy and yellow-lit, although it felt a little underheated. We took over one side of an extra-long booth, each of us assuming giant seating space and sprawling convivially. Our arms were spread and they connected us to one another like paper dolls.

We spent time with the menu, reading aloud what side stuff came with the "Wedding Pancake," or with the "Great American-French Toast." Willy wanted a Sliced Turkey Dinner Platter, but Terrence said, "Don't get that. It's frozen. I mean frozen when served, as you're eating and trying to chew." The waitress approached, order pad in hand. She wore a carnation-pink dress for a uniform. We fidgeted in irrelevant ways, as if finding more comfortable spots on the booth seat. But we didn't whisper our orders. We acted important about our need for food. We'd been through an emergency.

After the waitress, we discussed what we'd tell Mother and Father, exactly. They'd be so busy anyway, we said, with baby Jules. They'd been busy already. Father had painted the nursery again, same as he'd done for each of us.

We wondered if washing-machine cold-water soap might remove the bloodstains Sarah had left on the pillowcase.

"We'll tell them . . ." Terrence said, but he couldn't finish. We pressed him. We wanted to know.

"O.K.," he said at last. "We just give them the truth. Describe how we seized control."

We said, "They're going to ask Sarah, and she'll say, 'Ask Hazel.'"

Our parents asked Hazel. She told them everything—all that she knew. She said, "Share. . . . Admit who won. . . . People look different at different ages. . . . Providence is the capital of Rhode Island. . . . Stand still in line. . . . Mother and Father have been alive a long time. . . . Don't pet strange animals. . . . Get someone to go with you. . . . Hold tight to the bus railing. . . . It is never all right to hit. . . . We have Eastern Standard Time. . . . Put baking soda on your bee stings. . . . Whatever Mother and Father tell you, believe them."

Grace Paley

Grace Paley was born in New York City in 1922. A graduate of Hunter College, also in New York, she has taught at Columbia University, Syracuse University, and Sarah Lawrence College in Bronxville, New York. Her short stories have been published in such magazines as The New Yorker, The Atlantic, *and* Esquire. *She is the author of three short story collections, published in 1959, 1974, and 1985; her collected stories were published in 1994. The following story is from her first collection,* The Little Disturbances of Man.

The Pale Pink Roast

Pale green greeted him, grubby buds for nut trees. Packed with lunch, Peter strode into the park. He kicked aside the disappointed acorns and endowed a grand admiring grin to two young girls.

Anna saw him straddling the daffodils, a rosy man in about the third flush of youth. He got into Judy's eye too. Acquisitive and quick, she screamed, "There's Daddy!"

Well, that's who he was, mouth open, addled by visions. He was unsettled by a collusion of charm, a conspiracy of curly hairdos and shiny faces. A year ago, in plain view, Anna had begun to decline into withering years, just as he swelled to the maximum of manhood, spitting pipe smoke, patched with tweed, an advertisement of a lover who startled men and detained the ladies.

Now Judy leaped over the back of a bench and lunged into his arms. "Oh, Peter dear," she whispered, "I didn't even know you were going to meet us."

"God, you're getting big, kiddo. Where's your teeth?" he asked. He hugged her tightly, a fifty-pound sack of his very own. "Say, Judy, I'm glad you still have a pussycat's sniffy nose and a pussycat's soft white fur."

"I do not," she giggled.

"Oh yes," he said. He dropped her to her springy hind legs but held onto one smooth front paw. "But you'd better keep your claws in or I'll drop you right into the Hudson River."

"Aw, Peter," said Judy, "quit it."

Peter changed the subject and turned to Anna. "You don't look half bad, you know."

"Thank you," she replied politely, "neither do you."

"Look at me, I'm a real outdoorski these days."

She allowed thirty seconds of silence, into which he turned, singing like a summer bird, "We danced around the Maypole, the Maypole, the Maypole . . .

"Well, when'd you get in?" he asked.

"About a week ago."

"You never called."

"Yes, I did, Peter. I called you at least twenty-seven times. You're never home. Petey must be in love somewhere, I said to myself."

"What is this thing," he sang in tune, "called love?"

"Peter, I want you to do me a favor," she started again. "Peter, could you take Judy for the weekend? We've just moved to this new place and I have a lot of work to do. I just don't want her in my hair. Peter?"

"Ah, that's why you called."

"Oh, for godsakes," Anna said. "I really called to ask you to become my lover. That's the real reason."

"O.K., O.K. Don't be bitter, Anna." He stretched forth a benedicting arm. "Come in peace, go in peace. Of course I'll take her. I like her. She's my kid."

"Bitter?" she asked.

Peter sighed. He turned the palms of his hands up as though to guess at rain. Anna knew him, theme and choreography. The sunshiny spring afternoon seeped through his fingers. He looked up at the witnessing heavens to keep what he could. He dropped his arms and let the rest go.

"O.K.," he said. "Let's go. I'd like to see your place. I'm full of ideas. You should see my living room, Anna. I might even go into interior decorating if things don't pick up. Come on. I'll get the ladder out of the basement. I could move a couple of trunks. I'm crazy about heavy work. You get out of life what you put into it. Right? Let's ditch the kid. I'm not your enemy."

"Who is?" she asked.

"Off my back, Anna. I mean it. I'll get someone to keep an eye on Judy. Just shut up." He searched for a familiar face among the Sunday strollers. "Hey, you," he finally called to an old pal on whom two chicks were leaning. "Hey, you glass-eyed louse, c'mere."

"Not just any of your idiot friends," whispered Anna, enraged.

All three soft-shoed it over to Peter. They passed out happy hellos, also a bag of dried apricots. Peter spoke to one of the girls. He patted her little-boy haircut. "Well, well, baby, you have certainly changed. You must have had a very good winter."

"Oh yes, thanks," she admitted.

"Say, be my friend, doll, will you? There's Judy over there. Remember? She was nuts about you when she was little. How about it? Keep an eye on her about an hour or two?"

"Sure, Petey, I'd love to. I'm not busy today. Judy! She was cute. I was nuts about her."

"Anna," said Peter, "this is Louie; she was a real friend that year you worked. She helped me out with Judy. She was great, a lifesaver."

"You're Anna," Louie said hospitably. "Oh, I think Judy's cute. We were nuts about each other. You have one smart kid. She's *really* smart."

"Thank you," said Anna.

Judy had gone off to talk to the ice cream man. She returned licking a double-lime Popsicle. "You have to give him ten cents," she said. "He didn't even remember me to give me trust."

Suddenly she saw Louie. "Oooh!" she shrieked. "It's Louie. Louie, Louie, Louie!" They pinched each other's cheeks, rubbed noses like the Eskimoses, and fluttered lashes like kissing angels do. Louie looked around proudly. "Gee whiz, the kid didn't forget me. How do you like that?"

Peter fished in his pockets for some change. Louie said, "Don't be ridiculous. It's on me." "O.K., girls," Peter said. "You two go on. Live it up. Eat supper out. Enjoy yourselves. Keep in touch."

"I guess they do know each other," said Anna, absolutely dispirited, waving goodbye.

"There!" said Peter. "If you want to do things, do things."

He took her arm. His other elbow cut their way through a gathering clutter of men and boys. "Going, going, gone," he said. "So long, fellows."

Within five minutes Anna unlocked the door of her new apartment, her snappy city leasehold, with a brand-new key.

In the wide foyer, on the parquet path narrowed by rows of cardboard boxes, Peter stood stock-still and whistled a dozen bars of Beethoven's Fifth Symphony. "Mama," he moaned in joy, "let me live!"

A vista of rooms and doors to rooms, double glass doors, single hard-oak doors, narrow closet doors, a homeful of rooms wired with hallways stretched before. "Oh, Anna, it's a far cry . . . Who's paying for it?"

"Not you; don't worry."

"That's not the point, Mary and Joseph!" He waved his arms at a chandelier. "Now, Anna, I like to see my friends set up this way. You think I'm kidding."

"*I'm* kidding," said Anna.

"Come on, what's really cooking? You look so great, you look like a chick on the sincere make. Playing it cool and living it warm, you know . . ."

"Quit dreaming, Petey," she said irritably. But he had stripped his back to his undershirt and had started to move records into record cabinets. He stopped to say, "How about me putting up the Venetian blinds?" Then she softened and offered one kindness: "Peter, you're the one who really looks wonderful. You look just— well—healthy."

"I take care of myself, Anna. That's why. Vegetables, high proteins. I'm not the night owl I was. Grapefruits, sunlight, oh sunlight, that's my dear love now."

"You always did take care of yourself, Peter."

"No, Anna, this is different." He stopped and settled on a box of curtains. "I mean it's not egocentric and selfish, the way I used to be. Now it has a real philosophical basis. Don't mix me up with biology. Look at me, what do you see?"

Anna had read that cannibals, tasting man, saw him thereafter as the great pig, the pale pink roast.

"Peter, Peter, pumpkin eater," Anna said.

"Ah no, that's not what I mean. You know what you see? A structure of flesh. You know when it hit me? About two years ago, around the time we were breaking up, you and me. I took my grandpa to the bathroom one time when I was over there visiting—you remember him, Anna, that old jerk, the one that was so mad, he didn't want to die. . . . I was leaning on the door; he was sitting on the pot concentrating on his guts. Just to make conversation—I thought it'd help him relax—I said, 'Pop? Pop, if you had it all to do over again, what would you do different? Any real hot tips?'

"He came up with an answer right away. 'Peter,' he said, 'I'd go to a gym every goddamn day of my life; the hell with the job, the hell with the women. Peter, I'd build my body up till God hisself wouldn't know how to tear it apart. Look at me Peter,' he said. 'I been a mean sonofabitch the last fifteen years. Why? I'll tell you why. This structure, this . . . this thing'—he pinched himself across his stomach and his knees—'this me'—he cracked himself sidewise across his jaw—'this is got to be maintained. The reason is, Peter: *It is the dwelling place of the soul.* In the end, long life is the reward, strength, and beauty.'"

"Oh, Peter!" said Anna. "Are you working?"

"Man," said Peter, "you got the same itsy-bitsy motivations. Of course I'm working. How the hell do you think I live? Did you get your eight-fifty a week out in Scroungeville or not?"

"Eight-fifty is right."

"O.K., O.K. Then listen. I have a vitamin compound that costs me twelve-eighty a hundred. Fifty dollars a year for basic maintenance and repair."

"Did the old guy die?"

"Mother! Yes! Of course he died."

"I'm sorry. He wasn't so bad. He liked Judy."

"Bad or good, Anna, he got his time in, he lived long enough to teach the next generation. By the way, I don't think you've put on an ounce."

"Thanks."

"And the kid looks great. You do take good care of her. You were always a good mother. I'll bet you broil her stuff and all."

"Sometimes," she said.

"Let her live in the air," said Peter. "I bet you do. Let her love her body."

"Let her," said Anna sadly.

"To work, to work, where strike committees shirk," sang Peter. "*Is* the ladder in the cellar?"

"No, no, in that kitchen closet. The real tall closet."

Then Peter put up the Venetian blinds, followed by curtains. He distributed books among the available bookcases. He glued the second drawer of Judy's bureau. Although all the furniture had not been installed, there were shelves for Judy's toys. He had no trouble with them at all. He whistled while he worked.

Then he swept the debris into a corner of the kitchen. He put a pot of coffee on the stove. "Coffee?" he called. "In a minute," Anna said. He stabilized the swinging kitchen door and came upon Anna, winding a clock in the living room whose wide windows on the world he had personally draped. "Busy, busy," he said.

Like a good and happy man increasing his virtue, he kissed her. She did not move away from him. She remained in the embrace of his right arm, her face nuzzling his shoulder, her eyes closed. He tipped her chin to look and measure opportunity. She could not open her eyes. Honorably he searched, but on her face he met no quarrel.

She was faint and leaden, a sure sign in Anna, if he remembered correctly, of passion. "Shall we dance?" he asked softly, a family joke. With great care, a patient lover, he undid the sixteen tiny buttons of her pretty dress and in Judy's room on Judy's bed he took her at once without a word. Afterward, having established tenancy, he rewarded her with kisses. But he dressed quickly because he was obligated by the stories of his life to remind her of transience.

"Petey," Anna said, having drawn sheets and blankets to her chin. "Go on into the kitchen. I think the coffee's all boiled out."

He started a new pot. Then he returned to help her with the innumerable little cloth buttons. "Say, Anna, this dress is wild. It must've cost a dime."

"A quarter," she said.

"You know, we could have some pretty good times together every now and then if you weren't so damn resentful."

"Did you have a real good time, Petey?"

"Oh, the best," he said, kissing her lightly. "You know, I like the way your hair is now," he said.

"I have it done once a week."

"Hey, say it pays, baby. It does wonders. What's up, what's up? That's what I want to know. Where'd the classy TV come from? And that fabulous desk . . . Say, somebody's an operator."

"My husband is," said Anna.

Petey sat absolutely still, but frowned, marking his clear fore-head with vertical lines of pain. Consuming the black fact, gritting his teeth to retain it, he said, "My God, Anna! That was a terrible thing to do."

"I thought it was so great."

"Oh, Anna, that's not the point. You should have said something first. Where is he? Where is this stupid sonofabitch while his wife is getting laid?"

"He's in Rochester. That's where I met him. He's a lovely person. He's moving his business. It takes time. Peter, please. He'll be here in a couple of days."

"You're great, Anna. Man, you're great. You wiggle your ass. You make a donkey out of me and him both. You could've said no. No—excuse me, Petey—no. I'm not that hard up. Why'd you do it? Revenge? Meanness? Why?"

He buttoned his jacket and moved among the cardboard boxes and the new chairs, looking for a newspaper or a package. He hadn't brought a thing. He stopped before the hallway mirror to brush his hair. "That's it!" he said, and walked slowly to the door.

"Where are you going, Peter?" Anna called across the foyer, a place for noisy children and forgotten umbrellas. "Wait a minute, Peter. Honest to God, listen to me, I did it for love."

He stopped to look at her. He looked at her coldly.

Anna was crying. "I really mean it, Peter, I did it for love."

"Love?" he asked. "Really?" He smiled. He was embarrassed but happy. "Well!" he said. With the fingers of both hands he tossed her a kiss.

"Oh, Anna, then good night," he said. "You're a good kid. Hon-est, I wish you the best, the best of everything, the very best."

In no time at all his cheerful face appeared at the door of the spring dusk. In the street among peaceable strangers he did a handstand. Then easy and impervious, in full control, he cart-wheeled eastward into the source of night.

John Cheever

John Cheever was born in Quincy, Massachusetts, in 1912 and went to school at Thayer Academy in South Braintree. He is the author of six collections of stories and four novels, as well as a memoir published after his death in 1982. His collected stories, published in 1978, received both the National Book Critics' Circle Award and the Pulitzer Prize. "The Death of Justina" originally appeared in Esquire *in 1960.*

The Death of Justina

So help me God it gets more and more preposterous, it corresponds less and less to what I remember and what I expect as if the force of life were centrifugal and threw one further and further away from one's purest memories and ambitions; and I can barely recall the old house where I was raised, where in midwinter Parma violets bloomed in a cold frame near the kitchen door, and down the long corridor, past the seven views of Rome—up two steps and down three—one entered the library, where all the books were in order, the lamps were bright, where there was a fire and a dozen bottles of good bourbon locked in a cabinet with a veneer like tortoise shell whose silver key my father wore on his watch chain. Fiction is art and art is the triumph over chaos (no less) and we can accomplish this only by the most vigilant exercise of choice, but in a world that changes more swiftly than we can perceive there is always the danger that our powers of selection will be mistaken and that the vision we serve will come to nothing. We admire decency and we despise death but even the mountains seem to shift in the space of a night and perhaps the exhibitionist at the corner of Chestnut and Elm streets is more significant than the lovely woman with a bar of sunlight in her hair, putting a fresh piece of cuttlebone in the nightingale's cage. Just let me give you one example of chaos and if you disbelieve me look honestly into your own past and see if you can't find a comparable experience. . . .

On Saturday the doctor told me to stop smoking and drinking and I did. I won't go into the commonplace symptoms of withdrawal but I would like to point out that, standing at my window in the evening, watching the brilliant afterlight and the spread of darkness, I felt, through the lack of these humble stimulants, the force of some primitive memory in which the coming of night with its stars and its moon was apocalyptic. I thought suddenly of the neglected graves of my three brothers on the mountainside and that death is a loneliness much crueler than any loneliness hinted at in life. The soul (I thought) does not leave the body but lingers with it through every degrading stage of decomposition and neglect, through heat, through cold, through the long winter nights when no one comes with a wreath or a plant and no one says a prayer. This unpleasant premonition was followed by anxiety. We were going out for dinner and I thought that the oil burner would explode in our absence and burn the house. The cook would get drunk and attack my daughter with a carving knife or my wife and I would be killed in a collision on the main highway, leaving our children bewildered orphans with nothing in life to look forward to but sadness. I was able to observe, along with these foolish and terrifying anxieties, a definite impairment of my discretionary poles. I felt as if I were being lowered by ropes into the atmosphere of my childhood. I told my wife—when she passed through the living room—that I had stopped smoking and drinking but she didn't seem to care and who would reward me for my privations? Who cared about the bitter taste in my mouth and that my head seemed to be leaving my shoulders? It seemed to me that men had honored one another with medals, statuary, and cups for much less and that abstinence is a social matter. When I abstain from sin it is more often a fear of scandal than a private resolve to improve on the purity of my heart, but here was a call for abstinence without the worldly enforcement of society, and death is not the threat that scandal is. When it was time for us to go out I was so light-headed that I had to ask my wife to drive the car. On Sunday I sneaked seven cigarettes in various hiding places and drank two Martinis in the downstairs coat closet. At breakfast on Monday my English muffin stared up at me from the plate. I mean I *saw* a face there in the rough, toasted surface. The moment of recognition was fleeting, but it was deep, and I wondered who it had been. Was it a friend, an aunt, a sailor, a ski instructor, a bartender, or a conductor on a train? The smile faded off the muffin but it had been there for a second—the sense of a person, a life, a pure force of gentleness and censure—and I am convinced that the muffin had contained the presence of some spirit. As you can see, I was nervous.

On Monday my wife's old cousin, Justina, came to visit her. Justina was a lively guest although she must have been crowding eighty. On Tuesday my wife gave her a lunch party. The last guest left at three and a few minutes later Cousin Justina, sitting on the living-room sofa with a glass of good brandy, breathed her last. My wife called me at the office and I said that I would be right out. I was clearing my desk when my boss, MacPherson, came in.

"Spare me a minute," he asked. "I've been bird-dogging all over the place, trying to track you down. Pierce had to leave early and I want you to write the last Elixircol commercial."

"Oh, I can't, Mac," I said. "My wife just called. Cousin Justina is dead."

"You write that commercial," he said. His smile was satanic. "Pierce had to leave early because his grandmother fell off a stepladder."

Now, I don't like fictional accounts of office life. It seems to me that if you're going to write fiction you should write about mountain climbing and tempests at sea, and I will go over my predicament with MacPherson briefly, aggravated as it was by his refusal to respect and honor the death of dear old Justina. It was like MacPherson. It was a good example of the way I've been treated. He is, I might say, a tall, splendidly groomed man of about sixty who changes his shirt three times a day, romances his secretary every afternoon between two and two-thirty, and makes the habit of continuously chewing gum seem hygienic and elegant. I write his speeches for him and it has not been a happy arrangement for me. If the speeches are successful MacPherson takes all the credit. I can see that his presence, his tailor, and his fine voice are all a part of the performance but it makes me angry never to be given credit for what was said. On the other hand, if the speeches are unsuccessful—if his presence and his voice can't carry the hour— his threatening and sarcastic manner is surgical and I am obliged to contain myself in the role of a man who can do no good in spite of the piles of congratulatory mail that my eloquence sometimes brings in. I must pretend—I must, like an actor, study and improve on my pretension—to have nothing to do with his triumphs, and I must bow my head gracefully in shame when we have both failed. I am forced to appear grateful for injuries, to lie, to smile falsely, and to play out a role as inane and as unrelated to the facts as a minor prince in an operetta, but if I speak the truth it will be my wife and my children who will pay in hardships for my outspokenness. Now he refused to respect or even to admit the solemn fact of a death in our family and if I couldn't rebel it seemed as if I could at least hint at it.

The commercial he wanted me to write was for a tonic called Elixircol and was to be spoken on television by an actress who was neither young nor beautiful but who had an appearance of ready abandon and who was anyhow the mistress of one of the sponsor's uncles. *Are you growing old?* I wrote. *Are you falling out of love with your image in the looking glass? Does your face in the morning seem rucked and seamed with alcoholic and sexual excesses and does the rest of you appear to be a grayish-pink lump, covered all over with brindle hair? Walking in the autumn woods do you feel that a subtle distance has come between you and the smell of wood smoke? Have you drafted your obituary? Are you easily winded? Do you wear a girdle? Is your sense of smell fading, is your interest in gardening waning, is your fear of heights increasing, and are your sexual drives as ravening and intense as ever and does your wife look more and more to you like a stranger with sunken cheeks who has wandered into your bedroom by mistake? If this or any of this is true you need Elixircol, the true juice of youth. The small economy size (business with the bottle) costs seventy-five dollars and the giant family bottle comes at two hundred and fifty. It's a lot of scratch, God knows, but these are inflationary times and who can put a price on youth? If you don't have the cash borrow it from your neighborhood loan shark or hold up the local bank. The odds are three to one that with a ten-cent water pistol and a slip of paper you can shake ten thousand out of any fainthearted teller. Everybody's doing it. (Music up and out.)* I sent this in to MacPherson via Ralphie, the messenger boy, and took the 4:16 home, traveling through a landscape of utter desolation.

Now, my journey is a digression and has no real connection to Justina's death but what followed could only have happened in my country and in my time and since I was an American traveling across an American landscape the trip may be part of the sum. There are some Americans who, although their fathers emigrated from the Old World three centuries ago, never seem to have quite completed the voyage and I am one of these. I stand, figuratively, with one wet foot on Plymouth Rock, looking with some delicacy, not into a formidable and challenging wilderness but onto a half-finished civilization embracing glass towers, oil derricks, suburban continents, and abandoned movie houses and wondering why, in this most prosperous, equitable, and accomplished world—where even the cleaning women practice the Chopin preludes in their spare time—everyone should seem to be disappointed.

At Proxmire Manor I was the only passenger to get off the random, meandering, and profitless local that carried its shabby lights off into the dusk like some game-legged watchman or beadle making his appointed rounds. I went around to the front of the station to wait for my wife and to enjoy the traveler's fine sense of crisis. Above me on the hill were my home and the homes of my friends, all lighted and smelling of fragrant wood smoke like the temples in a sacred grove, dedicated to monogamy, feckless childhood, and domestic bliss but so like a dream that I felt the lack of viscera with much more than poignance—the absence of that inner dynamism we respond to in some European landscapes. In short, I was disappointed. It was my country, my beloved country, and there have been mornings when I could have kissed the earth that covers its many provinces and states. There was a hint of bliss; romantic and domestic bliss. I seemed to hear the jinglebells of the sleigh that would carry me to Grandmother's house although in fact Grandmother spent the last years of her life working as a hostess on an ocean liner and was lost in the tragic sinking of the S.S. *Lorelei* and I was responding to a memory that I had not experienced. But the hill of light rose like an answer to some primitive dream of homecoming. On one of the highest lawns I saw the remains of a snowman who still smoked a pipe and wore a scarf and a cap but whose form was wasting away and whose anthracite eyes stared out at the view with terrifying bitterness. I sensed some disappointing greenness of spirit in the scene although I knew in my bones, no less, how like yesterday it was that my father left the Old World to found a new; and I thought of the forces that had brought stamina to the image: the cruel towns of Calabria and their cruel princes, the badlands northwest of Dublin, ghettos, despots, whorehouses, bread lines, the graves of children, intolerable hunger, corruption, persecution, and despair had generated these faint and mellow lights and wasn't it all a part of the great migration that is the life of man?

My wife's cheeks were wet with tears when I kissed her. She was distressed, of course, and really quite sad. She had been attached to Justina. She drove me home, where Justina was still sitting on the sofa. I would like to spare you the unpleasant details but I will say that both her mouth and her eyes were wide open. I went into the pantry to telephone Dr. Hunter. His line was busy. I poured myself a drink—the first since Sunday—and lighted a cigarette. When I called the doctor again he answered and I told him what had happened. "Well, I'm awfully sorry to hear about it, Moses," he said. "I can't get over until after six and there isn't much that I can do. This sort of thing has come up before and I'll tell you all I know. You see, you live in Zone B—two-acre lots, no commercial enterprises and so forth. A couple of years ago some stranger bought the old Plewett mansion and it turned out that he was planning to operate it as a funeral home. We didn't have any zoning provision at the time that would protect us and one was rushed through the Village Council at midnight and they overdid it. It seems that you not only can't have a funeral home in Zone B—you can't bury anything there and you can't die there. Of course it's absurd, but we all make mistakes, don't we? Now there are two things you can do. I've had to deal with this before. You can take the old lady and put her into the car and drive her over to Chestnut Street, where Zone C begins. The boundary is just beyond the traffic light by the high school. As soon as you get her over to Zone C, it's all right. You can just say she died in the car. You can do that or if this seems distasteful you can call the Mayor and ask him to make an exception to the zoning laws. But I can't write you out a death certificate until you get her out of that neighborhood and of course no undertaker will touch her until you get a death certificate."

"I don't understand," I said, and I didn't, but then the possibility that there was some truth in what he had just told me broke against me or over me like a wave, exciting mostly indignation. "I've never heard such a lot of damned foolishness in my life," I said. "Do you mean to tell me that I can't die in one neighborhood and that I can't fall in love in another and that I can't eat . . ."

"Listen. Calm down, Moses. I'm not telling you anything but the facts and I have a lot of patients waiting. I don't have the time to listen to you fulminate. If you want to move her, call me as soon as you get her over to the traffic light. Otherwise, I'd advise you to get in touch with the Mayor or someone on the Village Council." He cut the connection. I was outraged but this did not change the fact that Justina was still sitting on the sofa. I poured a fresh drink and lit another cigarette.

Justina seemed to be waiting for me and to be changing from an inert into a demanding figure. I tried to imagine carrying her out to the station wagon but I couldn't complete the task in my imagination and I was sure that I couldn't complete it in fact. I then called the Mayor but this position in our village is mostly honorary and as I might have known he was in his New York law office and was not expected home until seven. I could cover her, I thought, that would be a decent thing to do, and I went up the back stairs to the linen closet and got a sheet. It was getting dark when I came back into the living room but this was no merciful twilight. Dusk seemed to be playing directly into her hands and she gained power and stature with the dark. I covered her with a sheet and turned on a lamp at the other end of the room but the rectitude of the place with its old furniture, flowers, paintings, etc., was demolished by her monumental shape. The next thing to worry about was the children, who would be home in a few minutes. Their knowledge of death, excepting their dreams and intuitions of which I know nothing, is zero and the bold figure in the parlor was bound to be traumatic. When I heard them coming up the walk I went out and told them what had happened and sent them up to their rooms. At seven I drove over to the Mayor's.

He had not come home but he was expected at any minute and I talked with his wife. She gave me a drink. By this time I was chain-smoking. When the Mayor came in we went into a little office or library, where he took up a position behind a desk, putting me in the low chair of a supplicant. "Of course I sympathize with you, Moses," he said, "it's an awful thing to have happened, but the trouble is that we can't give you a zoning exception without a majority vote of the Village Council and all the members of the Council happen to be out of town. Pete's in California and Jack's in Paris and Larry won't be back from Stowe until the end of the week."

I was sarcastic. "Then I suppose Cousin Justina will have to gracefully decompose in my parlor until Jack comes back from Paris."

"Oh no," he said, "oh *no*. Jack won't be back from Paris for another month but I think you might wait until Larry comes from

Stowe. Then we'd have a majority, assuming of course that they would agree to your appeal."

"For Christ's sake," I snarled.

"Yes, yes," he said, "it is difficult, but after all you must realize that this is the world you live in and the importance of zoning can't be overestimated. Why, if a single member of the Council could give out zoning exceptions, I could give you permission right now to open a saloon in your garage, put up neon lights, hire an orchestra, and destroy the neighborhood and all the human and commercial values we've worked so hard to protect."

"I don't want to open a saloon in my garage," I howled. "I don't want to hire an orchestra. I just want to bury Justina."

"I know, Moses, I know," he said. "I understand that. But it's just that it happened in the wrong zone and if I make an exception for you I'll have to make an exception for everyone and this kind of morbidity, when it gets out of hand, can be very depressing. People don't like to live in a neighborhood where this sort of thing goes on all the time."

"Listen to me," I said. "You give me an exception and you give it to me now or I'm going home and dig a hole in my garden and bury Justina myself."

"But you can't do that, Moses. You can't bury anything in Zone B. You can't even bury a cat."

"You're mistaken," I said. "I can and I will. I can't function as a doctor and I can't function as an undertaker, but I can dig a hole in the ground and if you don't give me my exception, that's what I'm going to do."

"Come back, Moses, come back," he said. "Please come back. Look, I'll give you an exception if you'll promise not to tell anyone. It's breaking the law, it's a forgery but I'll do it if you promise to keep it a secret."

I promised to keep it a secret, he gave me the documents, and I used his telephone to make the arrangements. Justina was removed a few minutes after I got home but that night I had the strangest dream. I dreamed that I was in a crowded supermarket. It must have been night because the windows were dark. The ceiling was paved with fluorescent light—brilliant, cheerful but, considering our prehistoric memories, a harsh link in the chain of light that binds us to the past. Music was playing and there must have been at least a thousand shoppers pushing their wagons among the long

corridors of comestibles and victuals. Now is there—or isn't there—
something about the posture we assume when we push a wagon
that unsexes us? Can it be done with gallantry? I bring this up because the multitude of shoppers seemed that evening, as they
pushed their wagons, penitential and unsexed. There were all
kinds, this being my beloved country. There were Italians, Finns,
Jews, Negroes, Shropshiremen, Cubans—anyone who had heeded
the voice of liberty—and they were dressed with that sumptuary
abandon that European caricaturists record with such bitter disgust. Yes, there were grandmothers in shorts, big-butted women in
knitted pants, and men wearing such an assortment of clothing
that it looked as if they had dressed hurriedly in a burning building. But this, as I say, is my own country and in my opinion the car-
icaturist who vilifies the old lady in shorts vilifies himself. I am a
native and I was wearing buckskin jump boots, chino pants cut so
tight that my sexual organs were discernible, and a rayon-acetate
pajama top printed with representations of the *Pinta*, the *Niña*, and
the *Santa María* in full sail. The scene was strange—the strangeness
of a dream where we see familiar objects in an unfamiliar light—
but as I looked more closely I saw that there were some irregulari-
ties. Nothing was labeled. Nothing was identified or known. The
cans and boxes were all bare. The frozen-food bins were full of
brown parcels but they were such odd shapes that you couldn't tell
if they contained a frozen turkey or a Chinese dinner. All the goods
at the vegetable and the bakery counters were concealed in brown
bags and even the books for sale had no titles. In spite of the fact
that the contents of nothing was known, my companions of the
dream—my thousands of bizarrely dressed compatriots—were de-
liberating gravely over these mysterious containers as if the choices
they made were critical. Like any dreamer, I was omniscient, I was
with them and I was withdrawn, and stepping above the scene for
a minute I noticed the men at the check-out counters. They were
brutes. Now, sometimes in a crowd, in a bar or a street, you will
see a face so full-blown in its obdurate resistance to the appeals of
love, reason, and decency, so lewd, so brutish and unregenerate,
that you turn away. Men like these were stationed at the only way
out and as the shoppers approached them they tore their packages
open—I still couldn't see what they contained—but in every case
the customer, at the sight of what he had chosen, showed all the
symptoms of the deepest guilt; that force that brings us to our

knees. Once their choice had been opened to their shame they were pushed—in some cases kicked—toward the door and beyond the door I saw dark water and heard a terrible noise of moaning and crying in the air. They waited at the door in groups to be taken away in some conveyance that I couldn't see. As I watched, thousands and thousands pushed their wagons through the market, made their careful and mysterious choices, and were reviled and taken away. What could be the meaning of this?

We buried Justina in the rain the next afternoon. The dead are not, God knows, a minority, but in Proxmire Manor their unexalted kingdom is on the outskirts, rather like a dump, where they are transported furtively as knaves and scoundrels and where they lie in an atmosphere of perfect neglect. Justina's life had been exemplary, but by ending it she seemed to have disgraced us all. The priest was a friend and a cheerful sight, but the undertaker and his helpers, hiding behind their limousines, were not; and aren't they at the root of most of our troubles, with their claim that death is a violet-flavored kiss? How can a people who do not mean to understand death hope to understand love, and who will sound the alarm?

I went from the cemetery back to my office. The commercial was on my desk and MacPherson had written across it in grease pencil: *Very funny, you broken-down bore. Do again.* I was tired but unrepentant and didn't seem able to force myself into a practical posture of usefulness and obedience. I did another commercial. *Don't lose your loved ones,* I wrote, *because of excessive radioactivity. Don't be a wallflower at the dance because of strontium 90 in your bones. Don't be a victim of fallout. When the tart on Thirty-sixth Street gives you the big eye does your body stride off in one direction and your imagination in another? Does your mind follow her up the stairs and taste her wares in revolting detail while your flesh goes off to Brooks Brothers or the foreign exchange desk of the Chase Manhattan Bank? Haven't you noticed the size of the ferns, the lushness of the grass, the bitterness of the string beans, and the brilliant markings on the new breeds of butterflies? You have been inhaling lethal atomic waste for the last twenty-five years and only Elixircol can save you.* I gave this to Ralphie and waited perhaps ten minutes, when it was returned, marked again with grease pencil. *Do,* he wrote, *or you'll be dead.* I felt very tired. I put another piece of paper into the machine and wrote: *The Lord is my shepherd; therefore can I lack nothing. He shall feed me in a green pasture and lead me forth beside the waters of comfort. He shall convert my soul and bring me forth in the paths of righteousness for his Name's sake. Yea, though I walk through the valley of the shadow of death I will fear no evil for thou art with me; thy rod and thy staff comfort me. Thou shalt prepare a table before me in the presence of them that trouble me; thou hast anointed my head with oil and my cup shall be full. Surely thy loving-kindness and mercy shall follow me all the days of my life and I will dwell in the house of the Lord for ever.* I gave this to Ralphie and went home.

ALTERNATIVE
FORMS OF FICTION

While the composition of short stories is the primary arena in which fiction writers develop their craft, you may choose to explore other forms. You may feel uncomfortable with the form of short fiction, or you may seek a distinct form for a particular project. For instance, a writer constructing a fiction in the form of a class-notes column in a university alumni magazine may produce a piece that is markedly shorter than most short fiction, that is, *short-short fiction*. Someone writing about the history of a Southern family may find the short-story form too restrictive, and turn instead to the *novel*.

SHORT-SHORT FICTION

The sole distinction between short fiction and short-short fiction is an obvious one: short-short fiction is shorter. Contemporary editors and writers place the average length of a short-short fiction somewhere between 1,250 and 2,300 words. For the sake of discussion, let's call a short-short piece of fiction any story with fewer than 1,500 words, and with no minimum limit.

Writers have always been writing short-shorts. Isaac Babel was perhaps the most noted and least self-conscious practitioner of the form. Tolstoy, author of *War and Peace* and *Anna Karenina,* wrote short-shorts. Joyce Carol Oates writes short-shorts, as does Denis Johnson. Perhaps writers write short-shorts because they give more of an immediate pay-off, or because they allow for greater experimentation. Interesting forms of fiction—such as a story in the form of an obituary, a resume, a recipe, or the acknowledgements section of a book—are easier to sustain in the length of a short-short.

While you can do almost anything with a short-short, it still has to be a story. A short-short generally contains all the elements of fiction that standard-length stories contain; it just accomplishes fiction in a shorter amount of space. In fact, if what most impresses you about a short-short is its brevity, then it probably is not a strong story. A good short-short contains all the music and complexity of longer fiction, and as such its length becomes practically unnoticeable: the story itself transcends the superficial limitation of its few pages. Successful practitioners of the short-short do not necessarily approach the blank page with a short-short in mind. As Stephen Dixon, author of a few novels, hundreds of short stories, and dozens of short-shorts, says, the story determines its own length, not the writer.

There are, however, several strategies for deliberate entry into the form. One approach is to choose a form of writing, any form, and work to create a fiction within it. Try to write a story in the form of a letter of complaint, the ingredients label of a canned good, or an explanatory sign at a landmark. The very nature of these forms makes it difficult to sustain them at length. The content of this approach can either work within the form, such as a letter of complaint about an imaginary product purchased; or it can work against the form, such as a letter of complaint about the weather. Either way, working in this form will reveal the character of the narrator that you have chosen, and in that way you can begin to tell a story. Consider, for example, the following excerpt from "Class Notes" by Lucas Cooper:

> RICHARD ENDERGEL phoned a few weeks ago from Houston, under arrest for possession of cocaine—third time since 1974. Richard thinks this is it. Unless a miracle happens he is looking at 15 years or more for dealing in a controlled substance. STANFORD CRIBBS, mangled practically beyond recognition in an automobile accident in 1979, took his own life on March 19, according to a clipping from the Kansas City *Star*. His former roommate, BRISTOL LANSFORD, has fared no better.

A second approach is to select an image and "overfocus" on it, either in depth or in breadth. A depth overfocus, for example, could examine the story behind a single chair or a single button or a single head of lettuce or a single loaf of bread (such as Joanna Wos explores in "The One Sitting There"). A breadth overfocus, on the other hand, could examine through association a number of chairs or a number of buttons or a number of heads of lettuce. Here's a portion of a short-short fiction by Lydia Davis called "The Sock":

> It was a small thing, but later I couldn't forget the sock, because here was this one sock in his back pocket in a strange neighborhood way out in the eastern part of the city in a Vietnamese ghetto, by the massage parlors, and none of us really knew this city but we were all here together and it was odd, because I still felt as though he and I were partners, we had been partners a long time, and I couldn't help thinking of all the other socks of his I had picked up, stiff with his sweat and threadbare on the sole, in all our life together from place to place, and then of his feet in those socks, how the skin shone through at the ball of the foot and the heel. . . .

Through overfocusing, other images can emerge, and allow the story to grow beyond its initial limitations.

Another strategy is to repeat a statement that requires elaboration. For example, if you begin a story with "I hate . . ." and elaborate on that, then return to "I hate" and elaborate again, and continue the process until you have exhausted yourself, then you may create a kind of short-short. The process creates the potential for other repetitions to emerge, such as in Jamaica Kincaid's "Girl," where the author uses numerous repetitive phrases to extend her story and reveal the character of the narrator.

A final exercise in short-short fiction is to compress time. Begin a story with a sentence regarding one time frame, then allow the next sentence to "leap" into another time frame, and the sentence beyond that to leap to a further time frame. For example, you can begin: "We are married. We have a baby boy. The girl is born without ears." Don't bother pointing out to the reader the actual time leapt—let that emerge implicitly through gesture and detail. The time leap can extend itself several ways. You can continue time leaping until you can go no further in time (for example, "I die" could be the last extension of the above attempt). You can continue time leaping until you find the frame of time within which the narrative wants to linger (the author of the above story fragment, for instance, could pause after "the girl was born without ears," and describe the reaction of the parents).

A number of intriguing exercises exist to edit any standard-length fiction into a shorter form. You could cut opening paragraphs until you reach the essential action of the story; or you could cut back from closing paragraphs until you reach a critical action and the mere hint of resolution. You could also cut both opening and closing paragraphs in order to isolate as much as possible the apex of Freytag's Triangle. Kate Chopin's "The Story of an Hour" and David Foster Wallace's "Everything Is Green" achieve this dramatic spareness. You could also cut the excess of paragraphs themselves, and allow the story to emerge through carefully or even randomly selected sentences: reconstruct a long story through only the opening sentence of each of its paragraphs, or only the most essential single sentence of each of its paragraphs, or only the closing sentence of each of its paragraphs. While a great short-short may not result from these deletions, the core of the story may reveal itself in a new way.

Short-shorts can also be useful in constructing longer work. You can use a voice or a technique from a short-short to tell a longer, entirely different story. You can use the short-short as a warm-up for a later approach to a longer piece of fiction. You can also take characters you've created in short-shorts and recreate them in longer stories. If your short-short contains any compression of time, you can get between these time sequences and slow down time, and thereby extend the short-short from within itself. Sequences such as "I hit him. He hit me," can be extended to allow more detail and gesture in between the words of each sentence and the space between sentences. You can also go beyond the initial ending of your short-short and release it into the world of a longer fiction.

Writing Strategies

1. Choose a form of writing, any form, and work to create a fiction within it. Try to write a story in the form of an office memorandum, assembly instructions for a piece of furniture, a newspaper article.

   a. Work with content true to the form, such as an office memo about using the photocopier.

b. Work with content that seems fantastic for the form, such as an office memo about how to cheat a client successfully.

What does the content of the form reveal about the personality of the narrator? In what way does the form tell a story? Does it tell enough of a story to move the reader?

2. Select an image and "overfocus" on it.

a. Try a depth overfocus, to examine the story behind a single table or a single glove or a single radish.

b. Try a breadth overfocus, to examine through association a number of tables or gloves or radishes.

Do other images emerge? Does the story grow beyond its initial limitation of just one image?

3. Observe how Jamaica Kincaid's "Girl" uses the device of repetition. In a story of your own, repeat a statement that requires elaboration. Does the process of repetition lead to an exhaustion of the phrase? Does it allow other repetitions to emerge? How is the result a story?

4. Begin a story with a sentence focusing on one time frame, then allow the next sentence to "leap" into another time frame, and the sentence beyond that to leap to a further time frame.

a. Continue time leaping until you can go no further in time.

b. Continue time leaping until you find the frame of time where you want the narrative to linger.

Do the time leaps emerge implicitly through gesture and detail? Does the process extend itself to a natural conclusion?

5. Consider the following strategies for shortening a story you have already written.

a. Cut opening paragraphs until you reach the essential action. Let the story start there and see how it reads.

b. Cut back from the closing paragraphs until you reach a critical apex of action and the hint of resolution.

c. Cut both opening and closing paragraphs to seek to isolate as much as possible the apex of Freytag's Triangle.

d. Cut the excess of paragraphs themselves, and allow the story to emerge through carefully or even randomly selected sentences.

e. Reconstruct a long story through only the opening sentence of each of its paragraphs.

   f. Reconstruct a long story taking only the most essential single
      sentence of each of its paragraphs.
   g. Reconstruct a long story taking only the closing sentence of
      each of its paragraphs.

What emerges from these exercises? Does one particular approach
seem more effective than others? How so?

6. Consider the following strategies for extending a short-short
fiction you have already written.

   a. Use the voice or a technique from a short-short you've writ-
      ten to tell a longer, entirely different story.
   b. Take characters you've created in short-shorts and recreate
      them in longer stories.
   c. If you have a short-short that contains any compression of
      time, get between these time sequences and slow down time,
      and thereby extend the short-short from within itself.
   d. Extend the initial ending of your short-short.

THE NOVEL

The novel is the longest form of fiction, and many writers have at-
tempted to make it even longer, through the development of mul-
tivolume narratives (Proust's *The Remembrance of Things Past,* for
instance) and novels that are linked to other novels (the trilogies of
Robertson Davies and Lawrence Durrell, the trilogy-in-progress
by Cormac McCarthy). Classic as well as contemporary novels have
also been as short as one hundred pages (*Candide,* by Voltaire; *Damage,* by Josephine Hart), and are sometimes defined as *novellas,* or
short novels.

   The best way to develop an understanding of novel construction
is to read widely and thoroughly in the form. All the distinctions
within the range of story-writing apply, but especially important
is that different novelists deal very differently with time. The first
pages of Jeanette Winterson's *Oranges Are Not the Only Fruit* occur
in a generalized time of early childhood, told from the point of
view of an older narrator. Scott Bradfield begins *The History of Luminous Motion* by offering a series of observations from a young
narrator about one particular summer. Whereas Winterson's first
chapter suggests a large coming-of-age time frame for the entire

book, Bradfield promises a novel that will deal with just one summer. Fitzgerald's *The Great Gatsby*, a relatively short novel, is also set over an entire summer, but for the most part examines only four particular days within that summer. Hart's *Damage*, an extraordinarily short novel, follows events that occur over a number of years, and touches down in brief key scenes that forward plot and extend character. Robert Stone's *A Flag for Sunrise* is, at 400-plus pages, a considerably longer novel, but details the events of only a single week. Scene selection and scene extension—in which critical interactions unfold more slowly and the reader is privy to a greater amount of sensory detail and interior thought—occur uniquely within each fiction's particular time frame, and have as much to do with the nature of the characters as with authorial vision. If fiction focuses on how characters act over time, the length of that time does not necessarily affect the length of the fiction.

While there will not be a novel that has the precise structure and voice as your intended novel, there will be approximations from which you can learn and build. You might read novels in your area of interest, such as coming-of-age stories, novels with exotic settings, or novels about family conflict. You can examine novels for technique, such as a first-person voice looking back on a period of a hundred years, or multiple first-person voices that drive the novel in present tense, or a third-person voice with multiple interiors. You might consider the impulses for writing a novel. What can the novel accomplish that a short story can't? What pressures exist in the Winterson and Bradfield excerpts that seem to call for a long work of fiction? How might your concerns or writing style be well suited to a longer work?

The majority of fiction writers attempt the novel at one point or another in their careers, and some even attempt *only* novels. Preeminent short-story writers (James Joyce, Ernest Hemingway, William Faulkner) have also distinguished themselves as novelists, while other fiction writers have met with limited success in switching between the forms. Ability in either form is based on any number of factors. Temperament is often cited: novelists are more patient writers inclined to dwell upon characters and scenes; short-story writers are in a rush to get to the essence of event and character. But as James Joyce, Edith Wharton, Denis Johnson, and any number of others have demonstrated, writers can be both good novelists and good short fictionists.

For story writers embarking on their first novels, a good piece of advice may be: Don't let the length of the form overwhelm you. If you are writing strong short fiction, take your technique with you. Proceed with the same mixture of caution and conviction that characterizes your other work. In *The Plague,* by Albert Camus, a tragicomic character agonizes about his own novel, and becomes so obsessed with making the first sentence perfect, that it is all he writes—the first sentence, hundreds of times, in hundreds of variations. Short-story writers can experience a similar block, becoming so overwhelmed by the immensity of the task, that they change their technique to suit the immensity. In the novel, it is not necessarily the voice of your writing that has to change to accomplish the task; it is the scope of your writing, your ability to develop characters in greater depth, and your ability to explore more of the world where they live.

If you do feel an inclination to overreach when switching from writing short fiction to the novel, you can try breaking up the draft of your novel into chapters or sections, not moving on with the next chapter until you're satisfied with the previous one. It may be a good idea to keep rewriting the first chapter or section of your novel until you are comfortable with the voice, because your confidence and control of the voice—your authority—are critical to the success of the story. You can also build a mosaic of structure that allows you to move from character to character, or scene to scene, spending a section on each—as if each were a contained fiction. In this vein, you can study story cycles, novels that build carefully on an arrangement of individual and yet connected stories, novels such as *Winesburg, Ohio* by Sherwood Anderson, or *Monkeys* by Susan Minot. Investigating how the story cycle differs from other novel structures, and assessing these approaches, will tell you much about how you feel about embarking on a novel and which type of novel you are inclined to write.

Beginning a novel, you might meditate on a particular idea for years before setting down a single word on the page. Or you might experience sudden inspiration and draft an entire novel quickly. Some writers laboriously research their novels and are careful to visit their settings, while others (such as Stanley Elkin) just get on with the writing. You can find your first novel in a brief scene you once witnessed, as William Styron did with

Sophie's Choice, or you can find it in a short story you've written that you want to extend (or dig to the core of, or explore within a time frame that occurs before the story even begins), or you can find it in a newspaper article (as Toni Morrison did with *Beloved*). An important point to consider is to write about characters and events that you care about, because you will be spending a lot of time with them.

From a writer's point of view, the most fundamental way that the novel differs from the short story is in the work process. Because of its length, the novel simply cannot be written over the relatively short period of time in which stories can be drafted. The time required for drafting a novel may cause you to reexamine your writing routine. Some novelists write daily, at the same time each day, to allow themselves access to the same frame of mind to ensure continuity of voice and of vision. Other novelists lock themselves away for as long as possible, in search of producing a more organic result. William Faulkner, for example, wrote *As I Lay Dying* in six weeks.

After composing and reading the first chapter or the first segment of your novel, you may discover that you need a new approach, that you have lost continuity. On the other hand, you may feel that rereading the novel during its composition would be unfruitful or potentially inhibiting, and that you prefer to wait until the end to see what you've got. Regardless of which approach you choose, you should allow yourself to step back, at one point or another, and evaluate as objectively as possible how the approach is working for you. "A novel is really like a symphony, you know," Katherine Anne Porter told *The Paris Review*, "where instrument after instrument has to come in at its own time, and no other." Your concern for overall dramatic structure, and for issues of time and pacing, will lead you to methods of evaluation throughout the writing process.

Writing Strategies

1. Take a character or set of characters from a story you've written and try to imagine them on a larger canvas.

    a. Consider your characters over a broader period of time, including both before the time in which the story occurs and after the ending of the story. Is there anything on either end of the temporal spectrum that strikes you as particularly appealing? How does this reenvisioning of your characters alter their development as set out in your story?

b. Consider the story occurring in a larger arena, one that incorporates a greater complexity of human life: the workplace, the family, leisure time, daily living with all its requirements. Does anything strike you as particularly compelling in this new breadth? Are there blank spaces between the actions of your story that offer opportunity?

c. Examine the possibility that more complex interaction might occur between the characters. Get into the spaces between lines of dialogue, between critical gestures, and consider expanding both the exterior and interior of your characters—including what they say, do, and think. Does the storyline have an ambitious enough character interplay to bear the weight of the novel?

2. Take a situation you've written about and try to enlarge it by adding a greater level of detail or more characters, or by slowing down the passage of time within which it takes place. What is happening to the characters, to the style, and to the vision of the piece? Does this type of approach enlarge your writing in a useful and effective way?

3. Look at a story you've written as a potential first chapter for a novel. What possibilities for the future lives of your characters can you imagine? What aspects of their pasts seem to unfold and deserve attention?

4. When writing a novel, vary your technique, just to see where it takes you. If you're writing page by page, try to see ahead to larger actions that await your characters. If you're writing from a carefully detailed outline, diverge from it, allowing your characters the opportunity to surprise you.

5. Read five different novels, making notes on each. How long is the time period each covers? In what context are specific scenes occurring? How is the novel proceeding from scene to scene? How would you characterize the voice and structure of each novel? What do the five novels seem to have in common? What distinguishes each of them from the others?

Jeanette Winterson

"Genesis" is the opening chapter of Jeanette Winterson's novel Oranges Are Not the Only Fruit, *winner of the Whitbread First Novel Award for England and Ireland in 1985. Winterson was born in 1959 in Manchester, England, and received a degree in English from St. Catherine's College, Oxford University. She also has written the novels* The Passion *(1987),* Sexing the Cherry *(winner of the E. M. Forster Award of the American Academy of Arts and Letters for 1989), and* Written on the Body *(1993).*

Genesis

Like most people I lived for a long time with my mother and father. My father liked to watch the wrestling, my mother liked to wrestle; it didn't matter what. She was in the white corner and that was that.

She hung out the largest sheets on the windiest days. She *wanted* the Mormons to knock on the door. At election time in a Labour mill town she put a picture of the Conservative candidate in the window.

She had never heard of mixed feelings. There were friends and there were enemies.

Enemies were:　The Devil (in his many forms)
　　　　　　　　Next Door
　　　　　　　　Sex (in its many forms)
　　　　　　　　Slugs
Friends were:　God
　　　　　　　　Our dog
　　　　　　　　Auntie Madge
　　　　　　　　The Novels of Charlotte Brontë
　　　　　　　　Slug pellets

and me, at first. I had been brought in to join her in a tag match against the Rest of the World. She had a mysterious attitude towards the begetting of children; it wasn't that she couldn't do it, more that she didn't want to do it. She was very bitter about the

Virgin Mary getting there first. So she did the next best thing and arranged for a foundling. That was me.

I cannot recall a time when I did not know that I was special. We had no Wise Men because she didn't believe there were any wise men, but we had sheep. One of my earliest memories is me sitting on a sheep at Easter while she told me the story of the Sacrificial Lamb. We had it on Sundays with potato.

Sunday was the Lord's day, the most vigorous day of the whole week; we had a radiogram at home with an imposing mahogany front and a fat Bakelite knob to twiddle for the stations. Usually we listened to the Light Programme, but on Sundays always the World Service, so that my mother could record the progress of our missionaries. Our Missionary Map was very fine. On the front were all the countries and on the back a number chart that told you about Tribes and their Peculiarities. My favourite was Number 16, *The Buzule of Carpathian.* They believed that if a mouse found your hair clippings and built a nest with them you got a headache. If the nest was big enough, you might go mad. As far as I knew no missionary had yet visited them.

My mother got up early on Sundays and allowed no one into the parlour until ten o'clock. It was her place of prayer and meditation. She always prayed standing up, because of her knees, just as Bonaparte always gave orders from his horse, because of his size. I do think that the relationship my mother enjoyed with God had a lot to do with positioning. She was Old Testament through and through. Not for her the meek and paschal Lamb, she was out there, up front with the prophets, and much given to sulking under trees when the appropriate destruction didn't materialise. Quite often it did, her will or the Lord's I can't say.

She always prayed in exactly the same way. First of all she thanked God that she had lived to see another day, and then she thanked God for sparing the world another day. Then she spoke of her enemies, which was the nearest thing she had to a catechism.

As soon as "Vengeance is mine saith the Lord" boomed through the wall into the kitchen, I put the kettle on. The time it took to boil the water and brew the tea was just about the length of her final item, the sick list. She was very regular. I put the milk in, in she came, and taking a great gulp of tea said one of three things.

"The Lord is good" (steely-eyed into the back yard).

"What sort of tea is this?" (steely-eyed at me).

"Who was the oldest man in the Bible?"

No. 3, of course, had a number of variations, but it was always a Bible quiz question. We had a lot of Bible quizzes at church and my mother liked me to win. If I knew the answer she asked me another, if I didn't she got cross, but luckily not for long, because we had to listen to the World Service. It was always the same; we sat down on either side of the radiogram, she with her tea, me with a pad and pencil; in front of us, the Missionary Map. The faraway voice in the middle of the set gave news of activities, converts and problems. At the end there was an appeal for YOUR PRAYERS. I had to write it all down so that my mother could deliver her church report that night. She was the Missionary Secretary. The Missionary Report was a great trial to me because our mid-day meal depended upon it. If it went well, no deaths and lots of converts, my mother cooked a joint. If the Godless had proved not only stubborn, but murderous, my mother spent the rest of the morning listening to the Jim Reeves Devotional Selection, and we had to have boiled eggs and toast soldiers. Her husband was an easy-going man, but I knew it depressed him. He would have cooked it himself but for my mother's complete conviction that she was the only person in our house who could tell a saucepan from a piano. She was wrong, as far as we were concerned, but right as far as she was concerned, and really, that's what mattered.

Somehow we got through those mornings, and in the afternoon she and I took the dog for a walk, while my father cleaned all the shoes. "You can tell someone by their shoes," my mother said. "Look at Next Door."

"Drink," said my mother grimly as we stepped out past their house. "That's why they buy everything from Maxi Ball's Catalogue Seconds. The Devil himself is a drunk" (sometimes my mother invented theology).

Maxi Ball owned a warehouse, his clothes were cheap but they didn't last, and they smelt of industrial glue. The desperate, the careless, the poorest, vied with one another on a Saturday morning to pick up what they could, and haggle over the price. My mother would rather not eat than be seen at Maxi Ball's. She had filled me with a horror of the place. Since so many people we knew went there, it was hardly fair of her but she never was particularly fair; she loved and she hated, and she hated Maxi Ball. Once, in winter, she had been forced to go there to buy a corset and in the middle of communion, that very Sunday, a piece of whalebone slipped out and stabbed her right in the stomach. There was nothing she could do for an hour. When we got home she tore up the corset and used the whalebone as supports for our geraniums, except for one piece that she gave to me. I still have it, and whenever I'm tempted to cut corners I think about that whalebone, and I know better.

My mother and I walked on towards the hill that stood at the top of our street. We lived in a town stolen from the valleys, a huddled place full of chimneys and little shops and back-to-back houses with no gardens. The hills surrounded us, and our own swept out into the Pennines, broken now and again with a farm or a relic from the war. There used to be a lot of old tanks but the council took them away. The town was a fat blot and the streets spread back from it into the green, steadily upwards. Our house was almost at the top of a long, stretchy street. A flagged street with a cobbly road. When you climb to the top of the hill and look down you can see everything, just like Jesus on the pinnacle except it's not very tempting. Over to the right was the viaduct and behind the viaduct Ellison's tenement, where we had the fair once a year. I was allowed to go there on condition I brought back a tub of black peas for my mother. Black peas look like rabbit droppings and they come in a thin gravy made of stock and gypsy mush. They taste wonderful. The gypsies made a mess and stayed up all night and my mother called them fornicators but on the whole we got on very well. They turned a blind eye to toffee apples going missing, and sometimes, if it was quiet and you didn't have enough money, they still let you have a ride on the dodgems. We used to have fights round the caravans, the ones like me, from the street, against the posh ones from the Avenue. The posh ones went to Brownies and didn't stay for school dinners.

Once, when I was collecting the black peas, about to go home, the old woman got hold of my hand. I thought she was going to bite me. She looked at my palm and laughed a bit. "You'll never marry," she said, "not you, and you'll never be still." She didn't take any money for the peas, and she told me to run home fast. I ran and ran, trying to understand what she meant. I hadn't thought about getting married anyway. There were two women I knew who didn't have husbands at all; they were old though, as old as my mother. They ran

the paper shop and sometimes, on a Wednesday, they gave me a banana bar with my comic. I liked them a lot, and talked about them
a lot to my mother. One day they asked me if I'd like to go to the
seaside with them. I ran home, gabbled it out, and was busy emptying my money box to buy a new spade, when my mother said
firmly and forever, no. I couldn't understand why not, and she
wouldn't explain. She didn't even let me go back to say I couldn't.
Then she cancelled my comic and told me to collect it from another
shop, further away. I was sorry about that. I never got a banana bar
from Grimsby's. A couple of weeks later I heard her telling Mrs
White about it. She said they dealt in unnatural passions. I thought
she meant they put chemicals in their sweets.

My mother and I climbed and climbed until the town fell away
and we reached the memorial stone at the very top. The wind was
always strong so that my mother had to wear extra hat pins. Usually she wore a headscarf, but not on Sunday. We sat on the stone's
base and she thanked the Lord we had managed the ascent. Then
she extemporised on the nature of the world, the folly of its peo-
ples, and the wrath of God inevitable. After that she told me a story
about a brave person who had despised the fruits of the flesh and
worked for the Lord instead. . . .

There was the story of the "converted sweep," a filthy degenerate,
given to drunkenness and vice, who suddenly found the Lord
whilst scraping the insides of a flue. He remained in the flue in a
state of rapture for so long that his friends thought he was uncon-
scious. After a great deal of difficulty they persuaded him to come
out; his face, they declared, though hardly visible for the grime,
shone like an angel's. He started to lead the Sunday School and died
some time later, bound for glory. There were many more; I particularly like the "Hallelujah Giant," a freak of nature, eight feet tall
shrunk to six foot three through the prayers of the faithful.

Now and again my mother liked to tell me her own conversion
story; it was very romantic. I sometimes think that if Mills and Boon
were at all revivalist in their policy my mother would be a star.

One night, by mistake, she had walked into Pastor Spratt's Glory
Crusade. It was in a tent on some spare land, and every evening
Pastor Spratt spoke of the fate of the damned, and performed healing miracles. He was very impressive. My mother said he looked
like Errol Flynn, but holy. A lot of women found the Lord that
week. Part of Pastor Spratt's charisma stemmed from his time

spent as an advertising manager for Rathbone's Wrought Iron. He knew about bait. "There is nothing wrong with bait," he said, when the *Chronicle* somewhat cynically asked him why he gave pot plants to the newly converted. "We are commanded to be Fishers of Men." When my mother heard the call, she was presented with a copy of the Psalms and asked to make her choice between a Christmas Cactus (non-flowering) and a lily of the valley. She had opted for the lily of the valley. When my father went the next night, she told him to be sure and go for the cactus, but by the time he got to the front they had all gone. "He's not one to push himself," she often said, and after a little pause, "Bless him."

Pastor Spratt came to stay with them for the rest of his time with the Glory Crusade, and it was then that my mother discovered her abiding interest in missionary work. The pastor himself spent most of his time out in the jungle and other hot places converting the Heathen. We have a picture of him surrounded by black men with spears. My mother keeps it by her bed. My mother is very like William Blake; she has visions and dreams and she cannot always distinguish a flea's head from a king. Luckily she can't paint.

She walked out one night and thought of her life and thought of what was possible. She thought of the things she couldn't be. Her uncle had been an actor. "A very fine Hamlet," said the *Chronicle*.

But the rags and the ribbons turn to years and then the years are gone. Uncle Will had died a pauper, she was not so young these days and people were not kind. She liked to speak French and to play the piano, but what do these things mean?

Once upon a time there was a brilliant and beautiful princess, so sensitive that the death of a moth could distress her for weeks on end. Her family knew of no solution. Advisers wrung their hands, sages shook their heads, brave kings left unsatisfied. So it happened for many years, until one day, out walking in the forest, the princess came to the hut of an old hunchback who knew the secrets of magic. This ancient creature perceived in the princess a woman of great energy and resourcefulness.

"My dear," she said, "you are in danger of being burned by your own flame."

The hunchback told the princess that she was old, and wished to die, but could not because of her many responsibilities. She had in her charge a small village of homely people, to whom she was advisor and friend. Perhaps the princess would like to take over? Her duties would be:

(1) To milk the goats
(2) To educate the people
(3) To compose songs for their festival

To assist her she would have a three-legged stool and all the books belonging to the hunchback. Best of all, the old woman's harmonium, an instrument of great antiquity and four octaves. The princess agreed to stay and forgot all about the palace and the moths. The old woman thanked her, and died at once.

My mother, out walking that night, dreamed a dream and sustained it in daylight. She would get a child, train it, build it, dedicate it to the Lord:

a missionary child,
a servant of God,
a blessing.

And so it was that on a particular day, some time later, she followed a star until it came to settle above an orphanage, and in that place was a crib, and in that crib, a child. A child with too much hair.
She said, "This child is mine from the Lord."
She took the child away and for seven days and seven nights the child cried out, for fear and not knowing. The mother sang to the child, and stabbed the demons. She understood how jealous the Spirit is of flesh.
Such warm tender flesh.
Her flesh now, sprung from her head.
Her vision.
Not the jolt beneath the hip bone, but water and the word.
She had a way out now, for years and years to come.

We stood on the hill and my mother said, "This world is full of sin."
We stood on the hill and my mother said, "You can change the world."

When we got home my father was watching television. It was the match between "Crusher Williams" and one-eyed Jonney Stott. My mother was furious; we always covered up the television on Sundays. We had a DEEDS OF THE OLD TESTAMENT tablecloth, given to us by a man who did house clearances. It was very grand, and we kept it in a special drawer with nothing else but a piece of Tiffany glass and some parchment from Lebanon. I don't know why we kept the parchment. We had thought it was a bit of the Old Testament but it was the lease to a sheep farm. My father hadn't even bothered to fold up the cloth, and I could just see "Moses Receiving the Ten Commandments" in a heap under the vertical hold. "There's going to be trouble," I thought, and announced my intention of going down to the Salvation Army place for a tambourine lesson.

Poor Dad, he was never quite good enough.

That night at church, we had a visiting speaker, Pastor Finch from Stockport. He was an expert in demons, and delivered a terrifying sermon on how easy it is to become demon-possessed. We were all very uneasy afterwards. Mrs White said she thought her next-door neighbours were probably possessed, they had all the signs. Pastor Finch said that the possessed are given to uncontrollable rages, sudden bursts of wild laughter, and are always, always, very cunning. The Devil himself, he reminded us, can come as an angel of light.

After the service we were having a banquet; my mother had made twenty trifles and her usual mound of cheese and onion sandwiches.

"You can always tell a good woman by her sandwiches," declared Pastor Finch.

My mother blushed.

Then he turned to me and said, "How old are you, little girl?"

"Seven," I replied.

"Ah, seven," he muttered. "How blessed, the seven days of creation, the seven-branched candlestick, the seven seals."

(Seven seals? I had not yet reached Revelation in my directed reading, and I thought he meant some Old Testament amphibians I had overlooked. I spent weeks trying to find them, in case they came up as a quiz question.)

"Yes," he went on, "how blessed," then his brow clouded. "But how cursed." At this word his fist hit the table and catapulted a cheese sandwich into the collection bag; I saw it happen, but I was so distracted I forgot to tell anyone. They found it in there the week after, at the Sisterhood meeting. The whole table had fallen silent, except for Mrs Rothwell who was stone deaf and very hungry.

"The demon can return SEVENFOLD." His eyes roamed the table. (Scrape, went Mrs Rothwell's spoon.)

"SEVENFOLD."

("Does anybody want this piece of cake?" asked Mrs Rothwell.)

"The best can become the worst,"—he took me by the hand— "This innocent child, this bloom of the Covenant."

"Well, I'll eat it then," announced Mrs Rothwell.

Pastor Finch glared at her, but he wasn't a man to be put off.

"This little lily could herself be a house of demons."

"Eh, steady on Roy," said Mrs Finch anxiously.

"Don't interrupt me Grace," he said firmly, "I mean this by way of example only. God has given me an opportunity and what God has given we must not presume to waste.

"It has been known for the most holy men to be suddenly filled with evil. And how much more a woman, and how much more a child. Parents, watch your children for the signs. Husbands, watch your wives. Blessed be the name of the Lord."

He let go of my hand, which was now crumpled and soggy.

He wiped his own on his trouser leg.

"You shouldn't tax yourself so, Roy," said Mrs Finch, "have some trifle, it's got sherry in it."

I felt a bit awkward so I went into the Sunday School Room. There was some Fuzzy Felt to make Bible scenes with, and I was just beginning to enjoy a rewrite of Daniel in the lions' den when Pastor Finch appeared. I put my hands into my pockets and looked at the lion.

"Little girl," he began, then he caught sight of the Fuzzy Felt.

"What's that?"

"Daniel," I answered.

"But that's not right," he said, aghast. "Don't you know that Daniel escaped? In your picture the lions are swallowing him."

"I'm sorry," I replied, putting on my best, blessed face. "I wanted to do Jonah and the whale, but they don't do whales in Fuzzy Felt. I'm pretending those lions are whales."

"You said it was Daniel." He was suspicious.

"I got mixed up."

He smiled. "Let's put it right, shall we?" And he carefully re-arranged the lions in one corner, and Daniel in the other. "What about Nebuchadnezzar? Let's do the Astonishment at Dawn scene next." He started to root through the Fuzzy Felt, looking for a king.

"Hopeless," I thought, Susan Green was sick on the tableau of the three Wise Men at Christmas, and you only get three kings to a box.

I left him to it. When I came back into the hall somebody asked me if I'd seen Pastor Finch.

"He's in the Sunday School Room playing with the Fuzzy Felt," I replied.

"Don't be fanciful Jeanette," said the voice. I looked up. It was Miss Jewsbury; she always talked like that, I think it was because she taught the oboe. It does something to your mouth.

"Time to go home," said my mother. "I think you've had enough excitement for one day."

It's odd, the things other people think are exciting.

We set off, my mother, Alice and May ("Auntie Alice, Auntie May, to you"). I lagged behind, thinking about Pastor Finch and how horrible he was. His teeth stuck out, and his voice was squeaky, even though he tried to make it deep and stern. Poor Mrs Finch. How did she live with him? Then I remembered the gypsy. "You'll never marry." That might not be such a bad thing after all. We walked along the Factory Bottoms to get home. The poorest people of all lived there, tied to the mills. There were hundreds of children and scraggy dogs. Next Door used to live down there, right by the glue works, but their cousin or someone had left them a house, next to our house. "The work of the Devil, if ever I saw it," said my mother, who always believed these things are sent to try us.

I wasn't allowed in the Factory Bottoms on my own, and that night as the rain began, I was sure I knew why. If the demons lived anywhere it was here. We went past the shop that sold flea collars and poisons. Arkwright's For Vermin it was called; I had been inside it once, when we had a run of cockroaches. Mrs Arkwright was there cashing up; she caught sight of May as we went past and shouted at her to come in. My mother wasn't very pleased, but muttering something about Jesus associating with tax collectors and sinners pushed me inside, in front of them all.

"Where've you been May," asked Mrs Arkwright, wiping her hand on a dishcloth, "not seen hide of you in a month."

"I've been in Blackpool."

"Ho, come in at some money have you?"

"It were at Bingo 'ousie 'ousie three times."

"No."

Mrs Arkwright was both admiring and bad-tempered.

The conversation continued like this for some time, Mrs Arkwright complaining that business was poor, that she'd have to close the shop, that there was no money in vermin any more.

"Let's hope we have a hot summer, that'll fetch them out."

My mother was visibly distressed.

"Remember that heatwave two years ago? Ooo, I did some trade then. Cockroaches, hard backs, rats, you name it, I poisoned it. No, it's not same any more."

We kept a respectful silence for a moment or two, then my mother coughed and said we should be getting along.

"Here, then," said Mrs Arkwright, "tek these furt nipper."

She meant me and, rummaging around somewhere behind the counter, pulled out a few different-shaped tins.

"It can keep its marbles and stuff in 'em," she explained.

"Ta," I said and smiled.

"Ey, it's all right that one, you knows," she smiled at me and, wiping her hand firmly on my hand, let us out of the shop.

"Look at these May." I held them up.

"Auntie May," snapped my mother.

May examined them with me.

"'Silver fish,'" she read. "'Sprinkle liberally behind sinks, toilets and other damp places.' Oh, very nice. What's this one: 'Lice, bed bugs, etc. Guaranteed effective or money back.'"

Eventually we got home, Goodnight May, Goodnight Alice, God Bless. My father had already gone to bed because he worked early shifts. My mother wouldn't be going to bed for hours.

As long as I have known them, my mother has gone to bed at four, and my father has got up at five. That was nice in a way because it meant I could come down in the middle of the night and not be lonely. Quite often we'd have bacon and eggs and she'd read me a bit of the Bible.

It was in this way that I began my education: she taught me to read from the Book of Deuteronomy, and she told me all about the lives of the saints, how they were really wicked, and given to nameless desires. Not fit for worship; this was yet another heresy of the Catholic Church and I was not to be misled by the smooth tongues of priests.

"But I never see any priests."

"A girl's motto is BE PREPARED."

I learnt that it rains when clouds collide with a high building, like a steeple, or a cathedral; the impact punctures them, and everybody underneath gets wet. This was why, in the old days, when the only tall buildings were holy, people used to say cleanliness is next to godliness. The more godly your town, the more high buildings you'd have, and the more rain you'd get.

"That's why all these Heathen places are so dry," explained my mother, then she looked into space, and her pencil quivered. "Poor Pastor Spratt."

I discovered that everything in the natural world was a symbol of the Great Struggle between good and evil. "Consider the mamba," said my mother. "Over short distances the mamba can outrun a horse." And she drew the race on a sheet of paper. She meant that in the short term, evil can triumph, but never for very long. We were very glad, and we sang our favourite hymn, *Yield Not to Temptation*.

I asked my mother to teach me French, but her face clouded over, and she said she couldn't.

"Why not?"

"It was nearly my downfall."

"What do you mean?" I persisted, whenever I could. But she only shook her head and muttered something about me being too young, that I'd find out all too soon, that it was nasty.

"One day," she said finally, "I'll tell you about Pierre," then she switched on the radio and ignored me for so long that I went back to bed.

Quite often, she'd start to tell me a story and then go on to something else in the middle, so I never found out what happened to the Earthly Paradise when it stopped being off the coast of India, and I was stuck at "six sevens are forty-two" for almost a week.

"Why don't I go to school?" I asked her. I was curious about school because my mother always called it a Breeding Ground. I didn't know what she meant, but I knew it was a bad thing, like Unnatural Passions. "They'll lead you astray," was the only answer I got.

I thought about all this in the toilet. It was outside, and I hated having to go at night because of the spiders that came over from the coal-shed. My dad and me always seemed to be in the toilet, me sitting on my hands and humming, and him standing up, I supposed. My mother got very angry.

"You come on in, it doesn't take that long."

But it was the only place to go. We all shared the same bedroom, because my mother was building us a bathroom in the back, and eventually, if she got the partition fitted, a little half-room for me. She worked very slowly though, because she said she had a lot on her mind. Sometimes Mrs White came round to help mix the grout, but then they'd both end up listening to Johnny Cash, or writing a new hand-out on Baptism by Total Immersion. She did finish eventually, but not for three years.

Meanwhile, my lessons continued. I learnt about Horticulture and Garden Pests via the slugs and my mother's seed catalogues, and I developed an understanding of Historical Process through the prophecies in the Book of Revelation, and a magazine called *The Plain Truth,* which my mother received each week.

"It's Elijah in our midst again," she declared.

And so I learned to interpret the signs and wonders that the unbeliever might never understand.

"You'll need to when you're out there on the mission field," she reminded me.

Then, one morning, when we had got up early to listen to Ivan Popov from behind the Iron Curtain, a fat brown envelope plopped through the letter box. My mother thought it was letters of thanks from those who had attended our Healing of the Sick crusade in the town hall. She ripped it open, then her face fell.

"What is it?" I asked her.

"It's about you."

"What about me?"

"I have to send you to school."

I whizzed into the toilet and sat on my hands; the Breeding Ground at last.

David Foster Wallace

*David Foster Wallace was born in Ithaca, New York, in 1962. He was edu-
cated at Amherst College and the University of Arizona at Tucson, and
currently lives in Boston. He is the author of one story collection,* Girl with
Curious Hair *(1989); one novel,* The Broom in the System *(1990); and
one nonfiction work,* Signifying Rappers *(1990). His stories have appeared in* Harper's, Playboy, *and* The Paris Review, *and were cited for
inclusion in the* O. Henry Prize Stories *collection for 1988 and the* Best
American Short Stories *collection for 1992. "Everything Is Green" was
first published in* Puerto Del Sol *and* Harper's, *and can be found in* Girl
with Curious Hair.

Everything Is Green

She says I do not care if you believe me or not, it is the truth, go on
and believe what you want to. So it is for sure that she is lying.
When it is the truth she will go crazy trying to get you to believe
her. So I feel like I know.

She lights up and looks off away from me, looking sly with her
cigarette in light through a wet window, and I can not feel what
to say.

I say Mayfly I can not feel what to do or say or believe you any
more. But there is things I know. I know I am older and you are
not. And I give to you all I got to give you, with my hands and my
heart both. Every thing that is inside me I have gave you. I have
been keeping it together and working steady every day. I have
made you the reason I got for what I always do. I have tried to make
a home to give to you, for you to be in, and for it to be nice.

I light up myself and I throw the match in the sink with other
matches and dishes and a sponge and such things.

I say Mayfly my heart has been down the road and back for you
but I am forty-eight years old. It is time I have got to not let things
just carry me by any more. I got to use some time that is still mine
to try to make everything feel right. I got to try to feel how I need
to. In me there is needs which you can not even see any more, because there is too many needs in you that are in the way.

She does not say any thing and I look at her window and I can
feel that she knows I know about it, and she shifts her self on my
sofa lounger. She brings her legs up underneath her in some shorts.

I say it really does not matter what I seen or what I think I seen. That is not it any more. I know I am older and you are not. But now I am feeling like there is all of me going in to you and nothing of you is coming back any more.

Her hair is up with a barret and pins and her chin is in her hand, it's early, she looks like she is dreaming out at the clean light through the wet window over my sofa lounger.

Everything is green she says. Look how green it all is Mitch. How can you say the things you say you feel like when everything outside is green like it is.

The window over the sink of my kitchenet is cleaned off from the hard rain last night and it is a morning with a sun, it is still early, and there is a mess of green out. The trees are green and some grass out past the speed bumps is green and slicked down. But every thing is not green. The other trailers are not green and my card table out with puddles in lines and beer cans and butts floating in the ash trays is not green, or my truck, or the gravel of the lot, or the big wheel toy that is on its side under the clothes line without clothes on it by the next trailer, where the guy has got him some kids.

Everything is green she is saying. She is whispering it and the whisper is not to me no more I know.

I chuck my smoke and turn hard from the morning with the taste of something true in my mouth. I turn hard toward her in the light on the sofa lounger.

She is looking outside, from where she is sitting, and I look at her, and there is something in me that can not close up, in that looking. Mayfly has a body. And she is my morning. Say her name.

Joanna H. Wos

Joanna H. Wos is the youngest daughter of Polish emigrants who came to the United States following World War II. She has worked in museums and literary organizations for twenty years. Wos was the Writers Series Coordinator for the Santa Fe Literary Center and currently works part-time for the Hudson Valley Writers Center. Her stories have appeared in over eighteen literary magazines including Permafrost, Kalliope, *and* American Writing, *and the anthology* Loss of the Groundnote: Women Writing

About the Loss of Their Mothers *(1992). "The One Sitting There" first appeared in* The Malahat Review, *and was reprinted in* Flash Fiction *(1992).*

The One Sitting There

I threw away the meat. The dollar ninety-eight a pound ground beef, the boneless chicken, the spareribs, the hamsteak. I threw the soggy vegetables into the trashcan: the carrots, broccoli, peas, the Brussels sprouts. I poured the milk down the drain of the stainless steel sink. The cheddar cheese I ground up in the disposal. The ice cream, now liquid, followed. All the groceries in the refrigerator had to be thrown away. The voice on the radio hinted of germs thriving on the food after the hours without power. Throwing the food away was rational and reasonable.

In our house, growing up, you were never allowed to throw food away. There was a reason. My mother saved peelings and spoiled things to put on the compost heap. That would go back into the garden to grow more vegetables. You could leave meat or potatoes to be used again in soup. But you were never allowed to throw food away.

I threw the bread away. The bread had gotten wet. I once saw my father pick up a piece of Wonder Bread he had dropped on the ground. He brushed his hand over the slice to remove the dirt and then kissed the bread. Even at six I knew why he did that. My sister was the reason. I was born after the war. She lived in a time before. I do not know much about her. My mother never talked about her. There are no pictures. The only time my father talked about her was when he described how she clutched the bread so tightly in her baby fist that the bread squeezed out between her fingers. She sucked at the bread that way.

So I threw the bread away last. I threw the bread away for all the times I sat crying over a bowl of cabbage soup my father said I had to eat. Because eating would not bring her back. Because I would still be the one sitting there. Now I had the bread. I had gotten it. I had bought it. I had put it in the refrigerator. I had earned it. It was mine to throw away.

So I threw the bread away for my sister. I threw the bread away and brought her back. She was twenty-one and had just come home from Christmas shopping. She had bought me a doll. She put the package on my dining room table and hung her coat smelling of perfume and the late fall air on the back of one of the chairs. I welcomed her as an honored guest. As if she were a Polish bride returning to her home, I greeted her with a plate of bread and salt. The bread, for prosperity, was wrapped in a white linen cloth. The salt, for tears, was in a small blue bowl. We sat down together and shared a piece of bread.

In a kitchen, where such an act was an ordinary thing, I threw away the bread. Because I could.

Jamaica Kincaid

Jamaica Kincaid was born in Antigua, the West Indies, in 1949, and currently resides in New York. She is the author of two collections of short stories, At the Bottom of the River *(winner of the Morton Dauwen Zabel Award from the American Academy and Institute of Arts and Letters in 1983) and* Annie John *(1988). "Girl" was first published in* The New Yorker, *and can be found in* At the Bottom of the River.

Girl

Wash the white clothes on Monday and put them on the stone heap; wash the color clothes on Tuesday and put them on the clothesline to dry; don't walk barehead in the hot sun; cook pumpkin fritters in very hot sweet oil; soak your little clothes right after you take them off; when buying cotton to make yourself a nice blouse, be sure that it doesn't have gum on it, because that way it won't hold up well after a wash; soak salt fish overnight before you cook it; is it true that you sing benna in Sunday school?; always eat your food in such a way that it won't turn someone else's stomach; on Sundays try to walk like a lady and not like the slut you are so bent on becoming; don't sing benna in Sunday school; you mustn't speak to wharf-rat boys, not even to give directions; don't eat fruits on the street—flies will follow you; *but I don't sing benna on Sundays at all and never in Sunday school*; this is how to sew on a button; this is how to make a button-hole for the button you have just sewed on; this is how to hem a dress when you see the hem coming down and so to prevent yourself from looking like the slut I know you are so bent on becoming; this is how you iron your father's khaki shirt so that it doesn't have a crease; this is how you iron your father's khaki pants so that they don't have a crease; this is how you grow okra— far from the house, because okra tree harbors red ants; when you are growing dasheen, make sure it gets plenty of water or else it makes your throat itch when you are eating it; this is how you sweep a corner; this is how you sweep a whole house; this is how you sweep a yard; this is how you smile to someone you don't like too much; this is how you smile to someone you don't like at all; this is how you smile to someone you like completely; this is how you set a table for tea; this is how you set a table for dinner; this is how you set a table for dinner with an important guest; this is how you set a table for lunch; this is how you set a table for breakfast; this is how to behave in the presence of men who don't know you very well, and this way they won't recognize immediately the slut I have warned you against becoming; be sure to wash every day, even if it is with your own spit; don't squat down to play marbles— you are not a boy, you know; don't pick people's flowers—you might catch something; don't throw stones at blackbirds, because it might not be a blackbird at all; this is how to make a bread pud- ding; this is how to make doukona; this is how to make pepper pot; this is how to make a good medicine for a cold; this is how to make a good medicine to throw away a child before it even becomes a child; this is how to catch a fish; this is how to throw back a fish you don't like, and that way something bad won't fall on you; this is how to bully a man; this is how a man bullies you; this is how to love a man, and if this doesn't work there are other ways, and if they don't work don't feel too bad about giving up; this is how to spit up in the air if you feel like it, and this is how to move quick so that it doesn't fall on you; this is how to make ends meet; always squeeze bread to make sure it's fresh; *but what if the baker won't let me feel the bread?*; you mean to say that after all you are really going to be the kind of woman who the baker won't let near the bread?

Scott Bradfield

"Motion" is the title of the opening section of Scott Bradfield's first novel,
The History of Luminous Motion *(1989). Born in California in 1955,*
Bradfield received a Ph.D. in literature from the University of California
at Irvine, and currently teaches at the University of Connecticut. He is
also the author of three collections of stories, Dreams of the Wolf, Greet-
ings from Earth, *and* The Secret Life of Houses, *and the critical work*
Dreaming Revolution: Transgression in the Development of American Romance.

Motion

Mom was a world all her own, filled with secret thoughts and mo-
tions nobody else could see. With Mom I easily forgot Dad, who
became little more than a premonition, a strange weighted tendency rather than a man, as if this was Mom's final retribution,
making Dad the future. Mom was always now. Mom was that
movement that never ceased. Mom lived in the world with me and
nobody else, and every few days or so it seemed she was driving
me to more strange new places in our untuned and ominously clattering beige Ford Rambler. It wasn't just motion, either. Mom possessed a certain geographical weight and mass; her motion was
itself a place, a voice, a state of repose. No matter where we went
we seemed to be where we had been before. We were more than a
family, Mom and I. We were a quality of landscape. We were the
map's name rather than some encoded or strategic position on it.
We were like an MX missile, always moving but always already exactly where we were supposed to be. There were many times when
I thought of Mom and me as a sort of weapon.

"Do you love your mother?" one of Mom's men asked me. We
were sitting at Sambo's, and I was drinking hot chocolate. Mom
had gone to the ladies' room to freshen up.

It seemed to me a spurious question. There was something
sedentary and covert about it, like the bad foundation of some
prospective home. I had, as always, one of my school texts open in
my lap. It was entitled *Our Biological Wonderland: 5th Edition,* and
I was contemplating the glossary to Chapter Three. I liked the

word "Chemotropism: Movement or growth of an organism, esp. a plant, in response to chemical stimuli." Chemotropic, I thought. Chemotropismal.

"Your mother is a very nice person," the man continued. He didn't like the silence sitting between us there at the table. I myself didn't mind. He smoked an endless succession of Marlboros, which he crushed out in his coffee saucer rather than the Sambo's glass ashtray resting conveniently beside his elbow. Nervously he was always glancing over his shoulder to see if Mom was back yet. I didn't tell him Mom could spend ages in the ladies' room; the ladies' room was one of Mom's special places. No matter where we were living or where we were traveling, Mom found a sort of uniform and patient atmosphere in the ladies' rooms where she went to make herself beautiful. Sometimes, when I accompanied her there like a privileged and confidential adviser, we would sit in front of the mirror for hours while she tried on different lipsticks and eye shadows, mascaras and blushes. Mom found silence in the ladies' room, and in the beauty of her own face. It was like the silence that sat at the tables between me and Mom's men, only by Mom and me it was more appreciated, and thus more profound.

"I love my mom," I said, holding the book open in my lap. Mom's man wasn't looking at me, though. He seemed to be thinking about something. It was as if the silence had actually moved into him too, something he had inherited from the still circulating memory of Mom's skin and Mom's scent. I looked into my book again, and we sat together drinking our coffee and hot chocolate, awaiting that elimination of our secret privacy which Mom carried around with her like a brilliant torch, or a large packet of money. Sometimes I felt as if I were a million years old that summer, and that Mom and I would continue traveling like that forever and ever, always together and never apart. I remember it as the summer of my millionth year, and I suspect I will always remember that summer very well.

Those were nights when we moved quickly, the nights when Mom found her men. Usually I would lie in the backseat of our car and read my faded textbooks, acquired from the moldering dime bargain boxes of surfeited and dusty used-book stores. I would read by means of the diffuse light of streetlamps, or the fluid and Dopplering light of passing automobiles. Sometimes I had to pause in the middle of paragraphs and sentences in order to await this sentient light. In those days I thought light was layered and textured like leaves in a tree. It moved and ruffled through the car. It felt gentle and imminent like snow. Eventually I would fall asleep, the light moving across and around me on some dark anonymous street, and I would hear the car door open and slam and Mom starting the ignition, and then we would be moving again, moving together into the light of cities and stars, Mom pulling her coat over me and whispering, "We'll have our own house someday, baby. Our own bedrooms, kitchen and TV, our own walls and ceilings and doors. We'll have a brand-new station wagon with a nice soft mattress in back so you can lie down and take a nap any time you want. We'll have a big yard and garden. We might even have a second house. In the mountains somewhere."

In the mornings I would awake in different cities, underneath different stars. Only they were the same cities, too, in a way. They were still the same stars.

Mom kept the credit cards in a plastic card file in the glove compartment, even the very old cards that we never used anymore. The file box also contained a few jeweled rings and gold bands which we sold sometimes at central city pawnshops, and a few random business cards with phone numbers and street maps urgently scrawled on their backs. These were the maps of Mom's men, and sometimes I preferred looking at them rather than at my own textbooks. These were names of things, people and places that possessed color, suspense and uniformity, like a globe of the world with textured mountain ranges on it. Lompoc, Burlingame, Half Moon Bay, Buellton, Stockton, Sacramento, Davis, San Luis Obispo. Real Estate, Plumbing, Fire Theft Auto, 24 Hour Bail, Good Used Cars, Cala Foods and Daybrite Cleaners. Mom's men were accumulations of words, like nails in a piece of wood. When I closed the plastic file again the lid's plastic clamp clacked hollowly. "That's Mom's Domesday Book you've got there," Mom said. "Her Dead Sea Scrolls, her *tabula fabula*. That's Mom's articulate past, borrowed and bought and certainly very blue. If they ever catch up with your old mom, you take that file box and toss it in the river—that is, if you can find a river. Head for the hills, and I'll get back to you in five to ten, though I'm afraid that's just a rough estimate. I've stopped keeping track of the felonies. I think that's the compensation that comes with age—not wisdom. You're allowed to stop keeping track of the felonies." Mom was wearing bright red lipstick, tight faded Levi's and a yellow blouse. She drank from a can of Budweiser braced between her knees. I didn't think Mom was old at all. I thought she was exceptionally young and beautiful.

Outside our dusty car windows lay the flat beating red plains of the San Fernando Valley. Dull gray metal water towers, red-and-white-striped radio transmitters, cows. "Emily Dickinson said she could find the entire universe in her backyard," Mom told me. "This, you see, is our backyard." Mom gestured at the orange groves and dilapidated, sunstruck fresh-fruit stands and fast-food restaurants aisling us along Highway 101. The freeway asphalt was cracked and pale, littered with refuse and the ruptured shells of overheated retread tires. Then Mom would light her cigarette with the dashboard lighter. I liked the way the lighter heated there silently for a while like some percolating threat and then, with a broken clinking sound, came suddenly unsprung. Mom's waiting hand would catch it—otherwise it would project itself onto the vinyl seat and add more charred streaks to the ones it had already made. There was even a telltale oval smudge against the inside thigh of Mom's faded Levi's. "Now, keep your eyes out for the Gilroy off-ramp," Mom said. "It's along here somewhere. We'll have a McDonaldburger and then I know this bar where maybe I'll get lucky. Maybe we'll both get lucky." And of course we always did.

Kate Chopin

Kate Chopin was born in St. Louis in 1851. Reading widely and attending convent school as a child, Chopin married in 1870 and moved to New Orleans, where she mingled broadly within Louisiana aristocratic circles. After her husband's death in 1883, she supervised the Chopin family plantation in Natchitoches Parish. She eventually returned to St. Louis and there began her writing career. Prior to her death in 1904, Chopin published two volumes of short fiction, Bayou Folk *(1894) and* A Night in Acadie *(1897), and two novels,* At Fault *(1890) and* The Awakening *(1899). The collec-*

tion A Vocation and a Voice *remained unpublished until 1991. "The Story of an Hour" was published in book form in* Bayou Folk.

The Story of an Hour

Knowing that Mrs. Mallard was afflicted with a heart trouble, great care was taken to break to her as gently as possible the news of her husband's death.

It was her sister Josephine who told her, in broken sentences; veiled hints that revealed in half concealing. Her husband's friend Richards was there, too, near her. It was he who had been in the newspaper office when intelligence of the railroad disaster was received, with Brently Mallard's name leading the list of "killed." He had only taken the time to assure himself of its truth by a second telegram, and had hastened to forestall any less careful, less tender friend in bearing the sad message.

She did not hear the story as many women have heard the same, with a paralyzed inability to accept its significance. She wept at once, with sudden, wild abandonment, in her sister's arms. When the storm of grief had spent itself she went away to her room alone. She would have no one follow her.

There stood, facing the open window, a comfortable, roomy armchair. Into this she sank, pressed down by a physical exhaustion that haunted her body and seemed to reach into her soul.

She could see in the open square before her house the tops of trees that were all aquiver with the new spring life. The delicious breath of rain was in the air. In the street below a peddler was crying his wares. The notes of a distant song which some one was singing reached her faintly, and countless sparrows were twittering in the eaves.

There were patches of blue sky showing here and there through the clouds that had met and piled one above the other in the west facing her window.

She sat with her head thrown back upon the cushion of the chair, quite motionless, except when a sob came up into her throat and shook her, as a child who has cried itself to sleep continues to sob in its dreams.

She was young, with a fair, calm face, whose lines bespoke repression and even a certain strength. But now there was a dull stare in her eyes, whose gaze was fixed away off yonder on one of those patches of blue sky. It was not a glance of reflection, but rather indicated a suspension of intelligent thought.

There was something coming to her and she was waiting for it, fearfully. What was it? She did not know; it was too subtle and elusive to name. But she felt it, creeping out of the sky, reaching toward her through the sounds, the scents, the color that filled the air.

Now her bosom rose and fell tumultuously. She was beginning to recognize this thing that was approaching to possess her, and she was striving to beat it back with her will—as powerless as her two white slender hands would have been.

When she abandoned herself a little whispered word escaped her slightly parted lips. She said it over and over under her breath: "free, free, free!" The vacant stare and the look of terror that had followed it went from her eyes. They stayed keen and bright. Her pulses beat fast, and the coursing blood warmed and relaxed every inch of her body.

She did not stop to ask if it were or were not a monstrous joy that held her. A clear and exalted perception enabled her to dismiss the suggestion as trivial.

She knew that she would weep again when she saw the kind, tender hands folded in death; the face that had never looked save with love upon her, fixed and gray and dead. But she saw beyond that bitter moment a long procession of years to come that would belong to her absolutely. And she opened and spread her arms out to them in welcome.

There would be no one to live for her during those coming years; she would live for herself. There would be no powerful will bending hers in that blind persistence with which men and women believe they have a right to impose a private will upon a fellow-creature. A kind intention or a cruel intention made the act seem no less a crime as she looked upon it in that brief moment of illumination.

And yet she had loved him—sometimes. Often she had not. What did it matter! What could love, the unsolved mystery, count for in face of this possession of self-assertion which she suddenly recognized as the strongest impulse of her being!

"Free! Body and soul free!" she kept whispering.

Josephine was kneeling before the closed door with her lips to the keyhole, imploring for admission. "Louise, open the door! I beg; open the door—you will make yourself ill. What are you doing, Louise? For heaven's sake open the door."

"Go away. I am not making myself ill." No; she was drinking in a very elixir of life through that open window.

Her fancy was running riot along those days ahead of her. Spring days, and summer days, and all sorts of days that would be her own. She breathed a quick prayer that life might be long. It was only yesterday she had thought with a shudder that life might be long.

She arose at length and opened the door to her sister's importunities. There was a feverish triumph in her eyes, and she carried herself unwittingly like a goddess of Victory. She clasped her sister's waist, and together they descended the stairs. Richards stood waiting for them at the bottom.

Some one was opening the front door with a latchkey. It was Brently Mallard who entered, a little travel-stained, composedly carrying his grip-sack and umbrella. He had been far from the scene of accident, and did not even know there had been one. He stood amazed at Josephine's piercing cry; at Richards' quick motion to screen him from the view of his wife.

But Richards was too late.

When the doctors came they said she had died of heart disease— of joy that kills.

PART

II

WRITING IN THE WORKSHOP

FIRST WORKSHOPS

Much of your best writing is done during solitary moments: Lorrie Moore, in "How to Become a Writer," eloquently describes "the only happiness" you have when you are "writing something new, in the middle of the night, armpits damp, heart pounding, something no one has yet seen." Jorge Luis Borges has written that the beginning writer needs friends, and lots of them. A fiction *workshop* can give you the best of both worlds: the solitude you need to do your best writing, and a network of readers to respond attentively to your work.

In a workshop, students provide the course material, in the form of their stories, and classroom commentary, in the form of responses to stories. The workshop gives you the freedom to write whatever you want, and in exchange asks you to take the responsibility for constructively evaluating the work of others. In addition, it asks you to allow your own work to be evaluated by other students.

PEER REVIEW

Written Comments

In some workshops, the teacher will read a story aloud to a class in order to obtain spontaneous responses, or suggest in-class writing exercises. In most workshops, however, a story that will be discussed during a given class period is distributed a few days or a week earlier, to give everyone the opportunity to read the manuscript and prepare comments. In these instances, you are usually expected to place written comments on the manuscript, and then return these marked copies to the writer.

In order for the workshopped manuscripts to be useful to the individual writer, it is essential that you make a thoughtful evaluation. Reading is an intensely personal act, and the kind of reading that will most assist a writer is probably the kind of reading that seems most native to each reader. During the first pass through a story, you should respond naturally and spontaneously to characters, plot, language. During a second pass, you will often discover how the story works; its strong points and weak points become clearer to recognize and easier to articulate. A second reading also provides the opportunity to confirm or rethink early impressions: if a dull story failed to disclose subtle layers of depth during the second reading, you can be that much more sure that your first opinion was reasonable. Contrarily, a second reading often reveals what a first reading may have missed.

In most workshops, written evaluation consists of comments written in the margins, and a longer, more narrative comment at the end. In general, most workshop teachers attempt to improve fiction on two different levels: first, by correcting minor flaws on a sentence-by-sentence, paragraph-by-paragraph level (what one teacher calls the "fix-its"), and second, by providing summary statements about the strengths and weaknesses of the story as a whole. Usually, the comments in the margin can include a variety of different forms of information. You can use the margin to offer grammatical advice or suggestions about sentences that seem awkward or out of place, paragraphs that run too long, or passages that seem particularly slow or confusing. You also can use the margins to compliment the author on a passage that is beautifully written, a plot turn that is surprising or powerful, or simply a line of dialogue that seems particularly funny. You can use the margins to indicate the exact point where a story goes awry, or where paragraphs should be moved around or cut.

The comments in the margin constitute a running discussion that you conduct with the story itself. As you read a story, you laugh, you grow irritated, you find yourself liking a character. These reactions naturally and unconsciously happen every time you read; the art of good margin comments is to provide a readable record of those responses. If a line makes you laugh, write "This is funny." If you grow irritated, write "At this point, I am having a hard time enjoying your story"; if you know *why* that has occurred, tell the author. If a sentence seems weakly written, write "weakly written" in the margin. If you know why the sentence is ineffective, say so; if you prefer, provide the writer with an alternative. The best criticism usually includes constructive advice; but if you like or dislike a section of a story without knowing exactly why, then you can still tell the writer *what* you felt.

In other words, your margin comments should constitute a record of the spontaneous responses you felt during the first reading, and the more informed observations that you made during the second reading. For instance, suggestions about story architecture can be made only during the second reading; while a passage might seem slow during a first reading, it sometimes requires a second reading to see the role that passage performs in setting up the finer passages that may follow. In many workshops, readers write their first-reading comments in one color, then write their second-reading comments in another. In general, it is always helpful to the writer if you indicate in the margins how additional readings affected your perception of a given story.

While margin comments provide a running record of how you felt as you read a story, *end comments* provide a summary of all those impressions, and emphasize those compliments and criticisms that seem most important. The ideal end comment performs two functions. First, it reflects the quality and quantity of your impressions of the story. If you loved a particular story, for instance, the end comments should be adoring. If a story produced mixed feelings, you should take pains to identify both the strong and weak points of the piece. If the story was unabashedly awful, you can choose to be blunt, bland, polite, silent, authentically encouraging, or whatever combination of these strategies you believe creates a context for future criticism.

The second function of end comments is to make suggestions about how to improve the story. At this point you can simply review the comments that have already been written in the margins, then summarize the most important or the most frequently repeated criticisms. Alternately, you can attempt to summarize general impressions that never found their way into a margin comment; an entire story can feel slow, for instance, without feeling slow at any one point. Furthermore, you can choose to call attention to a story's strong points, and suggest improvement by playing to a story's established strengths: perhaps, for instance, a good character could be given an expanded role. You can seek similarities between the story and the writer's previous stories, in order to make larger suggestions about the writer's style. You can deliberately limit the number of suggestions you make in the end comments, focusing on two or three major points, explaining each criticism carefully, and providing constructive alternatives. Or you can simply provide a list of criticisms or praises (or both) without explanation. While the function of the end comment (and work-shopping in general) is to make suggestions to improve a story, that does not mean that the end comment should consist solely of criticisms. Effective praise—the articulation of a story's sources of power—is a challenge for the critic and an inspiration for the writer. You should find a vocabulary for expressing satisfaction and pleasure, and use it often.

Spoken Comments

In theory the class workshop devoted to a particular story should be a place where people discuss the opinions they developed in private readings of that story, and present criticism and compliments in proportion to how much they appreciated the story's strong points or sensed its limitations. In fact, the workshop possesses a new and different dynamic. A criticism that was easy to write in the margin of a story late on Sunday night, for instance, will often be difficult to speak aloud on Wednesday afternoon with the author sitting at the end of the table. The first student who speaks in the workshop responds to the story; every student after that responds to the story, and to the other comments as well. One student who feels that the commentary might be too negative (or who feels empathy for the writer), might speak glowingly as an antidote to the preceding comments. Sometimes, students who disagree with the first two or three spoken criticisms will sit quietly, or find their opinions tending toward the majority. A reader who did not understand a story's enigmatic ending and wrote in the end comment that "the ending doesn't work for me" might find one reader after another praise that same ending for its subtlety. Other readers might find themselves swayed by a particularly intelligent and passionate reading by a fellow student. And lastly, as much as most creative writing teachers try to avoid it, it is generally true that the workshop leader's opinion will weigh a great deal, shifting the classroom discussion in a new direction on a moment's notice—without necessarily altering any student's private, unstated opinion.

A creative-writing workshop is probably the most fluid and personal classroom that most students will enter. In fact, the workshop format bears less resemblance to the standard classroom than it does to the kind of call-and-response, improvised creative interaction that takes place in church groups, corporate boardrooms, or screenwriting sessions. What emerges from the mix is largely dependent on the personalities of the students and the workshop leader. Very rarely does a workshop consist of students giving their opinions in a completely objective manner that is in no way influenced by their peers, their friends, or their teacher. This free flow of subjectivity, however—readers changing their minds, readers influencing one another—transforms the workshop into a vehicle for discovery, where new ideas about writing can occur spontaneously. What every member of the workshop invariably finds is an individual idiom for criticism that makes a contribution to the discussion. Every participant knows that the workshop is a place for creative expression. What few appreciate, however, is that this is as true for your criticism as it is for your stories.

WHEN YOUR STORY IS WORKSHOPPED

Written Comments

If the workshop operates like a Congress or a Parliament, where consensus is built as people discuss, argue, compromise, change their minds, and discuss some more, the written comments are a secret ballot, where what everybody thought of the story before they entered the classroom is recorded for the writer's benefit. As a result, these comments can often be more persuasive evidence of a story's strengths or flaws than the spoken contributions of the class. In fact, the process of reading through ten copies of your story and finding the same private, unbiased comment in the margin of the same page seven times can be far more convincing proof than hearing one student offer the same suggestion in class and interpreting the ensuing quiet as mass assent. It is a frequent practice for writing students to take every workshopped copy of a story and transcribe every comment onto one clean copy, to see where readers agreed or disagreed, and how often. Whether or not you choose to make this effort, however, it is always useful to carefully read these marked-up manuscripts to detect whether any patterns to the criticisms exist, and whether what readers thought in private differed from what they stated in public.

Spoken Comments

During a workshop, when your fellow students tell you that the quality of your memories, the private language with which you choose to express yourself, and the human issues you consider important mean little or nothing to them, it can be wholly frustrating. Oppositely, when your fellow students tell you that what you wrote moved them, made them happier, or touched a fundamental emotional truth with which they live daily, it gives you a profound feeling of gratification. At times like these, it feels like your fellow students have made a judgment about whether or not you are a sensitive person with vital things to say; it can be remarkably easy to forget that they have simply told you whether or not they liked your story.

The straightforward peer evaluation that a workshop offers can be illuminating, but it can also be nervewracking. In fact, nervousness is often a good sign: if you are nervous about having readers tell you what they thought of your story, it is an indication that you actually care about what you wrote, that you made an effort to communicate something that was important to you, and that you worked hard. There are many ways to ensure that the potentially tense experience of having a story workshopped remains a constructive one. Be sure to listen; try not to respond or you'll miss the discussion and miss potentially helpful suggestions. Take notes, so that you'll have a written record of the exchange of ideas, instead of a general impression. Write down any questions the discussion raised for you, to be considered later, or addressed at a student–teacher conference. The best way to make the workshopping of your story a constructive experience, however, is to make sure that you do what you can to make your classroom a good place to work, by discussing other students' stories with care and compassion.

Peer Review Strategies

When you receive another student's story, make a copy of that story, and use this second copy as a worksheet for these strategies.

1. Most stories, on any level, produce at least one "visceral" reaction in their readers: an image, character, or piece of dialogue makes the reader feel something powerful, although that something cannot be easily described in words supplied by any critical lexicon.

   a. Describe the effect of a powerful reading moment in terms of a "visceral" feeling, something in your body. Describe the *precise* feeling, without using a cliche (no chills down the spine, no sinking feelings in the stomach, unless these things actually happened).

   b. Do (a), but describe a powerful reading moment in terms of a powerful moment from life: the first taste of a sweet plum in summertime, the jarring shock of a bicycle crash at age twelve.

2. As you read through the story, circle sentences or passages that you find awkward, unclear, or poorly written. Do not attempt to explain why these sentences do not work. Choose three (or more) of these sentences and rewrite them.

3. Select three (or more) sentences, phrases, or passages that you believe could be deleted, thereby improving the story. If you believe that the story requires no deletions, select three (or more) sentences, phrases, or passages that could be cut without harming the story. If you believe that cannot be done, make three selections anyway. Block these passages with dark ink or white-out.

   Read the story again when rereading seems fresh (one day later, two days later, a week). Did your changes make a difference? Explain.

4. Select three aspects that you would add to the story: more in-depth treatment of a specific character, an extra character, more detail about setting, an extra scene or a longer treatment of a scene that might have been described in passing, or in a flashback.

   Indicate (in the margins) where you would like these additions to be made. Even if you believe no additions need to be made, make these selections anyway.

As in the third strategy, reread the story. Would you still make these recommendations?

5. As you read the story, mark places where you liked, or did not like, some aspect of the story. If you can describe your impressions in words, do so; if not, mark these places with checks or asterisks.

After you have finished the story, pick five of these marked places and increase the specificity of each of your comments.

    a. If you make a check or asterisk, replace that mark with a word or phrase.

    b. If you placed a word or a brief phrase, replace it with a more detailed word or phrase. Use a thesaurus, if necessary. For instance, if you wrote that a certain passage was "good," "excellent," or "funny," replace those words with a word that more precisely describes the experience of reading that passage: "good" becomes *vividly described, affecting, realistic,* "excellent" becomes *easy to picture, surprising but believable,* "funny" becomes *slapstick, witty.*

    c. If you wrote a detailed phrase, develop your thought into a short paragraph.

6. Choose one or more aspects of the story that you particularly enjoyed or found moving. Can you make one suggestion that would allow the writer to call attention to that strength, expand it, or make it a central part of the story? Place this comment at the end of the author's copy of the story.

7. Choose one or more aspects of the story that you did not particularly enjoy. Can you make one suggestion to deemphasize that trait, or remove it entirely? What will its removal do to other aspects of the story? Place this comment at the end of the author's copy of the story.

8. As you write your comments, pretend you are engaged in a conversation with the writer of the story. Respond to aspects of the story as though they were the author's half of the dialogue, and your comments in the margin were the other half. If the author writes something humorous, laugh. If the author talks too long, cut him or her off. If the author says something you didn't understand, ask him or her for clarification. If the author does something you enjoy, ask him or her to repeat it, or do it more

often. Use the same kind of language you would use in everyday conversation.

9. A checklist:

a. After finishing the story, reread the opening lines immediately. Do the first page and the last page of the story appear to belong to the same story? Does it look like the author knew what direction the story would take and how it would end when he or she began writing? Does the author's good "aim" (or, on the other hand, aimlessness) impress you as an asset to the story?

b. Knowing how the story begins and ends, do you feel that there are scenes or characters that do not advance the story, or have anything to do with the line that you could draw from the beginning to the end? Is the story the kind of writing where a phrase like "the line you could draw from beginning to end" makes any sense?

c. On a separate piece of paper, divide the story into "sections": a section consists of a scene, a passage devoted to a character, a passage of description, or a unit of time.

   Having selected scenes or descriptive passages, can you identify those that do and do not have anything to do with explaining, or setting up, the ending? Would you cut those elements of the story that do not seem "necessary"? Or did you enjoy reading them for other reasons? What reasons?

d. Were there specific aspects of the story—the dialogue, a specific character, the ending—that struck you as being borrowed from other narrative forms, like television, motion pictures, or popular music? Having identified these aspects, do you mind that they are borrowed?

e. Look carefully again at purely descriptive passages. Are there characters, places, or events that you would like to see described in deeper detail? Less detail?

f. Look carefully at the dialogue. Speak the dialogue out loud, if necessary. Is it "real" dialogue? If it is not real, is it enjoyable for other reasons? What reasons?

g. Did you consider the language—the selection of adjectives, the construction of sentences, the rhythm of dialogue—to be a strong point of the story? Select three places in the story where the language was particularly affecting, and mark those places for the author.

h. Did you feel that the story was told in the best voice possible? Would you change the voice or narrative point of view?

i. Does the story seem to start and end in the right places—in terms of time frame, characters, plot events?

10. Pick a character from the story, or a setting, for which relatively little information has been provided. Write a short description of this character (or setting). This description might be a brief history, or a physical description, or a missing scene where that character (or setting) plays a prominent role.

Do you think the author's story would be improved by including your additional description, or descriptions like them?

8

ADVANCED WORKSHOPS

WRITING IN THE LIGHT

Advanced workshops are marked by an even greater seriousness of discussion, greater purpose in the classroom, greater rigor in criticism, and, often, a greater degree of sociability. Almost everyone around the table has more at stake in their writing as their commitment to the craft has evolved, and this sense of shared commitment can be both inspiring and challenging. As advanced workshops seek to heighten the level of writing and criticism, more detailed discussions about the writer's and the writing's purposes are bound to occur. What is fiction attempting to accomplish, how does it accomplish it, and is the accomplishment worthwhile?

It can be exhilarating to hear your fiction discussed at length, as literature. It can also be challenging: the depth in which your story is analyzed may reveal problems or possibilities in it that you hadn't even considered. The criticism you receive in a workshop of high caliber can sustain you as a writer for years. The workshop convenes a group of writers who will be attentive readers of your fiction. Their insights, their nurturance of your sense of self as a writer, will support your work long after the class disbands. Accordingly, it is crucial to listen well, to have your questions addressed, and to retain interesting comments about your work and the work of others. Reading workshop pieces carefully and engaging in discussion will inevitably inform your own writing as well as create an atmosphere of communal ambition and care.

The effect of "writing in the light"—of writing in a public arena—can make you increasingly conscious of what writing means to you and of a higher level of expectation in the workshop; this may lead you to feel that you should show only your "safest" work. But if you resist the temptation to explore new forms, new voices, and new situations in the advanced workshop, then where will such experimentation take place? Such experiments become private writing, even though perhaps they could sustain a public discussion and be improved by it. By sharing the experiment with the workshop, you own up, in a way that most artists can't, to the fact that you have written it, that you have taken a risk and are now willing to hear about its effect on an audience. And yet, beyond that limited audience, nobody need know that you've done such a thing. In this way, despite how public a workshop may seem, it is still essentially private.

So what should you show your workshop? Should you try only experimentation? Should you try only polished pieces, because to hear tough criticism could discourage you at a tenuous stage in your writing? Should you show only first person, or third person? Or work that has already been published? Or work that has already been workshopped? It is safe to say that the workshop can best serve you—and that you can best serve the workshop—by submitting work that you are prepared to show, but work that is also your most recent, and, if not, is at least work you care about. To be sensitive to criticism is painful, but to feel no sting when someone says, "I don't see the point here" or a similarly critical comment, means that you are not engaged in the work at hand, that it does not matter. Writers who participate in many workshops remain as sensitive as ever if they consistently show work that represents their best talents and ambitions; hopefully they develop an awareness of which criticisms are useful to the story at hand.

The resistance to showing fresh work is certainly present in some workshops, and has reached such a level that some graduate programs now require that students submitting work for discussion note on their title page a "history" of the draft they are showing, including when it was initially written and whether and when the work has been workshopped before. The resistance to sharing fresh work is often productive, causing writers to edit rigorously before showing new stories.

Finally, it is important to remember that success in writing is more than relative. If success is defined by you, by what goals you set, and by how you go about achieving the goals, the workshop will work best for you. If you find satisfaction in reading, writing, and improving, then you will be more informed by any criticism the workshop offers. If, on the other hand, you look to the workshop either as the sole inspiration for writing or as the means for achieving professional success, then it can be a difficult experience.

Writing Strategies

1. Before your story is workshopped, make notes concerning its strengths and weaknesses. Line these up against what the workshop says about the story. How do they compare? Do you agree or disagree?

2. Before your story is workshopped, mark it up with line edits. Do these line edits jibe with your colleagues' responses? What are they missing that you've marked? What are you missing that they've marked?

3. Consider the history of your workshop submissions.

    a. Are there stories you've shown in workshop more than once? If so, did the multiple discussions yield substantial insight or change?

    b. Do you have stories that you've declined to share in workshop? If so, what distinguishes these stories from those you've shown? Are there ways in which your choice of submissions could better exploit the resource of a workshop?

THE VOICE OF THE WORKSHOP

Students engaged in the intensive atmosphere of an advanced workshop sometimes remark that, when they write, they can hear the voices of the workshop in their heads. Although it is not the intention of the workshop leader and the participants to accompany the writer in the solitary development of a first draft, if such a chorus can encourage ambitious writing, then the workshop succeeds. But if the voices inhibit the writer, it is then up to the writer to silence them, which is easier said than done. Anybody experiencing this kind of block may do well to recall how the workshop is a metaphor for the experience itself. In a workshop a number of well-meaning consultants provide you with tools. It is your task to sort through all the tools to find those that best serve the particular piece you're working on, and to leave the rest of the tools on the shelf for another time. Upon completion of the task at hand, even the useful tools have to go up on the shelf. When you feel a fresh short story emerging, you decide which tools to use, and when to pull them from the shelf.

If the next story you write has the quality of a stone, and you've got the saw of the workshop going in your ear, you must find a way to put aside the saw. You can try working in different environments, such as choosing a different room or a different building or even going outside to sit in a car or on a park bench. You can try a different writing process, such as writing directly on the word processor or in a notebook. You can try writing at a different time of day. You can try freewriting, journal writing, or any other casual kind of writing as a way of establishing your voice on the page.

A part of writing is inhibition—of getting beyond the barrier between you and language, and between imagined language and the way it gets set down on the page. In this sense, the dynamic of the workshop is really a metaphor for, and an extension of, the play of inhibition and inspiration that exists within every author. While some writers may find that they are simply not meant to write within the atmosphere of intensive workshops, most writers eventually succeed in reestablishing the priority of their own voices above all others and move on to the next level.

Writing Strategies

1. Make a list of some of the constructive criticisms and insights that fiction workshops have provided you. How have workshop discussions inspired you to strengthen content or technique? Is this list relevant to what you're writing now?

2. Try giving yourself an exercise, such as any of the strategies in this book, to free your voice. Try freewriting, or writing in a different form, or exploring a character that interests you.

3. Vary your writing routine through any or all of these methods: changing when you write, where you write, how long you write, or the instrument with which you write.

THE NOVEL IN THE WORKSHOP

Francine Prose once said that making a novel is like making Jell-O: sharing its beginning or middle with a workshop before it has taken its own full shape allows other people to apply their mold to your Jell-O. Indeed, perhaps even the act of workshop discussion will change the shape of your novel into something that you had not imagined, and perhaps even alter your creative process.

Workshop readers and leaders may resist the idea of the novel. They may want to see more before being able to discuss an opening section, or they may want to have more explained to feel comfortable in talking about a middle section, or they may need to have a summary of the novel's entire plot if shown only the closing twenty pages.

Whether they are shown Chapter One or Chapter Ten, workshop participants should be able to discuss the work. You can, for instance, provide plot synopses for missing chapters. Discussion can focus on the voice of the piece, or the techniques of dialogue, gesture and detail, or the overall narrative movement with which the piece impresses the reader. The novel writer may even supply a list of questions with the submission to indicate whether the best purpose of the workshop is to help improve what is on the page, or to provide input on what direction the novel can take beyond that being shown.

On the other hand, if you agree with Francine Prose's reasons for keeping the novel out of the workshop, you could instead show other kinds of work to fulfill the contract that you not only read other people's work, but also show your own. You could produce short-shorts, short stories, essays, or even a memoir fragment to serve as your contribution to the workshop. And you can gain from workshop discussion and your own criticism of short stories, because the elements of fiction that make successful short stories also make successful novels.

Writing Strategies

1. If selecting your own novel excerpt, read it thoroughly. Imagine coming to this excerpt as if you had no knowledge of what came before and what would come after. Does it seem to begin at a logical point and end at a logical point? Are there other places that you should be cutting to or cutting from?

2. When reading a colleague's novel excerpt, think about the voice. Does it engage you, entertain you, frustrate you? How so?

3. Consider the characters in the novel excerpt. Are they developing or changing over the pages that have been selected? Are there any gestures or details that are particularly strong or weak concerning these characters?

4. Consider the level of detail in the novel excerpt. Are you getting enough of a picture of the world in which the novel is set? Does the level of detail seem consistent with the pacing and the overall approach of the novel?

TEACHER–STUDENT CONFERENCES

The teacher–student conference provides you with an opportunity for dialogue about a particular piece of your writing and a chance to initiate a larger conversation. Some teachers will discuss your story in the same manner that they've discussed it in class, perhaps summarizing and supplementing the workshop discussion, and elucidating certain criticisms by giving specific suggestions. If you wish to discuss additional issues, such as the content of your story, your writing process, or your work as a whole, the conference is an opportunity for you to raise these questions.

The conference can also prove valuable in developing your reading list. You can ask about the books you've been reading—or the books the teacher has been reading—and gain suggestions for what you could read in the future. You may even have specific questions along these lines. Your interests, for example, could be in political fiction or magic realism, and your teacher may be able to help direct you to specific novels and story collections.

The teacher as writer can serve as a mentor, as well, someone whom you might ask for advice. Professional writers who are teachers are role models who represent possibilities for being a writer. Not only can they steer you to or away from further work-shops, but they can suggest ways that you can write while still earning a living—many of them have had such experiences, as taxi drivers, bartenders, high school teachers, copy editors, proofread-ers. They know what it takes to continue writing, and their exper-iences can inform you.

In short, use the conference to learn from your teacher any way you can. If you wonder about a weakness in your story that no one else has caught, bring it up. Come armed with questions, ideas, talking points.

Writing Strategies

1. Make a list of all the things that intrigue you and confound you about your story. Be prepared to discuss these with your teacher.

2. Make a list of the writers whom you're currently reading, whom you feel are influencing your work. Question your teacher about the nature and the range of this list.

3. Consider all of your work that your teacher has seen. What con-nections can you make among these pieces, in terms of subject and technique, and in terms of flaw and accomplishment? Bring up these connections in conference, and ask for advice about authors to read and writing strategies to use as you continue to write.

PART

III

ON YOUR OWN

WRITING WITHOUT
A WORKSHOP

The pressures of earning a living, or continuing in other educational arenas, can conspire to undermine your sense of yourself as a writer. In addition, friends and family may not always take your pursuit of the craft seriously; they may even refer to it as your hobby. A decidedly positive aspect of the workshop experience is that, in the classroom, peers treat each other as writers. But when you cease to attend workshop, or if the workshop has never played a part in your writing, who will treat you as a writer? If you're serious about writing, or if at least you are sure that you want to keep writing, you have to be the first one to see yourself as a writer.

SPACE AND TIME

First, there is the question of space and time. You must find an appropriate space for writing, available for a significant period of time in your day. The space could be a seat on a commuter train, as it has been for best-selling novelist Scott Turow, or it could be an isolated house in Brazil, as it was for renowned poet Elizabeth Bishop, or you may want to invest in your own small office, as John Cheever did. Your particular lifestyle will determine the suitable space and the suitable time. But you need space and time to get the work done. In a way it sounds simple and obvious, this issue of space and time, but consider your day. Can you easily imagine a time and a space in the day where you can write? It is up to you, regardless of the degree of difficulty, to carve out the space and time, to take thirty minutes of an hour lunch break to write, the way some people sneak off to gyms. Or to give up your weekends to writing.

In order to improve as a writer, you will need space and time that can be part of your routine, that can occur regularly—every day, every other day, every weekend. Frequency allows greater chance for improvement, and for the opportunity to experience inspiration and transform it into art. The discipline of maintaining a writing regimen can enable you to transcend your own artistic boundaries. A large part of writer's block is inhibition, and participation in a routine can break that inhibition. "I write every morning," novelist Virginia Woolf notes in her diary, "feeling each day's work like a fence which I have to ride at, my heart in my mouth till it's over, and I've cleared, or knocked the bar out."

Practical issues—how much time is required per writing session, how often the sessions should occur, and at which time of day— depend on your own writing process. Some writers can concentrate only in short bursts, while others need a few hours to work up to a productive session. Some writers need the almost addictive nature of the daily routine, while others find that time off refreshes them. Artistic temperaments vary widely, and writing routines are accordingly diverse. Try out a number of times and spaces, if you can, and allow yourself to choose through experience.

Writing Strategies

1. Write out your weekly schedule. Try to pinpoint a consistent, extended time (minimum forty-five minutes) for writing each day, or at consistent intervals (every other day, every weekend). Now think of a place you could write during this time—in your home or office, at a library, on the bus. Keep to your schedule; note how and when your routine is interrupted. Work to make it fail-safe.

APPROACHES TO THE BLANK PAGE

Concurrent with mapping out your routine is the essential difficulty of writing: approaching the blank page. There is probably nothing more terrifying than situating yourself at a desk with everything you need to write, and then finding yourself staring at an empty piece of paper not knowing whether you have anything to say, or if what you say is worthwhile or even interesting. Writes Sylvia Plath: "I have done, this year, what I said I would: overcome my fear of facing a blank page day after day, acknowledging myself, in my deepest emotions, a writer, come what may: rejections or curtailed budgets." To be a writer, and to face the blank page, is to face uncertainty on many levels. You don't even know if you'll be able to produce; and even if you are able, you won't at the time be sure that it'll be any good; and even if it is, you can't be certain that its strength will have any meaning to anyone but you.

The physical act of approaching the blank page is entangled with ambivalence and even fear. You can engage in rituals that allow for distractions to help you slide into the actual task of writing— you can prepare a cup of coffee, or sharpen a certain number of pencils. Or you can concentrate on somehow shrinking the task— you can use notebooks with smaller pages, to make filling the page seem less intimidating. You can reread what you've written the session before, or ignore it entirely, to give yourself a feeling of freshness. Rereading the previous day's writing, John Barth once told *The Paris Review*, "is to get to the rhythm partly, and partly it's a kind of magic: it *feels* like you're writing, though you're not." Frank Conroy, whenever he reached an impasse in writing his first book *Stop Time*, reread all that he had written up to that point, before beginning to write anew. Ritualizing the approach to the blank page allows you to feel comfortable with the process of starting to write. Regardless of whether you choose a ritual, the point is to know how you compose best, and to use that knowledge to allow you to compose more and to compose regularly. Consider the method used by Ernest Hemingway:

> When I am working on a book or a story I write every morning as soon after first light as possible. There is no one to disturb you and it is cool or cold and you come to your work and warm as you write. You read what you have written and, as you always stop when you know what is going to happen next, you go on from there. You write until you come to a place where you still have your juice and know what will happen next and you stop and try to live through until the next day when you hit it again. You have started at six in the morning, say, and may go on until noon or be through before that.

Hemingway also kept a word count of his daily production.

A schedule is crucial, in one way, but even more crucial is your desire to grasp at opportunities whenever and however they present themselves. The poet Jorie Graham, a recent recipient of a MacArthur Fellowship, sometimes writes poems while sitting in her car in the parking lot of her neighborhood supermarket, because that is where both the inspiration and the opportunity present themselves. A schedule can allow you to "keep in shape," so that when the inspiration strikes, you are prepared to work with it.

Writing Strategies

1. Develop a routine that works for you, that puts you in the right frame of mind for writing. Get coffee, or not. Play the radio, or not.

2. Develop a relationship to the previous session's writing that works for you—either reread, or not. But be consistent.

3. Keep a notebook or pad of paper within reach for taking down ideas, images, and specific lines that you can later use in your fiction.

4. Make yourself write something when you think you're least ready for it: when you're waiting in line, or getting ready to go to sleep at night.

LIVING WITH UNCERTAINTY

The process of writing, as Virginia Woolf notes, allows for both failure and achievement: "I write two pages of arrant nonsense, after straining; I write variations of every sentence; compromises; bad shots; possibilities; till my writing book is like a lunatic's dream. Then I trust to some inspiration on re-reading; and pencil them into sense." In order to write something good, you have to write. A good line or a good paragraph is only possible if the writing preceding and following it exists. All writers fail, and it can be liberating to know that Updike and Joyce and Kafka and Woolf and Tolstoy all failed. And they succeeded, in part, because they gave themselves the right to fail.

Living with uncertainty can be overwhelming. You block off a time in your day, turn off your phone, limit yourself to just your desk, and then find out that you have nothing to write. Or you write for weeks at a time, filling page after page, only to determine that the work is weak. No wonder the chronicles of the most renowned writers of our times are filled with alcoholism, depression, alienation, and suicide. But many acclaimed writers have also learned to live with the uncertainty, although sometimes their very sanity draws accusations—as if the public thinks that they are not so committed to their art as the stereotype of the insane writer suggests they need to be. "You write that the main character of my *Name-Day Party* is a figure who should be developed," Chekhov responded to one critic. "Good God, I am not a brute without feelings, I understand that. I understand that I cut up my characters and ruin them, that I ruin good material for nothing." Art, by its very nature, is imperfect, and struggling with the limits of imperfection is the ultimate grappling that writers must endure. In a way, your path through uncertainty lies in recognizing your limits, then pushing at them any way you can, while exercising as often as possible all the diversity of your strength as a writer.

Writing Strategies

1. Force yourself to write a minimum number of words every day. Don't be afraid to cut them, but allow them onto the page first.

2. If you're blocked for an extended period of time (depending on your own definition of *extended*), vary your routine. But keep allowing yourself a specific time in a separate space.

3. Try writing in a different form, such as a poem, journal entry, or essay, or recording dreams that you can recall. Examine what you've written for potential use in fiction. Who are the characters, what are the images, whose voices emerge?

4. Try writing in a vein you know you will fail at: if you're strong only in first person, try third person; if you're strong only in very short stories, try longer stories. What strengths are showing through the anticipated weaknesses? How can these strengths help you address the shortcomings?

READING

How can you tell if you're getting better as a writer, given all this uncertainty? What worth can you ascribe to your own work, and how does such evaluation take place, and what are the most important ways that you can contribute to your own improvement? The way to a writer's self-awareness is reading—reading the best work you know, reading the work of your colleagues, and reading your own work scrupulously.

Because reading is so important to the process of writing, it is essential to be as disciplined about it as you are about your own writing. You may want to create time and space for reading. You may want to be conscious of what you like to read and why—think about what you want to accomplish in comparison with authors you're reading. You can keep track of what you read, and when your writing is not coming along well, you can *on occasion* allow yourself to read during your writing time. You can also follow current fiction by reading literary magazines and book reviews, by going to bookstores to browse through books you've heard about, and by sharing your own work with others. If you're in the process of finishing a writing workshop, consider exchanging stories with the other participants even after the workshop ends. By continuing to hear their comments and giving them yours, you will remain sharp as a critic, which is essential to your own writing. It will also provide you with extensive feedback from someone who views your commitment as serious. If you find yourself missing the workshop experience, or if you want a chance to participate in a workshop for the first time, you can probably find a group in your town, free of charge—check local bookstores, libraries, universities, alternative and arts publications, and social organizations such as the Y.

While it is true that not everyone who writes really wants to be a better writer, it is certain that writing better requires seriousness, a dedication to the task, and an understanding that writing is a discipline. Many writers who commit themselves to writing view it as a way of life, and as a process that sustains them. For them, the act of writing in itself, as well as the insight and creation that accompanies it, is reward enough. "I write in service of illumination and writing," says Mark Helprin, author of two story collections and three novels. "I write to reach into 'the blind world where no one can help' [quoting Norman Maclean, author of *A River Runs Through It*]. I write because it is a way of glimpsing the truth. And I write to create something of beauty."

Writing, ultimately, is a process of discovery, and as such it is personal to each writer. These intimate qualities of your writing process will lead you to return to it again and again, even when you think that you may fail. The writing itself can become so particular to you, to who you are and how you want to live, that it will be essential for you to write in order to thrive. There is nothing wrong with having this kind of "biological need" to write: it just means that in writing you have found an essential process of thinking that has meaning to you, that informs you. Eudora Welty writes: "The events in our lives happen in a sequence in time, but in their significance to ourselves they find their own order, a timetable not necessarily—perhaps not possibly—chronological. The time as we know it subjectively is often the chronology that stories and novels follow: it is the continuous thread to revelation."

Writing Strategies

1. Develop a reading regimen that allows you to read carefully and critically without sacrificing your *writing* regimen. Try reading whenever you can—on public transportation, or during lunch breaks or coffee breaks.

2. Keep a log in which you write a brief comment on each book (or even each story) you read, noting the voice, the subject matter, or anything that strikes you as essential to the fiction. Read extensively in the particular approaches with which you identify strongly, but periodically review your annotations to ensure that you're reading a range of fiction, both current and older, by a wide variety of authors.

WRITING AS A CAREER

Few fiction-writing careers involve just writing fiction. Most professional writers also teach writing, or write for newspapers and magazines, or serve as editorial consultants on projects such as marketing manuals or corporate newsletters. But although a writing career involves more than just selling your fiction, and although publishing your work is tangential to your development as a writer, if you want to begin to make a living as a writer you will eventually need to publish. Franz Kafka wrote with a placard over his desk that said WAIT. But the fact is, you will need to pursue publication in order to obtain support for further writing through fellowships, lectureships, writing residencies, academic appointments, magazine article contracts, and book contracts. There are occasionally writers who, early in their development, sell their first stories to *The New Yorker* or *The Atlantic,* but for the most part gaining publication success happens gradually. Few fiction writers can live off what they actually want to write. Writing is an act of faith for many writers who aspire simply to write better and to write more.

Part of publishing is the sense of recognition, the knowledge that an audience can find you, share what you have cared about, and perhaps be moved by it. For this reason, you'll want to find a venue with an appropriate audience, which means a magazine or publishing house that publishes work similar to yours in some aspect, or work you admire. When pursuing publication, you should regularly read the fiction published by the magazines or publishing houses to which you aspire, and see if it makes sense for you to submit your work to them. If it does make sense, be sure to adhere to standard manuscript guidelines. Your work should be typed, double-spaced on eight-and-a-half by eleven-inch white paper, with your name and return address on the upper-right corner of the first page, the title centered on the page, and the text beginning a quadruple space from the title. If at all possible, you should submit your work to a specific editor; be sure to enclose a self-addressed stamped envelope for the editor to use when returning a story or sending you a contract.

If your return envelope comes back and it feels so thick that the story must be in it, be sure to open it anyway. Some editors will ask you to consider making changes before their final decision, and other editors, while declining your work, may write you a comment, and become a part of your "workshop beyond the workshop." Take these comments as you would any criticism; if it strikes a chord, you can develop a revision. Submit such a revision to the same magazine, however, only at the editor's invitation. Comments take only a minute or two for editors to write, and some writers recommend that you take only that much time to think about them. But editors are experienced readers, and often their hurried comments contain substantial insight. Issues such as whether or not to submit your story to more than one magazine at once are particular to each literary magazine; check the magazine's masthead, *Writer's Market,* or *Directory of Literary Magazines* for information on simultaneous submission. Richard Burgin's interview following this section will help give you a sense of exactly what a magazine editor looks for, and how the process of editing a literary magazine works.

It is important not to pay too much attention to the professional success of writers around you when it comes to measuring your own worth as a writer. Writers develop at different rates and in different ways, and if early publication was the only yardstick for success, then Franz Kafka (the majority of whose work was published posthumously), Bernard Malamud, and Toni Morrison (whose first books did not appear in print until the authors were in their late thirties), among others, could not be characterized as successes. Inevitably, it seems, some developing writers are likely to become distracted by their own success or by the success of others. Although there are any number of ways to gain solace along the writing career track, the best way to come to terms with careerism in writing is to reflect on a simple question: Why do you write? If you look solely for affirmation of your writing in the responses of editors and publishers and awards committees, and if your overriding purpose in writing is to gain that affirmation, then your answer to the question of why you write (and consequently the writing itself) may leave you dissatisfied. Great writers write to uncover, discover, reveal truths to themselves and, ultimately, to other people. The process of discovery in the act of writing is the first and most essential reward.

Writing Strategies

1. Read widely in magazines to which you're thinking of submitting your work.

    a. Note the range of the fiction that is published in each particular magazine, including the style, tone, length, and subject matter. Does the magazine, apart from what you've learned from the various market catalogs, seem to have a predilection for a certain length or subject or voice?

    b. Compare, as objectively as possible, the quality of your own work to the quality of the work in the magazine. Line edit and critically review a story in the magazine that you consider of similar quality to your own work. Then, almost immediately, line edit and review a story of your own. How does your story measure up?

2. Consider responses from editors.

   a. Are the encouraging remarks specific, and can they be useful in understanding when and how your writing works well for an audience?

   b. Are the critical remarks specific? Do they give you a fair sense of when and how your writing falls short in having its intended effect on an audience?

   c. If you have received more than one response on a story, compare all the notes. Is there an aspect of your story that the editors all agree on? Is it positive or negative? Do you sense any consensus that could be useful in helping you rewrite the story, or in furthering your writing in general?

3. Assemble a collection of quotes on the purposes and rewards of writing, including some of your own thoughts on the subject. How were you initially attracted to writing fiction? How does writing figure in your life now?

Richard Burgin

Richard Burgin is the author of Conversations with Jorge Luis Borges *(1969) and* Conversations with Isaac Bashevis Singer *(1985), as well as two short story collections,* Man Without Memory *(1989) and* Private Fame *(1991). He has received two Pushcart Prize citations for his short fiction, and regularly contributes to the* New York Times Book Review, Washington Post Book World, *and others. Burgin is the editor of* Boulevard *magazine, and serves on the faculty of Drexel University in Philadelphia.*

Emotional Real Estate:
An Interview with Richard Burgin

At Boulevard, *do you look for a certain kind of writing? How do you judge the writing that you receive?*

At *Boulevard* we're open to different styles of writing. We try to be eclectic in the best sense of the word and to be mindful of

Nabokov's dictum "there is only one school, the school of talent." Above all, when we consider the very diverse manuscripts submitted to us we value original sensibility—writing that causes the reader to experience a part of life in a new way. Originality, to us, has little to do with a writer intently trying to make each line or sentence odd, bizarre, or eccentric, merely for the sake of being "different" or "avant garde." Rather, originality is the result of the character or vision of the writer; the writer's singular outlook and voice as it shines through in the totality of his or her work.

As *Boulevard's* size and reputation have grown, its staff has increased and the processes used for evaluating submissions has somewhat altered. At present, the managing editor and I open the mail and decide after a cursory first reading of the thirty or so submissions we receive each day, which of our twelve to fifteen readers would be best equipped to read a particular piece. Our readers are a diverse group, themselves ranging from graduate students to a tenured professor, and including a housewife, a furniture painter, an arts administrator, and a practicing physician. Most of our readers are also working writers themselves, and all of them have an intense interest in and love for literature. Some, however, "only" read poetry, while others have a predilection for formally experimental work, and so on. We try to match the skills and interests of the readers (an all-volunteer group, incidentally) with the pieces in question. If the reader thinks a piece should be published, he or she passes the piece along to me and I make the final decision. It's through this simple process that we've published in recent issues such "unknown" writers as Frank Pike, Bruce Comens, Spencer Reece, and the then little known Kathleen Peirce and Melanie Sumner.

How does the rejection process work? What do you do about stories you like, but don't feel you can publish?

Sometimes, depending on just how poorly it's written, we'll reject a story after reading only a part of it. Much more often, though, decisions are difficult, sometimes agonizingly so. Often I'll end up reading a story or essay three or more times and taking longer than I probably should to make a final decision. This leads to the delicate question of how we write rejection letters. Our first rule is never, ever insult the writer's work. It is painful enough to have one's work rejected; there is no point in adding insult to injury. In those cases where the piece is clearly well below our standards, we send writers a polite rejection form thanking them for submitting their material. When we think the writer definitely has enough talent to publish in *Boulevard*, although the particular piece submitted to us is not quite good enough, we encourage them to submit to us again. I make sure in such cases that I tell the writers that I admire their work, and what specifically I liked about their piece. I add that it was difficult deciding against it and that I truly hope they'll send me more work to consider soon.

Generally I don't get too specific about what I don't like in a piece unless the writer requests such criticism. However, if I know that I will publish a piece if a writer will change certain things such as a melodramatic ending, or a particular event in a story that seems trite or insufficiently motivated, then I'll present them with that option and will be quite specific in my critique. I've sometimes spent a number of hours detailing my suggestions in letters and/or phone conversations but only when I'm convinced my suggestions will improve a piece to the point where I'll publish it. This happens just a few times a year, and of course the writers don't always agree with my suggestions, but I never regret making the effort when I believe in a piece's potential. In one case that ended happily, a writer sent me a fictional memoir about eighty pages long—way too long for what the piece and *Boulevard* needed. After extensive editing I proposed a thirty-page version, the writer agreed with me, worked on it with me, and *Boulevard* published the piece—which eventually was awarded a Pushcart Prize.

Do you think literary magazines in general have editorial biases? Do you think there is a way for a reader to tell what kinds of stories a given magazine publishes, or do you think these preferences are more or less covert?

There's little doubt that some magazines have an editorial bias and are therefore more likely to publish certain kinds of stories. Sometimes these publications are forthright enough to admit this bias and actually want you to know about it. For example, in the *Council of Literary Magazines and Presses Directory, Conjunctions* tells us that it "publishes formally innovative writing" while *The Long Story* says that it is "interested strictly in long stories—bias is left wing and concern for human struggle for dignity, etc."

Some magazines publish mainly women, others mainly gay writers or minorities. Some are devoted to publishing work from a particular part of the country—West Coast in the case of *Zyzzyva*. Consulting a good directory such as the *CLMP Directory, The International Directory of Little Magazines and Small Presses,* or *Novel and Short Story Writer's Market* can be a useful way to discover these "biases" and then decide if it is appropriate or not to send them work.

Of course an editor may have a covert bias that he or she may not wish to disclose or even be aware of. Some may prefer realistic stories in the third person with the traditional epiphany somewhere near the end; others may prefer first person confessional stories that are dramatic or shocking. Some may favor subtle Chekhovian stories, others stories with magic realism, etc. The theme you write about may attract or repel an editor because of experiences in his or her personal life. There's a fine line between "bias" and individual sensibility, and at a certain point to say "bias" is simply to say a different human being. Nevertheless, covert biases *do* exist, and that's important to remember in evaluating why a piece of yours may have been rejected. As far as discovering these covert editorial biases, the only thing I can think of is to read the fiction in a magazine over a period of time.

Do you have any advice for a serious beginning writer?

One of the charms and frustrations of being a serious writer is that there is no formula for becoming one. Important writers like Flannery O'Connor and Raymond Carver have come out of writing programs and equally important ones like William Faulkner, Edward Albee, Henry Miller, Isaac Bashevis Singer, and Tennessee Williams have never even graduated from college. Some, like John Updike, have supported themselves by writing their whole lives; others have had separate careers, like that well-known insurance lawyer Wallace Stevens or the good doctors Chekhov and William Carlos Williams. The only piece of advice I could give with a straight face is the socratic one of knowing yourself. Since there's little interest or point in copying others, and since all souls and lives are unique, self-knowledge about your own life and sensibility is the first step toward originality. Discover your own "emotional real estate"—that territory that is uniquely your own and that you are uniquely qualified to write about. And don't worry about publishing quickly. If there is one danger that may be an intrinsic part of many writing programs, it's that pressure—generally a peer pressure—to publish often and quickly. The artist should resist such pressure. The artist should devote him- or herself to discovering that territory that is his or her own, cultivate it, perfect it, and then try to share it with the world via publication.

Can you talk about the idea of influence in general? Who would you say has influenced you?

Because we have no other choice as writers but to draw from our own lives, everything that happens to us influences us. My parents (though my father died thirteen years ago) continue to be the strongest emotional, psychological, and—in many ways—intellectual influence on my life. After them, my sister, the friends of my childhood and adolescence, and all the people I've loved in my life are influential. If you want to understand yourself, study your parents, your family, and those people you chose to love. Explore what happened in those relationships and you'll begin to understand what your emotional real estate really is, and what it is you should probably be writing about.

As far as literary mentors go there hasn't been a single dominating one. Rather, different mentors have emerged to help me in valuable ways at different times in my life. When I was a sophomore at Brandeis I took a creative-writing class with the gifted poet Ruth Stone. She was the first accomplished writer to express a lot of enthusiasm for my work. She probably overpraised it, but it helped give me the confidence I needed to really begin not only writing longer works of fiction but reading literature far in excess of the works I was assigned in my college courses. When I mentioned to her once that one of my other professors had roundly criticized a story of mine that she was now praising, she said, "Maybe he isn't on your wavelength." Of course I was tremendously flattered by her quasi-subversive remark, but it stayed in my mind because this was the first time I'd really begun to realize that in literature, as opposed to science, it isn't always a question of a right or wrong critical response. I began to see that the reader as well as the writer brings to a work of literature his or her individual sensibility with all of its beauty and biases.

Ruth was also the first teacher to step outside the walls of the classroom and offer her friendship to me, as she did to a number of other students. I think her lasting legacy to me was to teach me to not hold back my enthusiasm for a writer if I feel it, and to err on the side of overenthusiasm rather than restraint. I have continued to try to apply this lesson in dealing with the writers who send work to me at *Boulevard,* and in my own classroom at Drexel University.

Nearly a decade later I met Isaac Bashevis Singer through a mutual friend in New York. I was then editing a magazine called *New York Arts Journal* and was fortunate enough to eventually publish two stories by Singer. A few months after I met Isaac and read everything he'd published in English, he agreed to work with me on an interview book similar to my *Conversations with Jorge Luis Borges.* Singer is a tremendously complex personality and my feelings about him are far from simple. Nevertheless he was a definite mentor, especially in the first years that we worked on *Conversations with Isaac Bashevis Singer.* In Isaac I found an unforgettable example of someone totally devoted to his art. At the same time he was intensely curious about other people and made himself available to anyone who wanted to meet him or had an interest in his work. His phone was always ringing and people were often knocking on his door. He didn't own an answering machine and answered the phone himself. Even after he won the Nobel Prize, he kept his New York phone number listed. The award didn't change him an iota; he never acted like a star. Consequently he often wrote between phone calls and visits by people, for (as he told me) in meeting new people and listening to them he learned more about life and got new ideas for stories. This was a valuable lesson for me.

Isaac was a perfectionist to a degree that sometimes frustrated me. That's why our book that began in 1976 was not published until 1985. He insisted on going over every word several times and kept adding or deleting material. When I published his story "The Death of Methusaleh" in the first issue of *Boulevard,* I had to make four trips from Philadelphia, where I was living, to his apartment in New York to go over every word of the translation with him. While it could be exasperating, I eventually came to value his perfectionism and ultimately to be inspired by it.

Toni Cade Bambara

Toni Cade Bambara is the author of two major short story collections, Go-rilla, My Love *(1972) and* The Sea Birds Are Still Alive *(1977), and one novel,* The Salt Eaters *(1980). Bambara was born in New York City in 1939. She received a degree in Theatre Arts and English at Queens College in 1959. From 1959 to 1969 Bambara was employed by the City of New York in a series of social work and neighborhood program positions, during which time she published stories in* Prairie Schooner, Redbook, *and other journals. She is also the editor of several anthologies of African-American literature, and has served on the faculty of several universities, including Livingston College in New Jersey and Spelman College in Georgia. "A Sort of Preface" is the preface to* Gorilla, My Love.

A Sort of Preface

It does no good to write autobiographical fiction cause the minute the book hits the stand here comes your mama screamin how could you and sighin death where is thy sting and she snatches you up out your bed to grill you about what was going down back there in Brooklyn where she was working three jobs and trying to improve the quality of your life and come to find on page 42 that you were messin around with that nasty boy up the block and breaks into sobs and quite naturally your family strolls in all sleepy-eyed to catch the floor show at 5:00 A.M. but as far as your mama is con-cerned, it is nineteen-forty-and-something and you ain't too grown to have your ass whipped.

And it's no use using bits and snatches even of real events and real people, even if you do cover, guise, switch-around and change-up cause next thing you know your best friend's laundry cart is squeaking past but your bell ain't ringing so you trot down the block after her and there's this drafty cold pressure front the weatherman surely did not predict and your friend says in this chilly way that it's really something when your own friend stabs you in the back with a pen and for the next two blocks you try to explain that the character is not her at all but just happens to be speaking one of her lines and right about the time you hit the laun-dromat and you're ready to just give it up and take the weight, she turns to you and says that seeing as how you have plundered her soul and walked off with a piece of her flesh, the least you can do is spin off half the royalties her way.

So I deal in straight-up fiction myself, cause I value my family and friends, and mostly cause I lie a lot anyway.

Lorrie Moore

Lorrie Moore's literary career began at the age of seventeen, when the magazine Seventeen *awarded her first prize in its short story contest in 1976 for her story "Raspberries." She has published two collections of short stories,* Self-Help *(1985) and* Like Life *(1990), one novel,* Anagrams, *and one work for children,* The Forgotten Helper. *She also contributes regularly to* Cosmopolitan, Ms., *and the* New York Times Book Review. *Moore is the editor of* I Know Some Things: Stories About Childhood by Contemporary Writers *(1992). She currently lives in Wisconsin and teaches at the University of Wisconsin–Madison. "How to Become a Writer" is collected in* Self-Help, *which won the Associated Writing Programs Award for short fiction.*

How to Become a Writer

First, try to be something, anything, else. A movie star/astronaut. A movie star/missionary. A movie star/kindergarten teacher. President of the World. Fail miserably. It is best if you fail at an early age—say, fourteen. Early, critical disillusionment is necessary so that at fifteen you can write long haiku sequences about thwarted desire. It is a pond, a cherry blossom, a wind brushing against sparrow wing leaving for mountain. Count the syllables. Show it to your mom. She is tough and practical. She has a son in Vietnam and a husband who may be having an affair. She believes in wearing brown because it hides spots. She'll look briefly at your writing, then back up at you with a face blank as a donut. She'll say: "How about emptying the dishwasher?" Look away. Shove the forks in the fork drawer. Accidentally break one of the freebie gas station glasses. This is the required pain and suffering. This is only for starters.

In your high school English class look at Mr. Killian's face. Decide faces are important. Write a villanelle about pores. Struggle. Write a sonnet. Count the syllables: nine, ten, eleven, thirteen. Decide to experiment with fiction. Here you don't have to count syllables. Write a short story about an elderly man and woman who accidentally shoot each other in the head, the result of an inexplicable malfunction of a shotgun which appears mysteriously in their living room one night. Give it to Mr. Killian as your final project. When you get it back, he has written on it: "Some of your images are quite nice, but you have no sense of plot." When you are home, in the privacy of your own room, faintly scrawl in pencil beneath his black-inked comments: "Plots are for dead people, pore-face."

Take all the babysitting jobs you can get. You are great with kids. They love you. You tell them stories about old people who die idiot deaths. You sing them songs like "Blue Bells of Scotland," which is their favorite. And when they are in their pajamas and have finally stopped pinching each other, when they are fast asleep, you read every sex manual in the house, and wonder how on earth anyone could ever do those things with someone they truly loved. Fall asleep in a chair reading Mr. McMurphy's *Playboy*. When the McMurphys come home, they will tap you on the shoulder, look at the magazine in your lap, and grin. You will want to die. They will ask you if Tracey took her medicine all right. Explain, yes, she did, that you promised her a story if she would take it like a big girl and that seemed to work out just fine. "Oh, marvelous," they will exclaim.

Try to smile proudly.

Apply to college as a child psychology major.

As a child psychology major, you have some electives. You've always liked birds. Sign up for something called "The Ornithological Field Trip." It meets Tuesdays and Thursdays at two. When you arrive at Room 134 on the first day of class, everyone is sitting around a seminar table talking about metaphors. You've heard of these. After a short, excruciating while, raise your hand and say diffidently, "Excuse me, isn't this Bird-watching One-oh-one?" The class stops and turns to look at you. They seem to all have one face—giant and blank as a vandalized clock. Someone with a beard booms out, "No, this is Creative Writing." Say: "Oh—right," as if perhaps you knew all along. Look down at your schedule. Wonder how the hell you ended up here. The computer, apparently, has made an error. You start to get up to leave and then don't. The lines at the registrar this week are huge. Perhaps you should stick with this mistake. Perhaps your creative writing isn't all that bad. Perhaps it is fate. Perhaps this is what your dad meant when he said, "It's the age of computers, Francie, it's the age of computers."

Decide that you like college life. In your dorm you meet many nice people. Some are smarter than you. And some, you notice, are dumber than you. You will continue, unfortunately, to view the world in exactly these terms for the rest of your life.

The assignment this week in creative writing is to narrate a violent happening. Turn in a story about driving with your Uncle Gordon and another one about two old people who are accidentally electrocuted when they go to turn on a badly wired desk lamp. The teacher will hand them back to you with comments: "Much of your writing is smooth and energetic. You have, however, a ludicrous notion of plot." Write another story about a man and a woman who, in the very first paragraph, have their lower torsos accidentally blitzed away by dynamite. In the second paragraph, with the insurance money, they buy a frozen yogurt stand together. There are six more paragraphs. You read the whole thing out loud in class. No one likes it. They say your sense of plot is outrageous and incompetent. After class someone asks you if you are crazy.

Decide that perhaps you should stick to comedies. Start dating someone who is funny, someone who has what in high school you called a "really great sense of humor" and what now your creative writing class calls "self-contempt giving rise to comic form." Write down all of his jokes, but don't tell him you are doing this. Make up anagrams of his old girlfriend's name and name all of your socially handicapped characters with them. Tell him his old girlfriend is in all of your stories and then watch how funny he can be, see what a really great sense of humor he can have.

Your child psychology advisor tells you you are neglecting courses in your major. What you spend the most time on should be what you're majoring in. Say yes, you understand.

In creative writing seminars over the next two years, everyone continues to smoke cigarettes and ask the same things: "But does it work?" "Why should we care about this character?" "Have you earned this cliché?" These seem like important questions.

On days when it is your turn, you look at the class hopefully as they scour your mimeographs for a plot. They look back up at you, drag deeply, and then smile in a sweet sort of way.

You spend too much time slouched and demoralized. Your boyfriend suggests bicycling. Your roommate suggests a new boyfriend. You are said to be self-mutilating and losing weight, but you continue writing. The only happiness you have is writing something new, in the middle of the night, armpits damp, heart pounding, something no one has yet seen. You have only those brief, fragile, untested moments of exhilaration when you know: you are a genius. Understand what you must do. Switch majors. The kids in your nursery project will be disappointed, but you have a calling, an urge, a delusion, an unfortunate habit. You have, as your mother would say, fallen in with a bad crowd.

Why write? Where does writing come from? These are questions to ask yourself. They are like: Where does dust come from? Or: Why is there war? Or: If there's a God, then why is my brother now a cripple?

These are questions that you keep in your wallet, like calling cards. These are questions, your creative writing teacher says, that are good to address in your journals but rarely in your fiction.

The writing professor this fall is stressing the Power of the Imagination. Which means he doesn't want long descriptive stories about your camping trip last July. He wants you to start in a realistic context but then to alter it. Like recombinant DNA. He wants you to let your imagination sail, to let it grow big-bellied in the wind. This is a quote from Shakespeare.

Tell your roommate your great idea, your great exercise of imaginative power: a transformation of Melville to contemporary life. It will be about monomania and the fish-eat-fish world of life insurance in Rochester, New York. The first line will be "Call me Fishmeal," and it will feature a menopausal suburban husband named

Richard, who because he is so depressed all the time is called "Mopey Dick" by his witty wife Elaine. Say to your roommate: "Mopey Dick, get it?" Your roommate looks at you, her face blank as a large Kleenex. She comes up to you, like a buddy, and puts an arm around your burdened shoulders. "Listen, Francie," she says, slow as speech therapy. "Let's go out and get a big beer."

The seminar doesn't like this one either. You suspect they are beginning to feel sorry for you. They say: "You have to think about what is happening. Where is the story here?"

The next semester the writing professor is obsessed with writing from personal experience. You must write from what you know, from what has happened to you. He wants deaths, he wants camping trips. Think about what has happened to you. In three years there have been three things: you lost your virginity; your parents got divorced; and your brother came home from a forest ten miles from the Cambodian border with only half a thigh, a permanent smirk nestled into one corner of his mouth.

About the first you write: "It created a new space, which hurt and cried in a voice that wasn't mine, 'I'm not the same anymore, but I'll be okay.'"

About the second you write an elaborate story of an old married couple who stumble upon an unknown land mine in their kitchen and accidentally blow themselves up. You call it: "For Better or for Liverwurst."

About the last you write nothing. There are no words for this. Your typewriter hums. You can find no words.

At undergraduate cocktail parties, people say, "Oh, you write? What do you write about?" Your roommate, who has consumed too much wine, too little cheese, and no crackers at all, blurts: "Oh, my god, she always writes about her dumb boyfriend."

Later on in life you will learn that writers are merely open, helpless texts with no real understanding of what they have written and therefore must half-believe anything and everything that is said of them. You, however, have not yet reached this stage of literary criticism. You stiffen and say, "I do not," the same way you said it when someone in the fourth grade accused you of really liking oboe lessons and your parents really weren't just making you take them.

Insist you are not very interested in any one subject at all, that you are interested in the music of language, that you are interested in—in—syllables, because they are the atoms of poetry, the cells of the mind, the breath of the soul. Begin to feel woozy. Stare into your plastic wine cup.

"Syllables?" you will hear someone ask, voice trailing off, as they glide slowly toward the reassuring white of the dip.

Begin to wonder what you do write about. Or if you have anything to say. Or if there even is such a thing as a thing to say. Limit these thoughts to no more than ten minutes a day; like sit-ups, they can make you thin.

You will read somewhere that all writing has to do with one's genitals. Don't dwell on this. It will make you nervous.

Your mother will come visit you. She will look at the circles under your eyes and hand you a brown book with a brown briefcase on the cover. It is entitled: *How to Become a Business Executive.* She has also brought the *Names for Baby* encyclopedia you asked for; one of your characters, the aging clown–school teacher, needs a new name. Your mother will shake her head and say: "Francie, Francie, remember when you were going to be a child psychology major?"

Say: "Mom, I like to write."

She'll say: "Sure you like to write. Of course. Sure you like to write."

Write a story about a confused music student and title it: "Schubert Was the One with the Glasses, Right?" It's not a big hit, although your roommate likes the part where the two violinists accidentally blow themselves up in a recital room. "I went out with a violinist once," she says, snapping her gum.

Thank god you are taking other courses. You can find sanctuary in nineteenth-century ontological snags and invertebrate courting rituals. Certain globular mollusks have what is called "Sex by the Arm." The male octopus, for instance, loses the end of one arm when placing it inside the female body during intercourse. Marine biologists call it "Seven Heaven." Be glad you know these things. Be glad you are not just a writer. Apply to law school.

From here on in, many things can happen. But the main one will be this: you decide not to go to law school after all, and, instead, you spend a good, big chunk of your adult life telling people how you decided not to go to law school after all. Somehow you end up writing again. Perhaps you go to graduate school. Perhaps you work odd jobs and take writing courses at night. Perhaps you are working on a novel and writing down all the clever remarks and intimate personal confessions you hear during the day. Perhaps you are losing your pals, your acquaintances, your balance.

You have broken up with your boyfriend. You now go out with men who, instead of whispering "I love you," shout: "Do it to me, baby." This is good for your writing.

Sooner or later you have a finished manuscript more or less. People look at it in a vaguely troubled sort of way and say, "I'll bet becoming a writer was always a fantasy of yours, wasn't it?" Your lips dry to salt. Say that of all the fantasies possible in the world, you can't imagine being a writer even making the top twenty. Tell them you were going to be a child psychology major. "I bet," they always sigh, "you'd be great with kids." Scowl fiercely. Tell them you're a walking blade.

Quit classes. Quit jobs. Cash in old savings bonds. Now you have time like warts on your hands. Slowly copy all of your friends' addresses into a new address book.

Vacuum. Chew cough drops. Keep a folder full of fragments.

An eyelid darkening sideways.

World as conspiracy.

Possible plot? A woman gets on a bus.

Suppose you threw a love affair and nobody came.

At home drink a lot of coffee. At Howard Johnson's order the cole slaw. Consider how it looks like the soggy confetti of a map: where you've been, where you're going—"You Are Here," says the red star on the back of the menu.

Occasionally a date with a face blank as a sheet of paper asks you whether writers often become discouraged. Say that sometimes they do and sometimes they do. Say it's a lot like having polio.

"Interesting," smiles your date, and then he looks down at his arm hairs and starts to smooth them, all, always, in the same direction.

RECOMMENDED READINGS

Leading Textbooks and Guidebooks

Ann Bernays and Pamela Painter. *What If? Writing Exercises for Fiction Writers.* New York: HarperCollins, 1990. A collection of detailed, thoroughly explained exercises designed by the authors and by contributing authors.

Carol Bly. *The Passionate, Accurate Story.* Minneapolis: Milkweed Editions, 1990. A formally innovative textbook (the book itself has narrative elements, which both explain and illustrate the lessons) that draws upon theories of psychoanalysis in a creative, not clinical, manner.

Rita Mae Brown. *Starting from Scratch: A Different Kind of Writer's Manual.* New York: Bantam, 1988. With chapters discussing topics ranging from "Computers and Other Expensive Knickknacks" to "Writing as a Moral Act," Brown considers the many different facets of the writer's life in expressive and sometimes autobiographical detail. *Starting from Scratch* also contains exercises, a recommended reading list and curricula, and professional advice.

Hallie and Whit Burnett. *The Fiction Writer's Handbook.* New York: HarperCollins, 1975. Broad-based, pragmatic chapters that emphasize neither technique nor inspiration at the expense of the other. Numerous author quotations and story excerpts. One of several textbooks considered "classic" in the field.

Janet Burroway. *Writing Fiction: A Guide to Narrative Craft.* New York: HarperCollins, 1992. 3rd edition. A popular textbook praised for its elegance, *Writing Fiction* focuses especially on issues of characterization and point of view, but also contains sections on revision, writing process, story form, and atmosphere, as well as directed exercises, twenty-five stories, and useful appendices.

Barnaby Conrad and the staff of the Santa Barbara Writer's Conference. *The Complete Guide to Writing Fiction.* Cincinnati: Writer's Digest, 1990. A collection of informal lectures on writing issues, each "keynoted" by a visiting author at the Santa Barbara Writer's Conference.

Natalie Goldberg. *Writing Down the Bones. Freeing the Writer Within.* Fore-word by Judith Guest. Boston: Shambhala, 1986. A series of short, in-terrelated essays on technique and the writing process, *Writing Down the Bones* encourages its reader to find methods of "letting go," while maintaining what could best be described as a Zen-like discipline. By the same author, see also *Wild Mind: Living the Writer's Life* (Boston: Shambhala, 1990).

Oakley Hall. *The Art & Craft of Novel Writing.* Cincinnati: Story Press, 1989. The first section of the book provides broad, accessible essays on topics such as "Characterization," "Plotting," and "Style." The second section describes the steps in the construction of a novel. Appendices include a simple novel synopsis and recommended reading list.

Rust Hills. *Writing in General and the Short Story in Particular. An Informal Textbook.* Boston: Houghton Mifflin, 1987. Rev. ed. Hills is the long-time fiction editor of *Esquire. Writing in General* offers a series of short, direct chapters on topics ranging from technique ("Techniques of Foreshadowing") to form ("Tension and Anticipation") to broader lit-erary issues ("The American Short Story 'Today'").

Robie Macauley and George Lanning. *Technique in Fiction.* New York: St. Martin's, 1987. 2nd edition. Shaped more like an informal, readable scholarly work (it contains footnotes and illustrative quotations from supporting texts), this successful textbook emphasizes technique and especially practice.

Victoria Nelson. *On Writer's Block: A New Approach to Creativity.* New York: Houghton Mifflin, 1993. Formerly called *Writer's Block and How to Use It.* As both titles suggest, Nelson's book emphasizes writer's block as a positive force in the development of the writer and the self. Especially recommended for writers on their own.

Jerome Stern. *Making Shapely Fiction.* New York: Norton, 1991. A self-described "tool box" of advice about narrative, *Making Shapely Fiction* offers a section on the shapes of stories, a recommended essay called "Write What You Know," and an alphabetically arranged se-ries of short essays on beginning writer's issues.

Writer's Digest Handbook of Short Story Writing. Preface by Joyce Carol Oates. Cincinnati: Writer's Digest, 1970. This handbook contains a collection of essays by different authors, emphasizing technical issues such as "Dialogue," "Description," and "Viewpoint." This book also contains advice on getting started and working with writer's block.

Personal Approaches

Some of these selections are textbooks or guidebooks that possess autobiographical elements. Others are autobiographical, and use the life of the author as a focus for reflection on the writing life. Others are collections of letters or interviews with an individual author.

Sherwood Anderson. *A Story Teller's Story.* New York: Penguin, 1989. Anderson's autobiography includes essayistic passages on the form of the short story and the development of the writer.

Dorothea Brande. *Becoming a Writer.* Foreword by John Gardner. New York: Jeremy Tarcher, 1981. Originally published in 1934, *Becoming a Writer* has been praised for its approach to what John Gardner calls the "root problems" of writing and writer's block.

John Cheever. *The Journals of John Cheever.* New York: Knopf, 1990. Cheever's journals, like Chekhov's letters or Woolf's diary (see below), provide an unusual portrait of the psychological interplay between a writer's life and his or her writing.

Anton Chekhov. *Anton Chekhov's Life and Thought: Selected Letters and Commentary.* Berkeley: University of California Press, 1975. Recommended source for Chekhov's letters.

Annie Dillard. *The Writing Life.* New York: HarperCollins, 1989. Like Eudora Welty's *One Writer's Beginnings* (see below), this work is a precisely remembered, insightful autobiography of the development of an individual writer's relationship to her art.

E. M. Forster. *Aspects of the Novel.* London: Arnold, 1927. An elegant, wise collection of essays on narrative form culled from lectures delivered at Trinity College, Cambridge, by the author.

John Gardner. *The Art of Fiction. Notes on Craft for Young Writers.* New York: Vintage, 1991. Gardner's influential text, a mix of principle, advice on technique, and the author's strong, guiding voice. Strongly recommended are the exercises found at the end of the book. By the same author, see also *On Becoming a Novelist* (New York: Harper & Row, 1983), *On Moral Fiction* (New York: Basic Books, 1978), and *On Writers and Writing* (Reading, MA: Addison-Wesley, 1994).

William H. Gass. *Fiction and the Figures of Life.* New York: Vintage, 1971. Diverse, richly composed collection of essays on the reading and writing of literature.

Richard Hugo. *The Triggering Town. Lectures and Essays on Poetry and Writing.* New York: Norton, 1979. While Hugo's book is written explicitly for poetry-writing students, many of his observations about inspiration and the creative-writing classroom are equally valuable to developing fiction writers.

David Lodge. *The Art of Fiction.* New York: Viking, 1993. The art of fiction is considered by this British novelist in fifty short and wide-ranging essays, including "The Intrusive Author," "The Reader in the Text,"

"Showing and Telling," "The Unreliable Narrator," and "The Non-Fiction Novel." Each topic is illustrated by a short passage or two taken from classic and modern fiction, citing authors such as E. M. Forster, J. D. Salinger, Jane Austen, Vladimir Nabokov, and Fay Weldon.

Flannery O'Connor. *Mystery and Manners.* Eds., Sally and Robert Fitzgerald. New York: Farrar, Straus & Giroux, 1961. Praised both for its writing style and substance. A mixture of autobiographical essays and essays on the nature of fiction, regionalism, religion, and teaching. O'Connor's letters are also recommended; see *The Habit of Being,* ed. Sally Fitzgerald (New York: Farrar, Straus & Giroux, 1979).

Brenda Ueland. *If You Want to Write. A Book About Art, Independence and Spirit.* St. Paul: Graywolf Press, 1987. Ueland's book, first published in 1938, emphasizes self-expression (a sample chapter title: "Be Careless, Reckless! Be a Lion! Be a Pirate! When You Write!"), imagination, and values over technical proficiency. Especially recommended for writers on their own.

Alice Walker. *In Search of Our Mothers' Gardens.* New York: Harcourt Brace Jovanovich, 1983. Walker's essays combine the personal and literary, and provide vivid and insightful essays on a writer's relationship to her influences. Especially recommended: "Looking for Zora" and the title essay.

Eudora Welty. *One Writer's Beginnings.* New York: Time Warner, 1984. Based on three lectures delivered at Harvard in 1983 ("Listening," "Learning to See," "Finding a Voice"), Welty's precise, fluid autobiography provides extraordinary insight into the development of the individual writer's literary imagination. See also the collection of interviews entitled *Conversations with Eudora Welty,* ed. Peggy Whitman Prenshaw (New York: Washington Square Press, 1984).

Edith Wharton. *The Writing of Fiction.* New York: Scribner's, 1925. As her own stories and novels illustrate, Edith Wharton approached the writing of fiction with rigorous aesthetic ideals about form, and a belief that narrative must possess moral vision. Especially recommended are the three middle chapters: "Telling a Short Story," "Constructing a Novel," and "Character and Situation in the Novel."

Virginia Woolf. *A Writer's Diary, Being Extracts from the Diary of Virginia Woolf.* Ed., Leonard Woolf. London: Hogarth Press, 1953. Specific passages about writing, culled from twenty-six volumes of Woolf's diaries.

Richard Wright. *Conversations with Richard Wright.* Eds., Michael Fabre and Kenneth Kinnamon. Jackson: University of Mississippi Press, 1993. A collection of interviews with Richard Wright. Among twentieth-century authors, few thought more about the marriage of political content and fiction writing style than did Wright. This work provides a comprehensive review of his insights on these, and other, writing issues.

Collections

Some of these collections include short stories or complete in-depth interviews with individual authors. Others gather quotations from well-known writers, or excerpt interviews.

Ann Charters, ed. *The Story and Its Writer. An Introduction to Short Fiction.* Boston: Bedford Books, 1992. 3rd edition. Charter's widely praised anthology of short stories also contains a prominent section featuring essays on writing and interviews from authors included within the book, as well as appendices featuring a glossary of literary terms and a history of the short story.

Nicholas Delbanco, ed. "A Symposium on Contemporary American Fiction." *Michigan Quarterly Review,* Fall 1987/Winter 1988. A two-part symposium on contemporary literature, culling short, thoughtful essays on fiction from eighty-three contemporary authors.

Paul Mandelbaum, ed. *First Words.* Chapel Hill: Algonquin, 1993. Forty-two well-known writers present their earliest childhood or adolescent writings; margin notes by the editor point to the connections between the juvenilia and each author's life or adult work. Participating authors include John Updike, Joyce Carol Oates, Ursula LeGuin, and Norman Mailer.

George Plimpton, ed. *Writers at Work. The Paris Review Interviews.* New York: Penguin. Six volumes (they are called "series") of interviews with celebrated authors. Each volume contains fourteen to sixteen interviews. The series is considered a vital and moving source of insight into the writer's art.

George Plimpton, ed. and intro. *The Writer's Chapbook. A Compendium of Fact, Opinion, Wit, and Advice from the 20th Century's Most Prominent Writers.* Excerpted from *The Paris Review* interviews.

William Safire and Leonard Safir, eds. *Good Advice on Writing. Great Quotations from Writers Past and Present on How to Write Well.* New York: Simon & Schuster, 1992. Divided alphabetically into subjects ("Cliches," "Coherence," "Complexity"), this collection features quotations from celebrated writers.

Susan Shaughnessy. *Walking on Alligators. A Book of Meditations for Writers.* San Francisco: HarperCollins, 1993. *Walking on Alligators* contains 200 short (one-page) essays on writing issues, each prefaced by a passage by a prominent author.

Sybil Steinberg, ed., John F. Baker, intro. *Writing for Your Life: Ninety-Two Contemporary Authors Talk About the Art of Writing and the Job of Publishing.* New York: Norton (Pushcart), 1992. Ninety-two contemporary authors are profiled and interviewed, and present their thoughts on the art and business of writing.

Janet Sternburg, ed. *The Writer on Her Work*. New York: Norton, 1980. Seventeen notable women writers examine their lives and their work in this series of essays, including Gail Godwin's "Becoming a Writer" and Joan Didion's "Why I Write."

Bill Strickland, ed., Will Blythe, intro. *On Being a Writer*. Cincinnati: Writer's Digest, 1989. Thirty-two in-depth interviews with important authors of the twentieth century.

Reference Sources for Publication Information

Reference information is available to the writer from many sources. *The Best American Short Stories, O. Henry Prize Stories,* and *Pushcart Prize* annual collections all provide listings of literary magazines. The *Associated Writing Programs Chronicle* and the *Poets and Writers, Inc.* newsletter also provide up-to-date information on conferences, contests, and other professional information. To contact AWP, write Old Dominion University, Norfolk, VA 23508. Poets and Writers, Inc. can be reached at 72 Spring Street, New York, NY 10012.

Council of Literary Magazines and Presses. *Directory of Literary Magazines*. New York: Moyer Bell, 1994. An annual catalog of the 500 U.S. and foreign magazines that publish poetry, fiction, and essays. This book contains clear descriptions of each magazine in the editors' own words, and lists useful information concerning submission and payment policies for each publication.

Len Fulton, ed. *International Directory of Little Magazines and Small Presses*. Paradise, CA: Dustbooks, 1993. 29th edition. Contains over 5,500 listings.

Mark Garvey, ed. *1994 Writer's Market*. Cincinnati: Writer's Digest, 1994. 4,000 listings. Includes advice about the business of publication.

Robin Gee, ed. *1994 Novel and Short Story Writers' Market*. Cincinnati: Writer's Digest, 1994. 1,900 markets listed. Includes advice on technique and publication.

The Guide to Writers' Conferences: Writers' Conferences, Workshops, Seminars, Residencies, Retreats, and Organizations. Coral Gables, FL: Shaw, 1993. 4th edition.

Advice on Revision

David Madden. *Revising Fiction: A Handbook for Writers*. New York: Penguin, 1988. 185 short chapters, each dealing with an important revision issue.

The appendices, presenting examples of revisions and a list of available revision examples, are strongly recommended.

Donald Murray. *The Craft of Revision.* New York: Harcourt Brace, 1995. 2nd ed. Murray, the author of more than a dozen books on writing, observes that "Writing Is Rewriting," and encourages his reader to think of revision in terms of concrete goals: "Re-Write to Focus," "Re-Write to Collect," "Re-Write to Shape," "Re-Write to Order," "Re-Write to Develop," "Re-Write with Voice," "Re-Write to Edit."

Jay Woodruff, ed. *A Piece of Work: Five Writers Discuss Their Revisions.* Iowa City: University of Iowa Press, 1993. Using early drafts, interviews, and final drafts of individual works by five contemporary authors (Tobias Wolff, Tess Gallagher, Robert Coles, Joyce Carol Oates, and Donald Hall), *A Piece of Work* provides five in-depth portraits of the revision process.

Advice on Teaching:
Unusual Approaches to the Workshop

Peter Elbow. *Writing Without Teachers.* New York: Oxford University Press, 1973. *Writing Without Teachers,* as the name suggests, offers innovative advice about writing and teaching writing, and is particularly well-suited for small groups attempting to design their own workshops.

Andrew Levy. *The Culture and Commerce of the American Short Story.* New York: Cambridge University Press, 1993. An account of the birth and development of the short story from the time of Poe, this book also contains a history of creative writing and the workshop. Although the focus is cultural, individual authors such as Poe and Wharton are examined.

Joseph Moxley, ed. *Creative Writing in America.* Urbana, IL: National Council of Teachers of English, 1989. This collection features essays on the theory and history of creative-writing workshops, the practice of teaching creative writing, and publishing. Especially recommended is Eve Shelnutt's "Transforming Experience into Fiction: An Alternative to the Workshop."

Eve Shelnutt, ed. *The Writing Room: Keys to the Craft of Fiction and Poetry.* Marietta, GA: Longstreet Press, 1989. *The Writing Room,* an open-ended textbook designed to appeal to both beginning and experienced writers, contains original essays by Shelnutt on both theoretical and pragmatic writing issues, as well as reading lists, suggestions for further study, exercises, and fiction, poetry, and essays by writing students and professional writers.

INDEX

COPYRIGHT ACKNOWLEDGMENTS